November 12, 1996

Dear June!

Best Wishes
on a great retirement.
Have fun at the
"family Picnic"!

Bob Hardcastle

More Praise for *Hardcastle's Money Talk*

"This straightforward presentation of the basic principals in developing a financial plan is outstanding. I regularly recommend to our investors the implementations of many of the long-term strategies presented in the book and believe it is rewarding to all investors."

—David A. Minella, President of GT Global Financial Services

"This book maps out a simple path in an easy-to-read narrative."

—William C. Freund, Ph.D., Professor of Economics, Pace University and former Chief Economist of the New York Stock Exchange

"*Money Talk*'s Uncle Bob hits the spot when he tells Benjamin Bigtimer that a better company is one that provides great benefits and leadership for its employees. Then, everyone profits."

—Ken Pontikes, President of ComDisco

"In *Hardcastle's Money Talk*, Bob Hardcastle deals with complex financial issues with clarity and in a manner which many of us can understand. I see myself and many of my friends in those seeking help from Uncle Bob."

—John C. Guyon, President of Southern Illinois University at Carbondale

"Popularized books to help individuals grow rich, plan their finances, become millionaires, and deal with wills and inheritance are often too complicated to be easily understood. Bob Hardcastle writes in a popular manner that will be understandable to the beginner as well as the seasoned investor. The book is fun to read, informative, and most of all helps the reader learn to ask the right questions. I plan to recommend it to professional planners, parents, colleagues, friends, and teachers and educators who wish to introduce money into the curriculum."

—Kate McKeown, Co-author with Lou Mobley of the best-selling book *Beyond IBM*

"In these turbulent times, we can surely appreciate sound financial advice from one who is experienced and successful. Bob Hardcastle has undertaken the challenge, and succeeded. I recommend *Hardcastle's Money Talk* as a practical, insightful, and seasoned approach to money management and investment."

—Rabbi Noah Weinberg, Founder and Dean of
Aish Hatorah College of Jewish Studies

"A terrific job in laying out the language so that people can understand."

—Harley Gordon, attorney and
author of *How to Protect Your Savings From Catastrophic Illnesses*

"I believe it will be very useful as a supplementary text in courses on personal finances. It is well written and organized in a manner so the reader progresses from simple to more complex problems."

—Larry K. Pettit, President of Indiana University of Pennsylvania

"One of the best financial primers I have read. Enjoyable reading in a unique storybook form. This book is definitely a must-read for young and old alike. Highly recommended."

—Ken Skala, author of *American Guidance for Seniors*

"This book offers a unique and interesting approach in explaining a variety of important financial- and estate-planning techniques. There is something for everyone in this book. It is an excellent source for many innovative and effective ideas."

—Renno Peterson, Co-Chairman of The Institute, Inc.

HARDCASTLE'S
MONEY
TALK

HARDCASTLE'S MONEY TALK

BOB HARDCASTLE

American Management Association

New York • Atlanta • Boston • Chicago • Kansas City • San Francisco • Washington, D.C.
Brussels • Mexico City • Tokyo • Toronto

This publication is designed to provide accurate and authoritative information in regard to the subject matter covered. It is sold with the
understanding that the publisher is not engaged in rendering legal,
accounting, or other professional service. If legal advice or other ex-
pert assistance is required, the services of a competent professional
person should be sought.

Library of Congress Cataloging-in-Publication Data

Hardcastle, Bob.
    Hardcastle's money talk / Bob Hardcastle.
        p.   cm.
    ISBN 0-8144-0234-8
    1. Finance, Personal.   2. Saving and investment.   3. Youth—
Finance, Personal—Case studies.   4. Widows—Finance, Personal—
Case studies.   5. Aged—Finance, Personal—Case studies.
    6. Married people—Finance, Personal—Case studies.   I. Title.
II. Title: Money talk.
HG179.H274   1994
332.024—dc20

                                                                    94-8693
                                                                       CIP

Printing number

10   9   8   7   6   5   4   3   2   1

To
"Mom and Dad,"
who are together forever

Contents

Acknowledgments

Throughout my investment career, many people have helped and guided me to understand the true value in investing and in the sharing of investment philosophies with others. There are simply too many to name here, but they have my profound gratitude.

Of these, there are a number who dedicated their time, effort, and expertise in helping me conceptualize, organize, and write this book. It is most appropriate that they be singled out and mentioned by name.

Jim Brabish originally organized the picnic theme and helped me pull out of my memory the many problems and experiences of literally thousands of those with whom I have been privileged to work. From these I have been able to create the composite individuals who form the cast of characters introduced in this book.

Kate McKeown has inspired me over the years to put down on paper what I have said in words to my clients, friends, and "Money Talk" listeners. It was she who introduced me to my publisher, AMACOM Books. It was also Kate who introduced me to Bob Maston, who has worked with the text to help make it concise, readable, and enjoyable.

My thanks also are due to my investment company staff for putting up with me during moments when nothing else seemed important but giving life to those who were being created for their roles in this book.

A very sincere expression of gratitude goes to Tony Vlamis at AMACOM for believing in me and in "Uncle Bob's Secrets."

Words fail when trying to express my heart-felt appreciation to my wife, Jan, who has been my partner since grade school. She not only typed the very first outline, but subsequently, every word of every page of the book—including every revision and the final version. Her often heard comment: "Not again?!" continued to inspire me to write the next revision more carefully and complete the project.

And, finally, I give thanks to all my clients and "Money Talk" listeners who have faithfully followed my investment views. I consider you my close friends. It is you who have given me the confidence to share my investment philosophy.

Introduction

The stories you are about to read are true. The only things changed are the identities of the people you will meet, their names, the settings, the way in which their individual problems are presented, the action as it's described, the dialogs as they are recorded, and the content of the problems dealt with. In fact, all those you will meet at the picinic are fictionalized descriptions of real people, real problems, real suggestions, and real secrets revealed.

The various characters you will meet at the picnic are presented to you by the author as seen through the eyes of "Uncle Bob." The author has selected this means and format to illustrate for you, the readers, many of those common problems you or someone you know may be experiencing. From his many years of dealing with such problems, the author reveals a variety of his "Secrets," by which such financial crises and challenges have been successfully met.

Although these relatives of Uncle Bob are really composites of numerous individuals he has helped during some thirty years of his professional career, they have been brought alive to help you avoid scholarly lectures and pedantic approaches. Uncle Bob's extended family includes individuals of all ages (from ten years up), and this book has been written to make solving problems, understanding money, and achieving financial health FUN.

Enjoy yourself at the picnic!

HARDCASTLE'S MONEY TALK

1

The Family Picnic

"Life is short. We work. We earn our money. We spend our
  money. Some people use their money well by saving, and
  some don't.

"We come into this world without money, and we leave this
  world without it. During our lifetimes, we use our money
  in three ways: We accumulate it; we preserve it; we distribute it.

"Everyone has a different idea of what accumulate, preserve,
  and distribute means. People handle money differently.

"Along the way we must learn that making money is fun,
  investing money is fun, and becoming wealthy is fun.
  Everyone can do it. It's easy. We just have to follow certain
  basic rules.

"With wise investing and saving, even a person of modest
  means can become a millionaire."

THESE THOUGHTS STIRRED IN BOB PROSPERITY'S MIND as he watched
family members arrive at the Prosperity family's annual reunion
picnic. Bob and Marge had moved from Goodvillage several years
ago. Each year they traveled back home for the big event of the
year.

Brothers, sisters, grandparents, aunts, uncles, and cousins
traveled from all over the country back to Goodvillage for these
reunions, which had been held for as long as anyone could remember. There would be over 100 people at the picnic today.

"Uncle Bob," liked and respected in the family, was a fixture
at these family gatherings.

What everyone liked most about Uncle Bob was the way he could talk about money. People went to Uncle Bob for help with how to save and stay out of debt. They knew he carried on the family tradition, the Secrets to Becoming a Millionaire. Bob had become a millionaire himself on a modest income from his office-supply business.

At the family picnic, it had become traditional for Uncle Bob to spend time talking to other family members about money. He was the one with the knowledge, the Secrets. And if you were lucky, you might be able to get some of Bob's time—a kind of free advice session.

From outward appearances, one would never know that Bob had the Secrets to Becoming a Millionaire. Slightly overweight and balding, he could pass for a university professor. To the picnic, Bob wore a St. Louis Cardinals T-shirt, a pair of baggy shorts, and a pair of well-traveled sneakers that most people would have already tossed on the trash heap.

Bob knew that the real measure of wealth was a person's inner character and his or her ability to achieve goals, so he did not put a lot of stock in outside appearance. He never wore $500 suits or $100 ties. He dressed casually and was always clean, and he felt good about himself. He could make himself look good with medium-price clothes; what he didn't spend on expensive clothes he used instead to develop his savings program.

What Bob did consider important was managing his money carefully to achieve the goal of financial security. This meant having sufficient money available to provide for emergencies and for retirement.

Bob found out early in life that the only things to buy were the things he, his family, and his business needed. He stayed away from buying things just because he wanted them. He stuck to just what he needed, and he bought only with cash. Naturally, he would take advantage of any offer of 60 or 90 days to pay without interest, but having the cash right now was what counted.

The key to his financial success was that he had started to save early in life and consistently saved every month—not big sums of money, but whatever he could save. There were months when he saved $50. There were months when he actually put away $10,000.

Whatever he could save, he did. Whenever he invested, he put his money only into those investments that he understood completely. Once Bob had set up his game plan for financial success, nothing could stop him from reaching his financial goals.

As a result, Uncle Bob today was a millionaire. He knew the Secrets. He had used the Secrets. They had worked for him. He hadn't become a millionaire by winning the lottery, or by having a wildly successful business. He had done it on an average income, just by wise saving and investing.

As Bob anticipated this year's picnic, he thought about the other family members, including all the cousins and even second cousins he would be seeing. Every year individuals came to him with questions about their money. But they all thought that becoming a millionaire was an unachievable goal.

This year, Bob was more aware than ever of other members of the family and their financial situations and financial needs. As Bob had grown older, he had become aware of how quickly life goes by. He had realized that everything that we put off until tomorrow financially would keep us from reaching our financial goals of becoming millionaires for many, many tomorrows.

Bob realized more than ever the truth of the words he had heard over and over again, which had been passed on to him from his great-grandfather, the family patriarch, Phillip Prosperity. These had become for Bob the Secrets to Becoming a Millionaire!

"Save."
"Start saving when you're young."
"Take advantage of the Magic of Compounding."
"Avoid debt."
"Use the Cookie Jar System to track your expenses."
"Invest your money wisely."
"Choose your investments by your own Sleep Syndrome, the ability to sleep at night and not worry about your investments."

"Plan your estate. Always be ready for financial emergencies."

"And most importantly, have fun investing!"

To Bob, the Secrets meant saving today to meet the needs of
tomorrow. People who save today will be able to meet financial
emergencies that arise, pay for their children's college education,
buy their homes, take nice vacations, retire comfortably, and
much more. Every day can be a happy day of saving as they look
forward to their days of retirement without financial worries.

Bob was concerned about the others in the family. He wondered about their futures. Did they know what their expenses
were? Were they staying out of debt? Were they buying only what
they needed with cash?

Were they saving systematically? Would they someday become millionaires? Were they setting aside funds to pay for the
education of their children?

Would they be able to retire successfully? Were they accumulating enough money and making it grow so that when they
retired, they could live off just the earnings, not the principal? Did
they have their estates set up properly?

These questions and many more were churning in Bob's head
as he watched the family members arrive for the annual picnic.

Today, Bob wanted to reach out to others in his family. As he
grew older, Bob saw the importance of Old Phillip's words on
saving and building an investment portfolio. Bob had achieved his
goal of becoming a millionaire through careful saving and investing, while also having fun along the way. Now he wanted others
to understand the importance of financial planning while they
were still able to start saving money and to get and stay out of
debt.

Today he was going to make sure he shared with others his
Secrets to Becoming a Millionaire. He knew this was going to be
a great day.

$ $ $ $ $

It was a beautiful summer Sunday morning in the park. Some members of the family had already been to early morning religious services and would soon be arriving at the park. A bright sun radiated its warmth, and the trees and fields glistened with the rich green of early summer. The temperature was already 75 degrees, on its way to a high of 90.

Prosperity Park was attractive and well cared for. Its 200 acres were divided into a natural area of lakes and fields, the 100-acre Fortune Forest, and open areas with picnic grounds and ball fields.

Life was visible everywhere. Squirrels were running up and down trees. Birds were soaring overhead. A rabbit was darting back and forth through an open field.

A man was running with his dog. A couple rode bicycles down the road.

The main picnic pavilion was the size of a small house. It was a distinctive building at the top of a hill, overlooking the rolling hills and valleys around. It had a steep, four-sided roof, peaking in the middle. It would afford plenty of protection for picnickers when a summer shower broke out. A parking lot and a baseball field adjoined the shelter. Decorating it was a banner declaring WELCOME PROSPERITY FAMILY.

Each year at the picnic, Bob spent so much time talking about money and answering investment questions that he never had much time to play. He very much enjoyed talking about investing, but he still liked to play some, too. Every year, Bob resolved to get in at least a game of horseshoes. He always ended up not having time.

This year, he vowed that things would be different. He resolved to get in a game of horseshoes and maybe even play softball or volleyball, although he didn't consider himself a star.

As Bob and Marge, his wife of 35 years, sat side by side on the playground swings, he thought how happy they had been together and how much of his success he owed to her. Marge was a good contrast to Bob. She was a systems analyst for a downtown bank. She complemented Bob's inner wisdom and kept him on track. She was organized and got things done. She shared his visions about money and worked with him to achieve the goal of becoming millionaires. Her frosted hair was short and neatly trimmed. She wore a dark blue T-shirt, white shorts, and white sneakers.

"This year I *must* get in a game of horseshoes, and I am going to play softball, too," said Bob.

"Horsefeathers," Marge replied. "Not as long as there's *The Wall Street Journal* and you have a tongue that speaks. People will find you, and you like to talk. Everyone wants to find out your Secrets to Becoming a Millionaire.

"And, besides, when was the last time you played softball?"

"Okay," Bob said, "let's leave it at horseshoes then. But, honey, I bet you that this year is different. If I don't get in at least a game of horseshoes this year, I owe you a dinner and a night on the town."

"It's a deal," she agreed.

As the people arrived for the picnic, Bob and Marge left the playground area and headed for the pavilion to meet the family, friends, and guests who were starting to arrive. A mood of celebration and fun was in the air.

"Should be a great day for a picnic," he said.

The pavilion was surrounded by green, rolling hills. On top of a far hill was the mansion of Bob's great-grandfather, Phillip Prosperity. He had settled in Goodvillage in the 1800s. He gained his wealth through working diligently in his country general store. It was there that he learned to buy, sell, and invest wisely for the long term.

The house was immense and grand. Its two and one-half stories encompassed 20 rooms. Its brick exterior was done in southern colonial style, complete with eight columns across the front. Side rooms jutted out with their own peaked roofs. The tallest brick tower had a stained glass window that glistened in the sun. Adjoining the house were a barn and stables. Today, the house was open for public tours, and served as the office of the local historical society. Some of the family who had never visited it would be able to take the tour during the picnic.

As a boy, Bob had heard stories about Old Phillip. His business was successful, and he wisely managed what he had. He always bought low and sold high.

Old Phillip said, "Most investors buy high and sell low. They run with the pack. They are afraid to make decisions on their own. Most investors buy and sell on emotion."

Phillip, on the other hand, made his investment purchases whenever the investment price was low or recently had dropped. And he usually sold when everyone else was buying and the price was going up.

He also paid himself first by taking earnings from his general store and placing them in a separate account, from which he then made profitable investments. With the balance he paid his bills and expenses.

It was said that he always chuckled when he proclaimed, "Most people pay their bills first, and they have nothing left to save." He always advocated, "Pay yourself first, then pay the bills."

After many years, he had built his mansion on the 200-acre plot that is now Prosperity Park. His general store had grown far beyond his wildest dreams. He was able to contribute regularly to many charities and donated his spare time helping others learn to have fun investing.

Old Phillip represented a great tradition of financial wisdom in the Prosperity family. Bob recalled the day when his mother, Annie, talked to him about this tradition.

She explained to Bob how his father, Bill, had for many years been helping people learn to save and invest. He had inherited this tradition from his own father, who, in turn, had learned it directly from Old Phillip.

"Your father transmitted Old Phillip's tradition to me, your mother. This was just before your dad died, when you were still very young. I have tried over the years, as you were growing up, to be faithful to what your dad and our family held as a sacred trust. And now, Bob, it is time for me to pass on to you what I have received from our dear family."

His mother then handed him a small, flat, unwrapped box. Bob knew from the way she was handling it that it must contain something very important. The box was covered with dust and looked as if it hadn't been opened for years. Bob blew off the dust gently, carefully lifted the lid, and gazed inside. Although he was still very young, he felt that something very special was happening at this moment.

He gently lifted out of the box a simple brown framed piece of cloth with the following words needlepointed on it:

SAVE TODAY AND PLAN FOR TOMORROW!

His mother said, as he examined the old, slightly brittle cloth, "This is something that I have kept all these years and want you to have. It hung on the wall in Old Phillip's private office for many years.

"When Phillip was a young man and first realized how important it was to save money regularly, he told his wife, Minnie, about it. On his next birthday just a few weeks later, Minnie presented him with this handmade needlepoint cloth. From then on, the cloth hung on Grandad's wall to remind him constantly to save every day.

"Just before Old Phillip died," Bob's mother continued, "he gave me this needlepoint. It has symbolized how we can take charge of our lives and our money through saving and investing. We can plan our own financial futures and become millionaires by following certain secret investment principles. Old Phillip became much wealthier than anyone would have ever thought possible judging by the size of his store. That's because he followed the secret principles of saving and investing."

Now the saying was in Bob's mind all the time: *Save today and plan for tomorrow!* He was proud of it, yet also intimidated by it. He knew he must be faithful to it for himself and for the sake of his family. But also, he must be faithful in sharing these principles with others and encouraging them to do likewise. If Bob could share the Secrets to Becoming a Millionaire, it would help everyone. Bob had been given a demanding and noble mandate.

Marge was in charge of invitations. Even though she and Bob had moved out of town several years ago, she was still in charge of organizing and keeping track of who was coming to the picnic. All those who had been invited to the picnic had been asked to return the short "tear-away" at the bottom of the invitation stating if they were coming (___) YES or (___) NO, how they were coming, and whether or not they needed a place to stay.

Some of those coming had added a note mentioning that they hoped to have an opportunity to visit with Bob. Others had phoned or written notes during the course of the year to make it known that they wanted to use some of Bob's time at the picnic to discuss investments.

$ $ $ $ $ $

As Bob and Marge reached the pavilion area, the excitement felt by all the arrivals was evident to them. They sat down on a bench which had a commanding view of the whole park, including the parking lot, which was close to the pavilion.

"This family is never short on challenges," Marge said. "I'm glad that it's you doing the talking and not me. I'm going to enjoy sitting in the sun, drinking cold drinks, and having some good conversation." As she said this, one of the young children walked up to her and Bob and handed each of them a tall glass of iced tea.

"Well, it's got to be done," Bob replied. "I don't want to see people ruined financially. The Secrets to Becoming a Millionaire are part of our family tradition. If only the others would come to understand. And, by the way, do you have these children trained, or is this a bit of your magic—talking about a cold drink and having one thrust into our hands?"

Bob had a favorite, descriptive, confidential name for each of his close relatives. He didn't mention that name to anyone else except Marge, who was both his wife and his confidant. For example, as Dan and Denise, his first cousins, arrived, Bob whispered to Marge, "Well, here come Mr. and Mrs. *Debt* themselves!"

Dan and Denise were parking their luxury car at that moment. Although they earned good salaries, they spent heavily and saved nothing. Almost everything they bought was on credit. Their wallets were filled with credit cards. Gold, silver, orange, green, you name it—they had the credit cards.

Bob remembered the time when Dan and Denise had gone on a spree of buying on credit, running up thousands of dollars in credit card debt. Bob had tried to talk to them then, but it was no use. They said they would get out of debt in time. Whatever they wanted, they always went out and bought. It didn't make any difference how much it cost. If they liked it, they bought it. They had no view of the future. They thought only about today. Instant gratification was their way of life.

As Dan and Denise and their children, Darlene, age 17, and Darin, age 10, were getting out of their Jaguar in the parking area, Bob remarked to Marge, "Do you think Dan and Denise realize the danger they are in? What if they lose their jobs? What if one of them gets sick? What are they setting aside for their kids' college and their own retirement?

"Before they know it, tomorrow will be today and it's going to be too late to save for all the things they are really going to need down the line. Instant gratification may be nice today, but it's like a kid with a piece of candy. Once you eat the candy, it's gone. When you're an adult, you can't just eat candy; you've got to do what the squirrels do and store some of the good things away for tomorrow. If you don't, when tomorrow comes, you'll have nothing. You must set aside for retirement."

"You've definitely got your hands full with them," Marge replied. "No horseshoe time there. That night on the town sounds like a sure thing. I'd better start thinking about where I want you to take me."

"Don't be so sure of yourself. This year is going to be different. I'm going to score big just by making my Secrets well known, have fun doing it, and still have time for horseshoes."

In contrast to Dan and Denise, Sam and Sally were conservative. Even as Marge was boasting that the dinner and night on the town appeared to be a sure thing, Sam and Sally were driving in.

"Aha," Marge said. "Another of your challenges has just arrived. And what is your descriptive name for them, Bob?"

"That's easy! They are Mr. and Mrs. *Save-It!*"

Sam and Sally and their children, Sarah and Shawn, had arrived in a nice enough car, but nothing extravagant. Sam and Sally always said, "We can only wear one dress or one pair of pants at a time. We live in one house at a time and drive one car at a time. We don't have to impress anyone. We're having fun today and saving for tomorrow."

Like all the other cars, Sam and Sally's car had four good tires, clean windows, comfortable seats, and a radio. It was good enough for them, and it certainly had not cost what Dan and Denise's luxury sedan had. Sam and Sally had paid for their car with cash. They didn't owe anything to anyone. Regardless of what might occur in the future, Sam and Sally wouldn't have to be concerned about someone knocking on their front door and announcing, "The chair you are sitting in is not fully paid for, so we are taking it back," or, "The car you drive is being repossessed," or "You're going to have to move out of the house you live in." Any debt was too much debt.

No, Sam and Sally were never in debt. That was the way it had been since the first time they talked to Uncle Bob. Things had changed quickly for them, and much for the better. They and their children were neat and well groomed, but they did not wear designer fashions like Dan and Denise.

"Maybe Dan and Denise can learn something from Mr. and Mrs. Save-It," Bob thought. A start would be how to get and stay out of debt.

Bob looked at the Hechts with satisfaction. He smiled broadly at Marge. "They're really doing great, aren't they, Marge? They're disciplined. They save systematically, only buy what they need, and always pay for it in cash. No question about it, Marge, they are going to be millionaires in no time."

As Sam, Sally, and the kids were unloading the car, Scott Franklin wheeled up on a brand-new motorcycle. As the cycle rumbled up the park road, he drew everyone's attention.

The lanky, six-foot youth parked the bike and removed his helmet to reveal his new punk hair style. His hair, somewhat mashed down from the helmet, popped back up high in the middle, but was shaved on the sides. He had an earring in his left ear. He wore black boots, baggy shorts, and an oversize T-shirt with the emblem of a rock band printed on the back.

"Who is that?" asked Marge.

"Why, that's Scott Franklin," said Bob, "who, just for your own information, I call Scott *Youth.*"

Marge continued in feigned shock, "But where did he get that far-out haircut?"

"More importantly, where did he get the money for such a luxurious-looking motorcycle?"

Bob would soon find out that Scott had just quit college and was working the night shift in a local restaurant. It was the first time he had ever had cash, and he was spending every penny on video games, dates, clothes, jewelry, his new apartment, and, of course, the motorcycle. Scott was making what Bob considered dangerous moves that could hurt his chances for a viable future.

Marge observed, "He's just a young kid, but with all that energy and a few of your investment secrets, he could get on the right path to success. You might help him become a real winner!"

Bob looked at her with a big, warm smile and said, "You're absolutely right. Of course Scott is going to become a millionaire. It's easy. I'll just start him down the right path and he'll zoom ahead!"

Bob's whole attitude shifted from hopeful elation to a much more serious tone. Bob drew nearer to Marge and whispered, "Look, Marge. Larry Franklin has just arrived. I can't help thinking of him as Larry *Lost.* I think he is teetering on the edge of disaster. He's been struggling through his divorce, and he has no idea what he has been spending or where his money is going. He has a new car, new clothes, and a new hairstyle. And in spite of outward appearances, he still has to work two jobs. To me, Marge, he just seems overwhelmed by expenses."

Marge then softly replied to Bob, "Yes, I've talked often with

Linda, and she confided to me that she had been paying all the bills, writing out the checks, and doing all the shopping at the grocery store. She told me it all fell on her to take care of the kids and keep the home shipshape."

"Yes," Bob continued, "and now besides paying for the car and the clothes, Larry has to pay for lawyers, therapists, his apartment, and child support. He doesn't even want to guess what is coming next. It is a very stressful time, a time of change, and most importantly, a time to evaluate and assess one's finances and values—in fact, to evaluate his whole life and where he wants to go. Our family secrets are certainly needed here!"

Bob and Marge saw Benjamin Blackstone step out of his special-edition Rolls Royce. The biggest Rolls ever built, it was trimmed in gold and even had a gold hood ornament. It also had three antennas for his phones and two-way radio. The windows were tinted dark so that no one could see the TV and bar in the back along with the other luxuries. It didn't take Marge many guesses to discover that Bob's secret name for Ben was Mr. *Bigtimer*! His personalized license plate read, BIGTIME. Another such license plate hanging from his neck would have seemed appropriate, since Mr. Bigtimer was wearing a silk shirt and designer jeans along with two gold neck chains and a gold bracelet. He was big, six feet five inches, and talked in a booming voice. He chomped a cigar.

Bob watched Bigtimer's gestures as he gave bosslike directions to his wife, Betty, and their children, Benjamin, Jr., and Bridget, as they got out of the car. The owner of his own construction company, Ben made it big by making sure everything was done *his* way.

"Stay out of his way," Marge said.

Bob responded, "Well, Marge, he certainly has all the attributes of one who is tough, unchanging, and apparently happy the way he is now—King of the Hill! I remember how extravagant I used to be when my store was on top of the market. But things can change real fast. Bigtimer's got to understand that nothing stays the same. Things are always changing. He isn't ready for emergencies. Things can happen anytime. There have been people who were on top of the world one day, only to find themselves down and out and in the gutter the next."

"You're right, Bob," Marge encouraged. "Maybe you can pass some secrets on to him."

"It'll be difficult. Ben usually doesn't listen. Maybe I can catch him in a listening mood. He thinks he knows it all. But he doesn't."

As Bob was watching many of his cousins and their guests arrive, Marge went into the picnic shelter and brought back a couple of large paper cups filled to the brim with cool lemonade. As she handed one to Bob and sank back into the rather comfortable lawn chair next to Bob's, she remarked, "Bob, I just saw Wilma walking up the path talking to friends."

Bob replied, "That Wilma is a prize! I wish we could tell everyone Wilma and Jerry's story. It's a classic!" When Jerry died, their affairs were in good order. Wilma now had no debt, the house was paid for, and the children, Warren and Wendy, soon would begin college. She seemed very comfortable, and no one understood how she did it.

Bob knew that Wilma and her husband had done a tremendous job of planning ahead, preparing for the future, and realizing that emergencies might arise. They did this early in their life together. Now Bob was concerned that she continue this good planning as she began to prepare for her retirement. With Wilma this would be easy; she always listened. Because of what had happened years ago when her husband died, and the results of their early planning, she already knew how important it was to plan ahead financially.

As they sipped their lemonades, Bob and Marge noticed George and Gail Randolph resting comfortably under the shade of a giant old oak tree. Bob whispered, "Marge, there's George and Gail—Mr. and Mrs. *Gotittogether*." A retiree couple, George and Gail have been married for 42 years. They have worked together, played together, raised their kids together, and planned their lives together. They are inseparable. And, they retired without debt.

"There's one couple that doesn't need your help," Marge said.

"Well, don't be so sure of that, Marge," said Bob. "There are important financial issues to deal with at every age.

"For example, Marge, have they checked into having their will updated? Do they have their estate set up correctly? When they die, will their loved ones receive everything the way George and Gail want? Do they realize that they need a trust now in addition to a will?

"Have they thought about how they would pay for nursing home care if either of them ever needed it? Their entire estate could be wiped out. Have they considered nursing home protection? Yes, Marge, it's unbelievable, but even people who save their money and plan ahead, who do a great job of preparing for retirement, still can lose it all by not continuing to plan during retirement.

"I also know that they want to make sure that their grandchildren get a college education. There are still a couple of things they can do to ensure a great retirement."

"That's quite a list," said Marge.

Bob added, "They've had many years of successful planning, but there's much to do yet."

"I get the point. Seems as if there are investment things to deal with at every age," said Marge.

Finally, Bob wondered about one person not here, Grandma Greenlove.

Squinting his eyes and shading them from the sun, Bob looked over everyone who had arrived up to now, but couldn't find Grandma Greenlove. "I wonder," Bob said as though talking to himself, "about Grandma." Turning toward Marge, he asked, "What about Grandma? It's been tough for Grandma the last few years. First Grandpa died, and then Grandma got sick. She seems to be letting go and not caring anymore."

"It's been hard for her," Marge said. "She always let Grandpa do everything."

"It's been hard on everyone," said Bob. "Grandma can't take care of herself anymore."

"Yeah, but that was Grandpa's fault. He told Grandma, 'You stay at home, you raise the kids, you keep the house clean, and I will do everything else.' And he did. He bought the groceries. He wrote the checks. He made sure that they had the proper insurance. He made all the investments. He negotiated the purchase of the house, and handled all major purchases. He bought them a farm without Grandma even knowing about it, then he surprised her with it. They were so happy.

"Everything was fine until Grandpa died. Grandma was devastated. She didn't know how to do anything. She didn't even know how to write a check. Now she just sits around and cries and tries to remember where she is and constantly thinks about the old days."

Bob wondered what he could do today to help Grandma's loved ones understand what faced them, now that Grandma's health was failing. It was a tough situation and a very delicate thing to talk about, but Bob had to find a way to help the family understand that they needed to do something soon, or everyone would suffer, including Grandma.

Bob was concerned about these people he and Marge had been discussing. As he reflected, he remembered one of the basic principles his mother had often shared with him:

ENJOY TODAY, BUT PLAN FOR TOMORROW, FOR VERY SHORTLY,
TOMORROW WILL BE TODAY.

How right Mom was, Bob thought. The years fly by. The children grow up, marry, and live their own lives. All of a sudden it's time to retire, either because we have to or because we want to. In many companies today, people are being let go before their normal retirement age. They lose their benefits and have to look for a job at an age when many companies prefer to hire younger people.

It is so important to save money. There are so many emergencies that can arise, but most people think these will never happen to them. When they do, and there is no money, it is a devastating situation. Yes, as Bob looked over the arriving family members, he remembered his mother's words.

She told him that most people outlive their money. Most people feel that by the time they reach their late 60s or early 70s, they have only a few years left. They say it is best to spend their money and not worry about the future. After all, they say, they are not going to be around too much longer.

However, one morning these people wake up and find out that they are still alive, but their savings are dead; their money is gone. They didn't live too long. They simply outlived their money. There is nothing a person can do once his or her money is gone. Social Security won't cover all the bills. The company benefit package won't pay all the expenses. People are forced to lower their living standards.

Financial security results from a combination of systematic savings throughout one's lifetime, planning ahead financially to meet emergencies, and providing for a fulfilling retirement. Many people who do not plan and save become broke sometime during retirement.

But Bob knew that if he followed Great-Grandfather Phillip Prosperity's secrets of saving, his money would grow, and there would always be plenty. He would never outlive his money, and after he died, his estate would go to his loved ones exactly as he had planned—to whom, in what way, and when.

"Mom and Great-Grandfather Phillip knew what they were talking about," Bob said to Marge. "So many peole today think that winning the lottery is the answer. They want that instant gratification. That's so foolish. Your chances of winning a lottery, Marge, are about the same as your chances of catching a fish in the Pacific Ocean off the coast of California while you're standing in New York City throwing the fishing line out. It's almost impossible."

"What are you talking about?" said Marge.

"Everyone needs to realize how terribly important it is to start saving as early in life as possible. How we save and where we invest will determine how long it takes us to become million-aires. I remember Mom's words: 'Enjoy living every moment, while planning for tomorrow.' I hate to see others make the same mistakes over and over again." He paused.

"The road to financial success starts with making this deci-sion: 'Yes, I will commit myself to saving today and staying out of debt forever.' "

Bob hoped he could have some influence on the family today. He was ready to share his Secrets to Becoming a Millionaire. If he could share his secrets with everyone today, maybe just maybe, everyone could become a millionaire.

And who knows, there might even be someone else at the picnic whom he had not seen yet who also wanted to become a millionaire. It was up to Bob to carry on the legacy. He was ready. It was a great day, and he hoped that it was going to be an even greater and more successful day than he could imagine. He was ready to share the family's secrets. He hoped everyone else was ready to learn.

2

Sam and Sally Save-It: The Value of Systematic Saving

ON A SOCCER FIELD NEAR THE PAVILION, two children played a one-on-one match.

Sarah Save-It and Darin Debt, both 10, skirmished as they both kicked at the ball, fighting for control. The ball squirted loose, and they ran after it. Sarah reached it first. Putting her foot on top of the ball, she skillfully rolled it backwards, faked Darin, and sped off for the goal. With a clear shot, she pulled her right foot back, pivoted on her left, and kicked a straight and strong shot into the net.

"That's best of three. I win," said Sarah, as she ran to the goal to retrieve the ball. She was a healthy-looking young girl, with long, thick, reddish-brown hair that glistened in the sun. Her fair skin was dotted with freckles. She was neatly attired in a pink T-shirt, turquoise shorts, and last year's red runabout shoes.

"Come on, best of five," retorted Darin. He was slightly over-weight and had a bit of a tattered look, although his shirt and shorts were decorated with the logo of a popular name brand. The shirt had some stains, and the shorts had a small rip in them. His sneakers were untied and worn-looking, masking their origi-nal $100-plus name-brand price.

"Okay, best of five," said Sarah, passing the ball to Darin. "My goal, so you start."

Sarah and Darin always felt as though they were best friends in many ways, even though they saw each other only once or twice a year. But their parents led opposite lifestyles, especially when it came to how they managed their money.

Sarah's parents were the Save-Its, who carefully saved and invested their money. They bought only what they needed. They never bought things on a whim. They always paid for their purchases immediately.

Darin's parents, the Debts, bought everything on credit. They were compulsive buyers. Whatever looked good, they bought right away. They didn't care whether they needed it or what it cost. Their attitude was, "If it gives us pleasure now, let's buy it. Who cares about tomorrow?"

Last year, Bob had worked with the Save-Its. He had helped them set up a savings program. He had encouraged Sarah to start her own savings account.

This year, Bob hoped to talk with the Debts. He was concerned that they were headed for financial trouble. Bob was sure they had already put themselves in a deep hole of debt. Before they knew it, they might be so deep in debt that they would never be able to get out. In the long run, they might never really achieve financial independence.

Looking at Sarah, Darin moved the ball between his feet, attempting to fake her. He went to the right, attempting to go around Sarah. She picked her moment, then kicked the ball from between Darin's feet. She took control, then started for the goal, where she scored again.

"How'd you get so good at this?" asked Darin. "Last year I beat you all the time."

Sarah explained, "Well, last fall I joined a soccer team. I learned how to play. I practiced every day. I got better and better as I practiced. I still practice a little almost every day, and I'm still improving. Look, I beat you!"

"Well, you were just lucky," said Darin.

"No, my dad said if I practice a little every day, I will get real good. Dad taught me to, as he says, 'Make your plans, set your goals, and then practice a little every day to reach your goals.' And it worked."

Darin replied, "We don't do things that way at my house. My dad likes to jump into something in a big way all at one time."

Sarah asked, "Like you were going to learn soccer last summer. Weren't you going to Pelé's soccer camp?"

"Yes, well, I did sign up for it. I went a couple of times, but I decided I didn't like it. The coaches were too bossy. They made us work really hard. Like we were in the Army or something."

"So you quit because you didn't want to work at it."

"Not their way. It wasn't any fun. Just work."

"That camp cost a lot of money, didn't it?"

"I don't know. I guess about $500. My mom and dad paid for it." Darin reached into his pocket. He asked Sarah, "Want some candy?" Out of a seemingly bottomless pocket, he pulled out a smashed chocolate bar, a sucker, a squashed pack of chewing gum, and a pack of jelly beans.

"No thanks, Darin, I just had an apple."

"An apple! Well, okay, but on a picnic I prefer jelly beans!"

"Darin, you always have so much candy. Where do you get it all?"

"Oh, I go buy candy every week when I get my allowance," Darin replied.

"Do you *save* any of your allowance?" Sarah asked.

"Save it? Why should I save it? I'm just a kid! We're both kids. We don't need to save money now. Whatever I want, my parents get for me. I can use my allowance for anything I want—candy, comic books, video games. All I have to do is name it and I get it."

"But Darin, saving is just like soccer."

"How so?"

"Last year, you were better than I was. But I practiced a little every day, and I got to where I can beat you. By putting in a little time and effort every day, I started getting better. I started my savings account the same way. Last year, Uncle Bob talked with me and Mom and Dad about saving money. Ever since then, I've been saving a little money every day. After a year now, I have a lot of money."

"Good for you, Sarah," said Darin with a hint of sarcasm. "How do you save, anyway? Do you have a piggy bank by your bed?"

"No, it's a lot neater than that," Sarah answered. "I have my own savings account at the bank. I go to the bank every couple of weeks, and I add money to my account."

Darin was not impressed. His thoughts turned to his newest toy. "Hey, I've got something I want to show you. It's in my backpack."

They ran to the edge of the field behind the left goal post, where his backpack lay. Sarah held the ball.

"You've got to see this," he said. He reached in a pulled out a 16-bit SuperFAST, the hottest new video system of the season.

"This is the most awesome video game you can get," he said.

"I've seen that advertised on TV," said Sarah. "Do you have Franklin the Frog? That's a cool game."

"Yeah, it came with the system. I also have Ancient Warriors. Wanna play it?"

"Sure." After a few rounds of Franklin the Frog and Ancient Warriors, Sarah's mind returned to the subject of money.

"Darin, did your mom and dad buy this for you?"

He replied, "Yeah. Neat, huh? I just kept telling them I wanted it. Finally, they bought it. I'm supposed to pay them back from my allowance."

"How long will it take you to pay them back?"

"I don't know. I think they forgot about it. Maybe I can get away without paying."

"So they bought it just because you said you wanted it?"

"Yeah."

"And you don't think they'll make you pay for it?"

"Right."

Sarah handed back the SuperFAST. "Darin, all you ever do is spend, spend, spend. You've got to start thinking about saving your money. Next year, a new video system will come out. The SuperFAST will be out of date. Then I guess they'll have a new one called UltraFAST. Everyone will want one. You won't be able to get $25 for your SuperFAST at a garage sale."

"That's a long way off. Besides, my mom and dad have lots of money. We buy whatever we want."

"*Where* do your mom and dad get all that money?" Sarah queried.

"I don't know. They just buy things. If they like it, they buy it. I do, too."

"Darin, have you ever talked to Uncle Bob? He really knows a lot about money. Last year at the picnic, he talked to me and to my mom and dad for a long time. He gave me the idea of having my own savings account. He's really fun to talk to. He says that saving money is fun. It can make you rich. That will make you happy."

Sarah paused for a moment and got excited. She said, "You know what the best thing is that Uncle Bob told me?"

"No, what?"

"I could be a millionaire when I grow up!"

"How? Are you going to be a movie star?"

"No! Uncle Bob showed me how I could be a millionaire. I'm not talking just about working or having a career. I'm going to be a millionaire by saving my money and one day investing it—whatever that means! Who knows how much money I'll have? But I'm going to be a millionaire just from saving my money. I've already started with my own savings account.

"It's great to save," Sarah continued. "Mom and Dad say I'm learning good habits about money. When I get older, I'll be a millionaire a lot sooner than any of my friends. If we talk to Uncle Bob, he can show you, too. Don't you want to be a millionaire?"

"Yeah! I want to be a millionaire! I want to be a *billionaire*! I want to have my own airplane, too," Darin chimed in. Now, he was excited, too.

She pulled on his arm, and pointed to the picnic pavilion. "Look, there's Uncle Bob. Let's go talk to him!"

$ $ $ $ $ $

Bob was sitting on top of a picnic table under the pavilion.

"Uncle Bob, Uncle Bob," cried Sarah. She ran up to him and gave him a big hug. Darin was alongside.

"Hi, kids."

"Uncle Bob, do you know how much I have in my savings account?" asked Sarah.

"How much?"

"$500."

"That's terrific!"

"I did just what you told me to do. I save some dimes and quarters every day. Mom and Dad helped me start a bank account. My money is growing. It's up to $500. Aren't you proud of me?"

"My goodness, Sarah. I'm *so* proud of you. That's just terrific."

"Now I go to the bank with Mom and Dad, and we check to see how much money we've got. I see my name on the computer screen with my own account number."

"Great!"

"Oh, it's so much fun, Uncle Bob. It's fun to save money. Just like you told me."

"Congratulations!"

"If I do exactly what you tell me to do, I'll become a millionaire, won't I, Uncle Bob?"

"You sure will, Sarah. If you keep saving money as you're doing, you'll be a millionaire some day."

"Uncle Bob, can you tell Darin how to be a millionaire?" She jumped on top of the table and took a seat next to Bob.

Darin echoed, "Uncle Bob, can I become a millionaire?"

"Sure you can," said Uncle Bob.

"When do I start?"

"Right now. Have a seat." Darin climbed onto the table and sat next to Bob, on the other side from Sarah. Bob put his arms around both of them.

"How do you become a millionaire?" asked Bob. "Very simple. You start saving money."

"What is saving? How do I do it?" asked Darin.

"Let me explain. First, Darin, how much allowance do you get?"

"$10 a week."

"Do you do anything else to make money? Sell lemonade? Mow lawns? Clean your room?"

"No."

Sarah jumped in. "Darin, you'd have even more money if you worked."

"Never thought of it," he replied. "Mom and Dad take care of everything. Why should I?"

Bob said, "Let's get back to saving. Darin, how much do you save now?"

"Nothing. Why?"

"You don't have any money left over from your allowance?"

"No, I spend it all on toys, candy, and things."

"Darin, listen up. The sooner you start saving your money, the sooner you are going to become a millionaire. Don't you want to become a millionaire?"

"Oh, yes, Uncle Bob. But before that I've got to get more video games. Look at my SuperFAST." He pulled it out of his backpack and showed Bob.

"That's nice," Bob said.

"I want to have fun doing all kinds of things. I just want to play all day long. You know, I'm just a kid. I want my own VCR. I want a cordless telephone. I want a Giants jacket. I want all of those things, and I want them now. I don't like to wait for things. Why should I wait? Isn't that the way everybody is, Uncle Bob? Mom and Dad buy whatever they want. They don't wait."

"Maybe that's the way it is in your house now. That's because your mom and dad take care of everything. But your mom and dad aren't always going to take care of you."

"You know what, Uncle Bob?"

"What?"

"When I grow up, I'm going to be rich."

"I hope so."

"I'm going to have my own airplane. I'll have a big house and a Ferrari."

"How are you going to get those things?" asked Bob.

"I'm going to play for the Los Angeles Dodgers."

"You have to be really good to play in the pros, you know," chided Sarah. "How are you going to get good enough at baseball? You wouldn't even finish soccer camp."

"Yes, but that's different."

"Darin," Uncle Bob continued, "no matter what you do, you'll never be rich unless you save your money. Ballplayers have made millions, only to blow it all. Some athletes end up poorer than they were when they started. I don't want that to happen to you."

"Me neither. How can I stay out of that mess?"

"By saving. Buy only what you need and only what you can afford. Let me show you how to save *and* get those things you want. How old do you want to be when you have your own airplane?"

"When I'm 25."

"If you are going to have your airplane when you are 25, you'd better start saving your money now."

"Now? Why so soon?"

"It will take that long for it to grow. Did you think you could just wake up when you're 25 and have that airplane?"

"Oh, Uncle Bob, I never thought about that."

"Well, I can understand that, Darin. Most young people don't think about saving money. Would you like me to let you in on a little secret?"

"Yeah, Uncle Bob, tell me."

"Yeah, Uncle Bob, tell Darin. Tell both of us," said Sarah.

"Well, the secret is this. Most people don't think about saving money until it's too late. They work all day, they pay the bills, they take care of all the expenses, they try to have a nice life, they try to make sure their children have a good education, and then, all of a sudden, they are at an age when they are getting ready to retire. They were so busy with other things, they never thought about saving money for themselves."

"People the age of my grandma and grandpa?" asked Darin.

"Yes."

"Gosh, Uncle Bob, what happens to those people?"

"Well, either they have to keep working or they have to change the way they live their lives."

"How would they change?"

"They can't live the same lifestyle as they did when they were working. There are a lot of people like that."

Bob paused for a moment. "You see, Darin, if you save your money, you're going to get rich. You're going to become a millionaire. When you retire, you'll still be able to have your airplane and all your nice things."

"You mean, Uncle Bob, I'll be able to have nice things when I grow up if I don't buy stuff and things today?"

"Yes. Basically that's right. You don't have to stop buying your candy and toys entirely. Just don't buy as much. Save the rest of your money. You can do that, can't you?"

"Yeah, I guess I can. But there are so many new games I want. And I always need something to snack on."

"Well, Darin, you'll just have to choose. Do you want to spend all your money on stuff and things? Or do you want to save money for that airplane?"

"Uncle Bob, I want that airplane."

"So, start saving today. Candy and gum get eaten, VCRs eventually break, and jackets get worn out. But saving money and investing it wisely will make you into a millionaire!"

"Investing? What's that?"

"Investing is what you do with your money after you save it."

"You don't just keep it in your piggy bank?"

"No, you find places to put your money. Places where your money will *make money* for you. That's right, your money will earn money for you apart from the money you will make by working or asking your mom and dad for it."

"Is that like interest?" asked Sarah.

"Precisely," said Uncle Bob.

"What's interest?" asked Darin.

Bob answered, "Interest is one way you can make money with your money. You get interest when you put your money in a bank account. You let the bank keep your money, and the bank pays you. It gives you back more money than you gave it. In the meantime, you don't have to stay at the bank and watch it use your money. You can go to school; you can play; you can do whatever you want. Your money keeps growing and growing."

"Just by putting some of my allowance in the bank?"

"That's right."

"Gee, that's neat, Uncle Bob. Really neat!"

"There are other ways you can invest, too."

"Tell me more. I'm getting excited about saving money. Wow, this is totally awesome, Sarah. Saving money is fun!"

"Let's say you buy a lawn mower. You could use it to mow lawns during the summer. You know what? If you spent $100 for a lawn mower, you probably would make more than $100 during the summer by mowing lawns."

"So I would make more than I spent."

"Right! Here's another idea. Do you like baseball cards?"

"Do I like baseball cards? I've got baseball cards, football cards, basketball cards, hockey cards. I've got all kinds of cards. I think they're neat. I've spent a lot of my allowance on cards."

Bob explained, "You could buy collector baseball cards and sell them to your friends. Buy only good players like Mickey Mantle, Ted Williams, Stan Musial—the Hall of Famers."

"I've got some good ones already," said Darin. "I have George Brett's rookie card. I've also got Nolan Ryan and Dwight Gooden. And Willie Mays and Sandy Koufax."

"Sounds as if you have a good collection already."

"I've gone out and bought all the best players in every sport. In hockey, I've got Wayne Gretzky and Mario Lemieux. In basketball, I have Michael Jordan and Larry Bird. In football, it's Joe Montana."

"Darin, those cards could be good investments. You made a good investment and didn't know it. You probably just bought your cards for fun."

"I did."

"Keep buying, but just the good players. Look for cards that will increase in value. Don't let yourself get stuck with dogs."

"Do they have dog cards now?"

Bob laughed. "No, I don't mean 'dogs' like your pet. A dog is a card that no one wants, one you can't sell."

"I'm wasting money if I buy a dog."

"Right. Be selective in the cards that you buy. Then make sure that you sell the cards for more than you paid for them."

"That really sounds good. But you know, Uncle Bob, I still like my candy and everything now. Do I really have to save money and wait for it to grow?"

"It will never grow if you don't save. What better time than right now to start saving? Do you really want that airplane when you're 25?"

"Yeah, I do, Uncle Bob."

"Then you'd better start saving something now. You don't have to save a lot, just something."

"You mean I can save nickels and quarters?"

"That's how I got started," Sarah chimed in. "I put them all in my coin bank. When that was filled, I took them to the real bank and started my savings account."

"Okay, Sarah. Okay, Uncle Bob. I'll do it. I'm going to start saving tomorrow."

"No, Darin, you've got to start today."

"How can I do that?" Darin asked.

"Darin, do you have any money with you now?" asked Bob.

"Yes." He reached into his pocket and pulled out a handful of change. "Let's see . . . 87 cents."

"Okay. Darin, why don't you take that quarter and put it into your other pocket?"

"All right." He did as Bob said.

"That's the start of your savings account."

"So this is how I'll get rich?"

"Right. Do you miss that quarter yet?"

"No, not really. I never count how much I have. I just spend what I have."

"That's the point. When you first get your allowance, set aside your saving money. That way, you won't miss it. By the way, when you get home, do you have some place to keep the money you save?"

"Yes. I'll get an empty jar."

"It takes time to get used to saving. Sometimes you may forget. But just keep doing it. Save. As you save more and more, you'll start to have fun saving."

"Okay, Uncle Bob, I'll do it!"

"Make sure you watch your money grow. You'll be a millionaire."

Sarah jumped in, "Uncle Bob, Uncle Bob. Tell us the story about Willie Wolf and the animals. That'll show Darin how to save and why he should save."

Darin asked, "What's the big deal about Willie Wolf?"

Uncle Bob explained, "Darin, it's a story, a real neat story about animals that live in Fortune Forest."

"Where's Fortune Forest?"

"It's not very far from here. And the animals are kind of like people."

"What do you mean, Uncle Bob?"

"Well, some of these animals know exactly what they want out of life and go and get it. Others don't have any idea what's going on and just kind of exist from day to day. They have no idea what their purpose in life is. Some of the animals are leaders, some are followers, and some are just lost. Some of the animals are stubborn and won't listen to anyone. Those are some of the reasons why I say the animals are like people."

Sarah added, "It's the best story. When you hear Uncle Bob's story about the animals, you'll know exactly why you need to save money."

Darin, looking at Sarah, said, "How could an animal story show me how to save money?"

"You'll see, Darin. Please, Uncle Bob, please."

"Not just yet. I'll tell you the story later."

"You will tell it today?" asked Sarah in a firm voice.

"Yes, yes," Bob agreed. "Why don't you two run over to the basketball court and shoot some baskets? Or, better yet, does anyone want to play some horseshoes?"

Darin and Sarah looked over to the basketball court on the other side of the soccer field.

"Oh, look, there's Jennifer and Jason." "Come on, Sarah, let's go play with them."

Darin and Sarah got down from the picnic bench.

"Thanks, Uncle Bob," said Darin.

"Thanks, Uncle Bob," said Sarah, smiling.

"I'll beat you there!" yelled Darin.

The two raced across the field, leaving a cloud of dust behind. Bob was pleased as he watched them run. He smiled when he saw Darin pat his right pants pocket, which held the quarter that would be the start of Darin's savings account and million-dollar fortune.

$ $ $ $ $ $

As Bob watched Sarah and Darin run to the basketball court, Sarah's parents, Sam and Sally Save-It, walked up behind him.

Sally greeted Bob.

"Oh, Sally, Sam, how are you?"

Sally asked, "Was Sarah bugging you about her savings account? That's all we ever hear about. She's so proud."

"She's doing great. *You* should be proud," Bob said. "You're giving her a great start."

"You should hear her. She tells everyone she's going to be a millionaire."

Bob said, laughing, "Just now she was working on Darin to start a savings account. She wants him to stop spending so much money on candy and video games."

Sally explained, "Darin's just like his parents, Dan and Denise. They just spend, spend, spend. They buy whatever they feel like buying. It doesn't make any difference whether they really need it. I don't know *where* they get the money. Did you see that jewelry that Denise is wearing?"

"Yes," Bob answered. "It must be quite expensive."

"I'm really worried about them," Sally continued. "Could you talk to them today, Bob?"

"I'm planning to. Incidentally, thanks for the card you sent. I enjoyed our talk last year also!"

Sam spoke up. "Bob, I just want to tell you how much we appreciate what you did for us last year. We've really gotten control of our finances. Our company business is down, and I didn't get a raise this year. But do you know, it *feels* as if we have more money than we ever had before? We're putting our money where we want to put it. We don't spend aimlessly anymore."

Sally added, "It feels good to know that we are preparing

now for Sarah's college education. And for our retirement, too. I know that's many years away. But you showed us how to save money early in life. It puts time on our side."

"Yes," Sam concurred. "Time is so valuable. You showed us the importance of time and how compounding works. Wow, we are going to be millionaires some day. It may not be soon, but there's no doubt in our minds that it's going to happen. It's so much easier to save when you don't have any debt and you really have a handle on your expenses."

"Gosh, Bob, how do other people make it? I can't believe we didn't know what our expenses were," said Sally.

"Yes, Sally. Most people don't know what their expenses are. That's why my Cookie Jar Expense Checklist really makes sense."

"It made a lot of sense for Sam and me, Bob. I'm sure it will make sense for others, too," Sally said.

"It's a lot easier to save, now that we are getting out of debt and know what our expenses really are," Sam said, reaching over and touching Sally's shoulder.

"Good deal," Bob agreed.

"The first thing you told us to do was to get our finances in order. We did a complete analysis of our income and expenses," Sally remarked.

"We were shocked," confessed Sam. "We had no idea that we were spending as much money as we were."

"And once we found out *where* we were spending some of that money, we were shocked," Sally added. "Then you told us to get out of debt as quickly as possible."

"Bob, Sally and I had no idea we had so much debt," said Sam. "We totaled up the amount of money we owed. It was staggering. The car, my college loan, the mortgage on the house, the boat that we bought three years ago. We owed a lot of money. We had bought living room furniture last year, right before the picnic."

"We didn't think we would ever get out of debt, Bob," Sally said and sighed.

Sam went on, "We sold the boat to clear up that debt. It gave us a little extra money on top. Then we used that each month to pay off my college loan faster. We also added a small amount to the principal each month to get the living room furniture paid off quicker. Last month, we paid off the college loan. In four more months, the furniture will be completely paid off, and it will be ours."

"You know, Bob, what the most important thing is?" asked Sally.

"No. What is it?"

"It's knowing that we can go to sleep at night and not have to worry about our debt. We had no idea that we had a black cloud hanging over us. It was a debt cloud. It was stopping us from being able to reach our financial goals, and we didn't even know about it. Now we go to bed at night and don't worry about the debt. It's as you told us, Bob. A person has to have a good Sleep Syndrome. Your Sleep Syndrome idea sure works out great for us. If we were worrying about something in our finances, we couldn't sleep at night. We'd toss and turn, roll and kick, and talk about it and discuss it and even argue about it sometimes, but now that our debt is almost completely gone, we sleep very soundly."

"That's right," Bob agreed. "Sleep Syndrome is the only way to go—You have to be able to go to bed at night and not worry about your investments. Some people say, 'Well, I've got to make more money on my investments.' They go into something that is high risk, totally out of their Sleep Syndrome. And what do they do? It doesn't make any difference whether they are making money or losing money, they worry about it all the time. They watch the newspaper; they follow the ups and downs in the market; they think about it all night long. That's terrible. That's not the way to have fun with your money. If you're in an investment that doesn't allow you to sleep well at night, get out now."

Sam seemed relaxed. "We sleep well at night. We choose investments we are comfortable with."

Sally asked, "Bob, do you know what meant the most to us?"

"No. What was it, Sally?"

Sam jumped in. "Sally, let me tell Bob. Paying ourselves first, that was the thing. We paid ourselves first, the way you told us to. Before, when one of our paychecks came, we turned around and paid all the bills. By the end of the month there was nothing left to save. Then all of a sudden, the beginning of the month was here again. There were more bills, and there went the paycheck again. There was no money left over for us. No money left over to save. It just flew out the door to pay all the bills, and we were still getting deeper in debt. We weren't going anyplace financially.

"Then after we talked to you at the picnic last year, we decided to pay ourselves first, just as you said. We followed your instructions and we opened up another checking account. When a paycheck came in, we took 10% a month right out of it and wrote a check into our second checking account. Then we paid all the bills and expenses with the balance of the money. We started sleeping soundly at night. Our money was growing."

Sally continued, "If there were still some bills we couldn't pay, we looked into our expenses carefully. We found places where we had spent some money that month that we really didn't need to spend. Following it on a day-by-day basis really made sense. Your Cookie Jar Expense Checklist worked out great for us."

Sam went on, "You know, Bob, it's really easy to plan ahead. You told us to start planning ahead for college education for Sarah and Shawn, and to have funds set aside for emergencies, and to save for retirement. It's easy when you start doing it. If we think about it all the time, it's really fun."

"I know," Bob responded. "It really is fun, isn't it? Saving money, making money, investing money, and knowing all about your money are really fun. It's exciting. I'm so happy for your family.

"Sally and Sam, I want you to be buddies with your money. Think about it all the time. I don't mean be a miser. I don't mean make money the focus of your life. But I do want you to always think about what you're spending your money on. Where is the best place to put your money? What do you really need to spend?

How much can you save? What things can you do without today so you can have more happiness and fun tomorrow?"

Sally said, "One thing I was wondering about, Uncle Bob, was what you said about using other people's money to help us retire."

"Yes. There are three savings systems you can use in retirement. One is your individual savings. Another is Social Security. The third is one many people aren't aware of. That's your company benefits package."

"I know all about that," Sam explained.

"Good for you."

"There are some great programs I hadn't known about. Besides the hospitalization plan, our company has a savings program. It lets us invest up to 15% of our income. The company matches up to half of whatever I invest. It's like a gift, Bob. They give us money for saving. And all of the money accumulates on a tax-deferred basis. We can even borrow some of it in the future for emergencies or for Sarah's education."

"It's like having other people save money for us," Sally answered her own question.

Sarah returned from the basketball game and listened as Bob, Sam, and Sally continued their conversation.

Sam was talking. "Another thing that has really helped was getting rid of the credit cards."

"We had a clipping party," Sarah interjected. "We cut them all in half and threw them away."

Sam said, "Yes, we tore them all up. Except for one, for emergencies. We normally pay cash. Once in a while, if something is on sale and the store offers 90 days same as cash, then maybe we'll use our credit card. But we always pay the credit card bill before interest is charged. No debt, no bills. We sleep soundly at night; we have a great Sleep Syndrome. What a great feeling!"

"I know, Daddy. The only time we buy anything now is when we really need it. You always say to pay for it with money, not plastic."

"That's right, honey, just as Uncle Bob explained. Don't buy anything that you can't afford to pay for today. If you can't pay for it today, you don't need it now."

"That's right," Bob concluded. "By staying out of debt, knowing what your expenses are, saving every penny you can, and planning ahead, you're following the right path to financial success and becoming millionaires."

The Save-Its continued to thank Bob for his help.

Sam appeared pleased. "Bob, we have gotten to where it's fun each month to do our Cookie Jar Expense Checklist and update our financial profile."

"If everyone knew about the Cookie Jar Expense Checklist and how to do a financial profile, no one would have to worry about what their expenses were, or go into debt, or have to guess how much they were spending each month. They'd be in complete control of their financial destiny," agreed Bob.

Sally said, "Just think, Bob, Sam and I know all this because we told you we were afraid to invest."

"It will pay big dividends for you down the line," Bob replied.

"It already has. We are so happy knowing that we will be able to send Sarah and Shawn to college, and meet emergencies, and have a great retirement."

With Sam and Sally happy with their finances, Bob sensed that this might be his opportunity for horseshoes. He asked, "Can I interest anyone in a game of horseshoes? How about it, Sally? How about it, Sam?"

"Um, well, . . . no, I don't think so, not right now," Sam stammered. "We need to get the volleyball net set up." He looked at Sally. "Right, Sally?"

"Oh, yes, uh, that's right," she replied.

"Can I help?" Bob asked.

Sam replied, "Sounds like a great idea, Bob, but I'm sure there are some other people you should talk to today."

"Yes, you're right. I'll leave you alone to struggle with this by yourself."

Bob turned and started walking toward the softball diamond.

Sarah yelled out, "See you later, Uncle Bob." She gave him a thumbs up sign.

Bob turned and smiled and stuck his thumbs up in the air, repeating Sarah's gesture.

3

Dan and Denise Debt: Things Don't Buy Happiness

DAN AND DENISE DEBT walked by the picnic shelter on their way to warm up for volleyball. They noticed families bringing food and leaving it on the tables.

"Dan, we need to get the soft drinks out of the car," said Denise.

"Yeah, people will start wanting some."

"What's a picnic without soft drinks?"

"You did pack them, didn't you?" Dan asked.

Denise halted and turned to Dan. "What? I thought you did."

He looked at her. "Well, I thought you did."

She looked up and away, and gritted her teeth. Shaking her head, she said, "Another mess! Here we go again!"

Denise was an attractive, slightly overweight woman in her early-30s. She had brown hair, permed and almost shoulder length. She wore a knit shirt sporting a designer logo, and her athletic shoes were an exclusive brand. She wore a gold necklace and earrings. Her wedding ring carried a huge diamond.

Dan was a six-footer who looked as though he had been athletic in his earlier years, before his waist grew. He wore a Chicago Cubs jersey and shorts.

He responded to Denise, "Don't blame me. You were bringing the drinks. You got the invitation. You talked to the Hechts."

Denise defended herself. "All I can go by is what you told me. Remember, we talked about this three weeks ago."

"I don't remember."

"You know I called you at the office that day. You said you would get the soft drinks. And ice and a cooler. And cups."

"I thought you said you were getting all that," he insisted.

"Here we go, running around all the time. You're just too busy. You never remember anything," she argued.

"Yes, we're on the go. We've had something every night for the past two weeks. You've just got us booked to the hilt. You try to be in so many places, you forget things. You did promise to take care of everything for this picnic."

Their 16-year-old daughter, Darlene, had been just behind them, hoping to play volleyball. She heard the bickering and interrupted, "Mom, Dad! Will you knock it off?"

"Darlene, you stay out of this," said Denise. "If you want us to get you that Mazda Miata convertible, you'll have to be on your best behavior."

"Yes, Mom," agreed Darlene as she obediently walked away.

Looking back at Dan, Denise said, "This is terrible. A picnic with no soda. What's a picnic without soda? Why did you screw this up?"

"I didn't screw up. You screwed up."

"You never take responsibility for anything."

"All right, enough!" Dan commanded. "We don't have to sit here and stew about it. Let's just take care of the problem. Let's go buy soda."

"And cups and a cooler and ice," added Denise. "Did you bring any credit cards?"

"Of course I did. All of them!" As he said this, he pulled out his wallet to show his wife that he had all his cards with him. They were his security blanket. Without his credit cards, he would be in dire straits. He opened his wallet and unfolded a two-foot-long accordion strand of clear plastic sleeves bulging with credit cards—bank cards, affinity cards, ATM cards, department store cards, hardware store cards, specialty store cards, telephone cards, and more. They came in all colors, and they all had heavy interest charges. He waved these at his wife. "Well, let's go!"

"One of us should stay here," countered Denise. "I'll stay; you go."

"Okay, fine."

"But you'd better get the right things. *Diet* soda, and get a mix of flavors."

"You and your diet soda. Do you know how many chemicals that stuff has?"

"It's better for you," countered Denise.

"Not everyone likes diet soda, Denise," Dan said.

"Just get it. And be sure to get cups. Good cups. Don't get cheap ones that fall apart."

Dan got into their black Jaguar sedan. The tires squealed defiantly as he sped away.

$ $ $ $ $ $

"Dan and Denise are the American Dream . . . and nightmare," Bob remarked to Marge, who was sitting beside him at the picnic table not far from where Denise and Dan had staged their little one-act episode.

"You know, Bob," Marge said as she fumbled through the stack of papers on her lap, "when Denise and Dan returned their slip saying they definitely were coming with the children, they wrote a short note . . . let me find it . . . Ah, here it is. Just below where they mention that there will be four of them and that they've already made accommodations for the night, Denise wrote:

Please tell Bob that we're all coming and look forward to another visit with him like last year. Actually we are doing fantastically well in the money game. We happen to have loads of credit and are living very well! But we do like Bob and anticipate a good chat with him and you.

Love, Denise"

They were the "smiling" consumers we see in magazine and television advertising. Consumption was their favorite activity. They had all the outward signs of success—a nice home, new luxury cars, and good clothes. But it was all a paper castle, built on a mountain of debt.

They earned good incomes: she as a systems analyst for the telephone company, he as a vice president with a large pharmaceutical company. They made lots of money and had a lavish lifestyle to show for it.

They lived in an elegant $600,000 suburban home they had built four years ago. The colonial brick, two and one-half story house had five bedrooms and a lavish two-level living room with a double fireplace and huge picture windows. It had a three-car garage and a circular driveway in front. In the basement, there was a game room and a sauna. The master bathroom was as large as three normal bedrooms, with two sinks, an oversize bathtub, a shower, and a Jacuzzi. The children's rooms were packed with toys, video games, and the latest hi-tech equipment.

Dan drove the Jaguar, Denise the Jeep Grand Cherokee. They also had a boat at their condo on the lake.

All of this luxury had been garnered with a minimum of cash. They put the minimum down on the house, and they leased the cars.

Dan prided himself on his ability to manipulate money. He had taught himself about tax shelters and a variety of devices to stretch his cash. He preferred to buy tax shelters rather than other investments, even though others might give better yields.

His personal finances were a bomb ready to explode. Dan and Denise surrounded themselves with expensive things, all acquired with little or no cash out of pocket. Everything was bought on credit.

Their philosophy was, "Let's live for now. Have fun today. Tomorrow will take care of itself. Why wait until we're too old to enjoy these things?"

While they consumed at a fast pace, Dan and Denise also ran a fast pace in their daily lives. They worked long hours, then rushed to pick up the kids from the neighbors. From there they hurried them to soccer practice and dance lessons. Dan and Denise didn't spend much time with each other, and the entire family was seldom home together.

They were smart people, but appeared scatterbrained from living the good life they couldn't afford. They were always rushing from one place or thing to another. They bought on impulse and spent without thought. Someone was always forgetting something or someone.

Dan and Denise were like habitual smokers or hard drinkers. They had to buy something every day and charge it! They didn't realize how much debt they were in and how deep this financial hole was growing. Bob had to try to do something today to stop them from plummeting into a pit of debt where their only companions would be collection agencies and bankruptcy lawyers.

$$\$ \$ \$ \$ \$ \$$$

Just after Dan drove away to the store, Bob walked over to greet Denise, leaving Marge in charge of arranging the serving area in the pavilion.

"Hi, Denise! You certainly look great! Marge and I did appreciate the note you put in your RSVP." With that, both Bob and Denise sat down on the comfortable lawn not far from the pavilion. "And so, Denise, how's everything getting along?"

"Oh, it's the same old thing, Bob. We're always bickering about something. I tell him something, he forgets. He says he tells me something. I don't remember. We always go our own way; we never seem to get together. We're always hassling about something." And with that she reached out and picked one of the many beautiful yellow dandelions that dotted much of the area.

Bob responded, "It sounds as if everything you do is a cri-sis."

"Bob, what's wrong with us? I don't understand it. Every-thing turns into a mess."

"You and Dan seem to be going in different directions. You're so busy; you have so much going on. Do you ever communicate?" asked Bob.

"No, we don't. We don't have much family time, and we don't have much time as a couple. But that's just because of where we are in life. Things will change as the kids get older. Besides, we have a nice home, we live well, we don't have any worries. Anytime we need something, we go out and buy it."

Bob replied, "Denise, there are many people who don't have the worries and frustrations that you and Dan have. They're at the same period in their lives as you are. You aren't unorganized and unable to communicate with each other because of your time of life. It's probably because the two of you don't have any direc-tion and don't focus on where you are today and where you want to be tomorrow."

Denise replied, "I don't really know what you mean, Bob. We really do have everything we want."

"Yes, but do you own those things? Are they really yours?"

"What do you mean, Bob?"

"What if someone knocked on your door today, and told you that you would have to pay back all the money you owe? If you couldn't pay it back, you would have to give back your house, your jewelry, your furniture, and some of the other nice things that you own!"

"Oh, that won't happen, Bob."

"It might happen, Denise, if you continue to buy without actually paying for it in cash. Denise, I know you and Dan well enough to know that you spend a lot. You have two very expen-sive cars, a big house, a summer house, and a time-sharing unit. When do you find time to enjoy it all?"

"Oh, we do. Not as much as we'd like, but it's nice just to know it's there."

"You and Dan make good money. But can you really afford all this?" asked Bob.

"We just get a loan or charge it. We'll pay it off later."

"But that's the problem, Denise. When are you going to pay it off? And what are you going to pay it off with? What happens if you or Dan loses your job? What happens if you become sick or disabled, or what if one of you dies? Who's going to pay the bills then? Who's going to bring in the money? Who's going to take care of all the debt? Who's going to make sure your kids have a good college education? Who's going to take care of the emergencies?"

"Wait a minute, Bob. Nothing like that is going to happen."

"But it might, Denise, it might. What else are you buying?"

"We're having the downstairs finished. I can't wait for you and Marge to come over and see it. It's going to be beautiful. There will be an office, a family room, and a rec room. We'll have a pinball machine, a pool table, and a video game center."

Bob asked, "How are you paying for it?"

"We have a home equity loan."

She continued. "Let's see, what else are we doing? Oh, I'm getting a new dining room set. It was a great bargain, only half price. You just have to take advantage of sales like that when they come up—even if you have to buy on credit."

"You bought that on credit, too?"

"Yes. It cost $3,000, but one of our cards just raised our credit limit to $12,000. They said we were valued customers, and thanked us for our good payment record."

"They want you to expand your spending on credit and increase your debt."

"The credit card companies make us feel important. They are always sending us notices upping our credit limit. They give us books of checks and special discounts."

"You're the credit card companies' favorite customers. They like people who carry a balance from month to month."

Denise continued. "One more thing we're doing—we're taking a cruise at the end of the month. It's a surprise. I haven't even told Dan. The kids are going, too."

"How are you paying for the cruise?"

Denise paused, a little embarrassed. "I charged it all yesterday. It's a great deal."

"What would you two do without those credit cards? You know, I'm really concerned about you and Dan. You're overextending yourselves financially."

"How can you say that?"

"Have you ever added up all the monthly payments you have for this loan or that loan and for your various credit cards?"

"No. Do you think Dan and I could ever sit down and *manage* our money together?" she asked with a hint of sarcasm. "I do my thing and he does his. I'm confident that with his money skills, he has this all figured out."

Bob replied, "Don't count on it. You two could be in big trouble right now. You need to do a financial profile."

"What's that?"

"It's finding out where you are financially. It's finding out what your expenses are. It's finding out if you have any money left over at the end of the month. I doubt if you know."

"How so?"

"You could be paying out more in loan and credit card payments than you're making. It sounds as if you have huge credit card balances that will take months and maybe years to pay off. And those credit cards keep adding interest at the rate of 18% to 21% per year.

"You're living in a paper castle—built with money that's not yours. It could come tumbling down at any moment."

She became subdued. "You mean collection agencies? Bankruptcy?"

"Yes," Bob said. "You've got to stop spending and start paying down your debt. No more spending. Stop now. And any spending you do should be for those things you really need. You should pay for everything with cash."

"But we need all the things we're getting, Bob."

"No, you don't, Denise. You like all those things, but you don't need them. Do you need to go on the cruise?"

"We need to get away. But I guess it doesn't have to be a cruise."

"Do you have to redo the downstairs?"

"No, but it will be great for the kids and the family."

"I'm sure it will be, but do you have to do it?"

"No."

"Did you have to buy the new furniture?"

"No. Gee, I've heard about bankruptcy happening to other people. It's pretty scary. I'd hate to end up that way. Last time Dan went to the bank, they didn't want to lend him more money."

"That's not all," Bob added. "You're creating some serious problems for yourselves down the line."

"What do you mean, down the line?"

"When I say down the line, I mean in the future. What about college education? Won't your daughter Darlene be ready for college in two years? Have you saved any money? Have you made any investments to pay for her education?"

"No, not really," Denise answered. "But I'm sure we can borrow."

Bob interrupted, "I'm sure you can borrow some money or get a loan. Or win the lottery. Maybe you'll be lucky enough to get some kind of scholarship for Darlene. Has she done well in school?"

"Well, she has been kind of lost the last couple of years. We just don't seem to have time for her."

"You see what I mean, Denise. Your family is going in different directions. No one is on course. You have to get it back together, or you're going to end up going nowhere. Have you started saving for retirement yet?"

"Retirement? Who thinks about that? Bob, I'm telling you

everything will be okay. We just take care of today. Tomorrow has always taken care of itself for us so far."

"So far. That's a big 'so far,' " said Bob. "Maybe those 'so far' days will come to an abrupt end faster than you think."

"I just figured everything would take care of itself," Denise said. "Dan is a master at manipulating money."

"When Dan comes back, let's have a talk with him," Bob said.

"Good luck, Bob. You know how hard-headed he can be."

"You see, if you don't get rid of this debt, you aren't going to be able to send your kids to college or meet emergencies that arise in the future. Or retire. You see, when you retire and you have debt, *you* may retire, but your debt won't. This simply means that when you go to sleep at night, you'll have to worry about your bills. Is that what you want?"

"No, of course not, but I don't really worry about them now. Dan will tell you, it will all be fine."

"I can't wait," Bob answered, anticipating a lively discussion.

$$\$ \$ \$ \$ \$ \$$

Dan returned with a carload of soft drinks, ice, cups, and three brand-new coolers. Bob and Denise helped him unload his purchases and carry them up to the pavilion. It took several trips.

"The picnic is saved," declared Dan, raising his clasped hands above his head as if to say, "I've just saved the world!"

Bob, clapping for the hero, gestured for Dan to sit down with him on the end of the bench away from where Marge and Denise were laying things out on the table.

"Dan," Bob started, "Marge and I were happy to get the note suggesting that you and Denise would like to talk about your finances."

"Well, sure, Bob, we always like to talk to you about money. Actually, we don't have much to say, since everything is going great with us."

"Yes, Denise has been telling me that you feel good about

your present financial condition. This would probably be a good time for us to talk—in other words, before we get deluged with picnic activities. Okay?"

Denise, joining her husband on the bench, agreed with Dan that this would probably be a good time to visit—just as their son, Darin, ran up to them with his friend Sarah Hecht.

"Hi, Mom. Hi, Dad. Hi, Uncle Bob. Hi, Aunt Marge. Uncle Bob, can you show me how to open a savings account?"

Denise replied, "Darin, that's a nice idea. But you don't need a savings account. We give you an allowance. Just enjoy it."

"But Uncle Bob told me I could be a millionaire by saving my money," Darin pleaded. "Are you going to make me a millionaire?"

Dan asked, "Bob, aren't you exaggerating?" He turned to Darin and said, "Saving nickels and dimes won't make you a millionaire, son. It takes big money. But I do hope you're a millionaire someday."

"Dan, I don't want to say you're wrong. But I want to explain to you the same formula for financial success that I showed Darin and Sarah. Anyone can become a millionaire."

Looking over at Darin, Bob reiterated, "Darin, you *can* become a millionaire by saving nickels and dimes."

Denise interrupted. "Darin and Sarah, why don't you run along? Go play on the swings."

"But I want to find out about becoming a millionaire," Darin demanded, looking at his mom. "You never told me about how much fun it is to save money. You always buy me things. Why don't we save money together? It'll really be fun. Uncle Bob says so. I want to become a millionaire."

"I'm going to be a millionaire," said Sarah. "Uncle Bob told me so. Right, Uncle Bob?"

"Right, Sarah!"

"Let's talk about this some other time," Denise interrupted. "Now, run along and play."

Darin and Sarah looked at each other and shrugged their

shoulders. They looked at Uncle Bob. Darin declared, "We'll see you later, Uncle Bob."

Sarah added, "Don't forget, Uncle Bob, we want you to tell us the story about Billy Bear, Dan Donkey, and Willie Wolf."

"Okay, kids, I will. Just a little later."

Then both of them turned and raced toward the swings.

"I'll beat you."

"I'll get there first."

Bob saw his work with Darin nearly undone by just a few words from the boy's mom and dad. It was amazing how some parents could be so out of touch with reality. Dan and Denise, Bob thought, needed to be talked with right now. They needed to be given constructive criticism, to say the least. Despite all their natural ability and ambition, they could end up with nothing if they didn't change immediately. Darin would go right back to his old spending and consuming habits. Bob would straighten out Darin later, but he knew that right now he had to focus his attention on Denise and Dan.

He looked at Dan and said, "Denise tells me you have some exciting things going on. She says you're remodeling the basement. You're getting a pinball machine and a pool table."

"And a large-screen TV and video center," Dan added. "It will be dynamite. We'll be the talk of the neighborhood. No one else will have what we have. Everyone will want to have a recreation area like ours."

"Sounds as if Denise caught a good sale on the dining room set," said Bob.

"Dining room set? That's news to me."

"I thought I told you about that," Denise said.

Dan shrugged his shoulders. "First I ever heard of it."

"Bob, here we go again!" Denise sighed.

Bob said, "I don't mean to start an argument." He paused for a moment. "Well, you're sure going to have fun on that cruise."

Dan looked surprised. "What cruise? What are you talking

about, Bob?" Then Bob remembered that Denise had said it was a surprise. Well, the surprise was out. He now had both of them looking at him.

"Bob, I told you that was going to be a surprise."

Dan did seem surprised. "We're going on a cruise?"

"Yeah, honey, at the end of the month. We're going to take the kids."

"Hey, that sounds great. When is it?"

"The 25th through the 30th," said Denise.

"Oh, wow, I'm supposed to be at a conference on the 27th. I might have to stay here."

"You'd better go. It's all paid for," she said. "On the credit card, that is."

Bob said, "Dan and Denise, I want to talk to you about something very important."

"Okay, Bob," Dan said. "What do you want to talk about?"

"Well, Dan, you expressed your interest in talking about your finances. And frankly, I'm really concerned about you two. You're spending money—the basement, the furniture, the cruise. And I know that's not all. How do you pay for it? It looks to me as if you're spending a lot of plastic."

"What do you mean, 'plastic'?" Denise asked.

"He means credit cards," Dan explained. "The plastic credit cards. We get a loan, or we charge it on a credit card. We have major credit cards, plus department store cards, gasoline company cards, and who knows what else. The offers come in the mail; they say we're preapproved for $5,000. They're good deals. We don't have a problem, Bob."

Denise looked at Dan and asked, "Dan, why don't you listen to Bob? He might have something here. Maybe we should listen."

Dan's voice became tense. "What are you talking about? Aren't you happy? Don't you go out and buy jewelry and anything you want? We go to Vegas whenever we want."

Bob's eyes lit up. "Vegas? What do you do in Vegas?"

"What do you think we do in Vegas? We go out to eat, we go to the shows, and we gamble."

"Tell me about how you gamble."

"We go out there and sign a ticket and have a great time. We spend a couple of thousand dollars."

Denise corrected him. "Last time you spent $5,000 plus some, remember? We had to come back home and borrow from the bank to pay off the excess."

"Denise, we don't need to talk about this." Dan's voice appeared to be very tense.

"Well, isn't it the truth?"

"So I let it get a little out of hand."

"Dan, do you know how much money you owe?" asked Bob.

"Of course I know."

"Have you added it up?"

"Well, no, not recently."

Denise added, "He's too busy doing everything else. Sometimes he doesn't pay much attention to our money."

"Hey, Denise, it's your problem, too," cautioned Dan.

Bob interrupted them. "Let's take some time right now. Let's work on this. All three of us. Now. At the picnic. We'll start with a financial profile." He looked at Denise. "Okay, Denise?"

"Okay."

He looked at Dan. "Okay, Dan?"

"All right."

Bob reached into his pocket. "I've got my calculator; let's get started."

"Wait a minute," interrupted Dan. "We aren't going to do this on a calculator. I've got my laptop computer in the car. It's got a built-in laser printer."

With that he jumped up and ran to the car. Denise looked over at Bob. "Bob, now I'm starting to worry. I was never concerned about the debt before. But if you think someone could come knocking at our door and take everything away from us, that would be terrible."

"I know you've worked hard to get what you have. Now what I want you to do is to make sure that you keep everything—that nothing gets repossessed."

Dan was back in a flash and set up his laptop computer on top of the picnic table. It was the latest model, of course; IBM 486 compatible with a color screen, printer, and Microsoft Windows.

"Where do we start, Bob?" Dan actually seemed eager to use his latest acquisition.

"Well, let's take a look at the house. Denise says you bought the house four years ago for $600,000. What do you think it's worth today?"

"Well," Dan said, "that's kind of a problem. When I went to the bank the last time to borrow money, they said I couldn't borrow any additional money on the house. With the flat housing market, it's only worth about $480,000 right now. And we owe $480,000 on the mortgage. That includes the home equity loan that we took out last year for the furniture we bought for our condo. Our monthly payment right now is about $2,600."

Denise added, "There's another note of $30,000 on the house, taken out last year to consolidate some debts. It's $650 per month for five years. This last loan for the basement remodeling adds another $20,000, charged out at $220 per month over 20 years."

"If we total that up on my calculator, you'll be paying $39,000 on the $30,000 note; $52,800 on the $20,000 note. Denise, that's $91,800 on something that you don't need anyway. Any other debts?" asked Bob.

"We have a condominium in Florida. It's worth $200,000. We owe $160,000 on it. We pay $1,400 per month over 15 years," said Dan.

"Tell him about the time-sharing unit," said Denise.

"It's worth $60,000. We pay $700 per month on it."

Denise gasped. "I didn't know that place cost so much. That's a lot of money for the little time we use it."

"What about your credit cards?" Bob asked. "How much do you owe on those?"

"I'm guessing about $30,000," said Dan. "It's hard to say, because it's spread over so many cards. That works out to about $400 per month."

Bob asked, "Do you know what kind of interest rates you're paying on those balances? Let me tell you. Very high. Your debts will continue to soar. You pay thousands a year in interest."

"That's shocking," said Denise.

"I wanted to point it out to you," said Bob. "What else is there?"

Dan said, "Well, there's $26,000 on Denise's jewelry . . . $19,000 on art and collectibles . . . $75,000 on our new boat."

"That adds about another $1,500 a month, Dan and Denise, to your monthly obligations. What about your two cars?"

"I lease both of those, and it runs about $1,600 a month."

Bob pulled out his calculator. Dan totaled on the computer. They got their answers at about the same time.

As he finished his calculations, Bob said, "Okay, your monthly obligations on these loans and the car leases total over $9,000. That's about $111,600 per year."

Denise turned as white as a sheet. "Oh, my gosh." She held her hands to her forehead, looked down, and sighed. "$100,000 a year in debt. We're mortgaged to our ears. We're living for today and sacrificing tomorrow. Dan, what are we going to do?"

Dan was silent.

"Bob, how are we going to get out of this?" asked Denise.

"We're getting to that," Bob said. "First, we have to see how much you make. Then we can figure out what you can afford. We can set up a budget that will allow you to pay off your debts. That's assuming, of course, that you don't take on more debt."

"That means we have to stop spending," said Denise.

"Right!"

Dan was silent. He looked away from Bob and Denise, signaling that he was not comfortable with the direction of the conversation.

"Okay, let's get to the budget. First of all, what is your income?"

Dan said, "I make $80,000 and Denise makes $55,000."

"Now, that's with our bonuses," said Denise.

"That's a lot of money, isn't it, Bob?" asked Dan. "It totals $135,000."

"You're right, that's a real good income. But it's your spending that has to be brought under control. It looks here as if you're spending over $100,000."

"$111,600 to be exact," said Dan, looking at the screen on his laptop.

"No, that's not quite all of it, Dan."

"What do you mean, Bob?" Denise asked.

"We aren't even counting your entertainment, the times you go to the show, when you eat out, your vacations, the video games, your food, and all your personal necessities around the house, your clothes—"

"Wait a minute, Bob, stop," said Denise. "If we haven't added those expenses yet, where is the money coming from?"

"Quite simply, you're both overspending. At the end of every year, your debts are higher. Your credit card balances keep going up."

"I guess they are higher every year."

Bob continued. "If you add up all your personal expenses, your utility bills, telephone, entertainment, and everything else that goes along with it, I bet you're spending another $30,000 a year."

"Oh, it can't be that much," Dan protested.

"Yes, it can. You have to remember, Dan, that you have $135,000 coming in. You have at least $30,000 to $35,000 worth of other expenses. That's on top of the debts we've already talked about. The list goes on and on. Groceries, medical bills, insurance, entertainment, clothes—it never stops."

"Well, wait a minute, we have cut our insurance costs down."

"You what?" Bob winced.

"Yeah, we got rid of the life insurance on Denise and me. We don't need it right now. It cost too much money."

"Oh, wow! Of all the things to get rid of! What if anything happens to you or Denise?"

"We're not going to die."

"But what happens if you do? Do you know for sure that you're not going to die?"

"Well, nobody knows that, Bob. But we are young."

"I know a lot of people who have died young. I know a lot of people who have become disabled, who have gotten sick and couldn't continue to work. You might fall into that category."

"I hope not."

"But something might happen. What would you do then?"

"Gosh, Bob, this whole thing is shocking. I can't believe it. There must be a mistake somewhere. I'm going to recheck these figures in the computer."

He paused for a minute and punched some keys on his laptop. He waited for the machine to respond, then punched some more keys. After the machine gave him its answer, he slapped his hand on the table. He looked puzzled.

"Same total, right, Dan?"

Dan agreed with a nod.

"There's no mistake, Dan. My calculator doesn't lie. And neither does your computer."

"Okay, Bob. You're right."

Bob said, "You have $135,000 coming in. You know what? We haven't even talked about taxes yet. What are your taxes?"

"Oh, I'm in good shape there," Dan answered. "I have some

great tax shelters. They haven't done real well in the way of returns, but the tax deductions are good."

"There are a lot of investments like that," Bob agreed. "They give you great tax benefits, but you lose your money."

"Well, I haven't lost my money yet; they just aren't giving me the returns I thought I would get. But they will."

"Well, never mind," said Bob. "We'll talk about that later. What are your taxes?"

"Last year, Bob, they were about $42,000."

"That sounds about right. Let's add it all up. $116,000 for debts and $30,000 for living expenses. $42,000 for taxes. What do you get, Dan?"

"$183,600. This is impossible. This must be twisted in some way."

"Bob, is there a mistake here?" pleaded Denise.

"I'm sorry, but this is the truth. Cold, hard facts. You let your credit cards fool you into believing that you could afford all this. $10,000 preapproved credit limit. Low-cost, tax-deductible home equity loan. No money down. Easy credit."

"It seemed like the way to go," Denise confessed.

"Today's pleasure, paid for with tomorrow's money. You have everything, all these *things*, but you own none of them. They could disappear tomorrow."

"I still think there's a mistake somewhere," Dan said, checking his figures again.

"Dan, do you know what a debt ratio is?"

"No."

"A debt ratio is the percentage of your debts to your total assets."

"Explain, please."

"You add up all of your assets—your house, your cars, all of your collectibles, everything you own. Then add up all the debts that you have. Then, divide the total of your assets by the total of your debts. What we are looking for is your *debt ratio*."

"What's that, Bob?" asked Denise.

"Debt ratio is that amount of your assets that someone else owns. You subtract your debts from your assets and that number equals your net assets. The average debt ratio, which is the percentage of your assets that is debt, is somewhere between 20% and 25% for most people. Believe it or not, some people have a zero debt ratio."

"You mean, Bob, they don't have any debt at all?"

"That's right. They sleep very well at night."

"I bet they do," said Dan. "This is really starting to get to me. If I add up all of our assets and all our debts, and figure the debt ratio, I don't even want to tell you what it comes to."

"Dan, can you do a printout?"

"Sure."

"Well, let's take a look at the totals," said Bob.

Dan pushed a key on the keyboard and the printer started printing and pushing out the balance sheet. Dan looked at the totals for a long minute without saying a thing to anyone. His lower jaw dropped in utter disbelief.

ASSETS

Assets		Liabilities	
House	$480,000	Home mortgage	$480,000
Condo–Florida	200,000	Second mortgage	30,000
Time share	60,000	Loan on basement	20,000
Jewelry	26,000	Condo mortgage	160,000
Art & collectibles	19,000	Credit cards	30,000
Boat	75,000	Jewelry	18,000
		Art & collectibles	14,000
		Boat	60,000
	$860,000		$812,000
Net Worth			$48,000

"I can just about guess what it says, Dan. The answer is, you are in financial trouble."

They all took a look. Denise's eyes started watering. She was trembling as she turned toward her husband. "Dan, what do we do? I don't want to lose our home and everything else."

Then she turned to Bob. "Bob, what do we do? Help us."

"Do you want to get out of this mess?"

"Yes," they both said. "Tell us what you think we can do!"

"Okay," said Bob. "You aren't going to like what I tell you. But if you follow my suggestions, I believe you can get back on track toward financial security."

"Bob, a little while ago, Darin and Sarah said they wanted to be millionaires. I guess Dan and I have always wanted to be millionaires, too. But we thought a millionaire was someone who just looked rich."

"You are not alone, Dan and Denise. Many people think that having a bigger home, driving a more expensive car, or going on vacations makes them millionaires because they live like them. However, people who stay out of debt often are much better off than those who have millions of dollars worth of assets alongside millions of dollars worth of debt."

$$\$ \, \$ \, \$ \, \$ \, \$ \, \$$$

"First, you are in immediate danger of falling behind in your payments. Quite simply, you have overextended yourselves."

Dan replied, "The banks check all this out, don't they? They said I was okay up until the last couple of months. Why do they make it so easy to get credit? We get these notices from the credit card companies about what good customers we are. They raise our credit limit, so we just charge it on up! I don't get it. The financial institutions are telling us we are in good shape. You are telling us we are in bad shape financially."

"Remember, Dan and Denise, the credit card companies and your banks are in the business of lending money. They make their money off the interest they charge you. With the amount of profit that the credit card companies get from people like you, they sure ought to call you valued customers.

"I heard a story one time about financial institutions and credit card companies. They give you an umbrella when the sun is shining and then, when it's raining, they take it away. They make you pay it off, one way or another."

"And I think it's raining disaster on us right now," confessed Denise. "Maybe we should cancel that cruise. I think we can still get a refund if we cancel within 10 days."

"That's probably a good idea," Bob agreed.

"I'll agree to that *only* because of my conference," said Dan. "Denise, I'm still not convinced that Bob hasn't manipulated the figures to suit his argument. You know how he's always trying to talk people into saving money."

"Dan, let's listen to what he has to say. Bob, tell us more."

"You also should consider selling some assets, such as the condo, the time-sharing unit, and the boat. If you put them up for sale now before you start getting hammered by collection agencies, you can hold out for a fair price. Once people know you're forced to sell, you're going to end up getting very little for your assets. Remember, in bad times, regardless of how much something might mean to you, it's not going to mean as much to someone else. When people know you're hurting financially, they'll offer you rock-bottom prices."

Dan, Denise, and Bob talked about what assets to sell. Despite Dan's reluctance, they worked up a plan to pay off the credit card debts over a three-year period.

"For all these loans you two have, think about how much interest you are paying. The condominium, the basement remodeling, and the debt-consolidation loan will cost two to three times the value of the loan principal just because of the interest you are paying."

"That's a hidden cost," Dan surmised.

"Right," Bob said. "The invisible debt is sometimes worse than the visible debt. Interest is invisible debt. And a lot of the debt is spread over 20 to 30 years. Would you still have your basement remodeled if you knew the real cost was over $40,000?"

"In current dollars," Dan argued. "That doesn't account for inflation. If we waited 10 years and paid cash, the basement would still cost us $40,000 because of inflation."

"You're right again, Dan! But, if you can't afford it, don't do it. That's like going out and buying things you like simply because you like them. Don't buy anything that you just like. Don't buy it unless you need it. And don't buy anything unless you can pay cash for it."

They both shook their heads from side to side and stared at the computer printout sheet as if it were going to change numbers and give them some magic formula. Bob looked at them and could almost guess what they were thinking. "There is no magic formula. There is no easy way out. You've got to stop spending and start paying off you debt now.

"Another thing," Bob continued. "About those credit cards. Do you know that at 18%, you could pay twice the initial price over a five-year period? Denise, if you buy a $300 pair of earrings and make minimum payments for two years, that's 20% more than those earrings cost you retail. To pay off the credit card balance, those earrings will have cost you over $360."

"Wow! What a steep price! I could've bought another pair for that."

"Just cut the word *debt* out of your vocabulary and your pocketbook. Start thinking *save* and *pay off debt*. If you just keep adding to your debt, you're digging yourselves into a deeper and deeper financial hole."

$ $ $ $ $ $

Bob brought up another issue. "Do you have cash reserves?" Bob asked.

"What do you mean by cash reserves?"

"Money saved."

"Not really," Dan said. "Well, we've got some, probably $500. But we've never had an emergency, Bob. I've got a good job, and besides, if something did happen, I'd figure out a way to borrow the money. Wait a minute, I'm fooling myself. Maybe I couldn't borrow any more money now."

"I don't think you could!"

"Wow, Bob, I guess we are in real financial trouble."

"What happens if you lose your job? What happens if you get sick and you can't work and they have to let you go?"

"Well, that's not going to happen."

"Why not?"

"Well, because . . . I'm not going to get sick."

"But what if you do?"

"Well, if I do, the company has a benefits package. They'll keep sending my paychecks if I'm sick."

"Yeah, but how long will that last?"

"Oh, I'm sure it would last a long time."

"Don't bet on it, Dan."

Denise jumped in. "Dan, do you know how long they will pay if you get sick?"

"No, but I'd better find out."

"Most companies don't pay for longer than three to six months maximum. If you got sick right now, Dan, and you couldn't work for six months, with the way your lifestyle is today, you're talking about over $70,000 of expenses, not counting taxes. So you can't say nothing will happen.

"People do get disabled, you know. People do get sick and can't go back to work. People have accidents. Have you ever been sick?" asked Bob.

"No, I'm healthy."

Denise differed. "Remember, Dan, last year when you had to go to the hospital with kidney stones?"

"Yes, but they paid the bill and I got my paycheck."

"We had insurance then. Remember, you canceled the insurance."

"You what!" Bob sounded shocked.

Dan said, "We canceled our health insurance three months ago. The cost was too high. We had to increase the payments on one of our loans, so I just dropped the health insurance."

"That's a terrible mistake." Bob calmed himself down. "If

you had a hospital bill for $10,000 or $20,000 or $50,000, how would you pay it?"

"If we couldn't get a loan, I don't know."

"It could ruin you."

"You're right, Bob. That was kind of a silly thing to do. We'll get that insurance back right away."

"Do it first thing Monday morning," Bob insisted.

Denise was beginning to understand the seriousness of their situation. "You know, Bob, maybe we do have spending problems." She looked at Dan. "What would happen if you or I do get sick? How in heck would we pay all our bills?"

Bob answered, "I can tell you what would happen. You might have to move out of your house. You might even have to sell the house along with all the other assets you're going to have to sell anyway. You might have to sell a lot of other things that we haven't even talked about—your jewelry, your furniture. You might be in a situation where you were totally bankrupt, without anything left. When you started selling, it would be a fire sale, at desperation prices. You'd get pennies on the dollar in order to pay off your bills before your creditors took everything."

"I never thought about it that way, Bob," Dan admitted. "We'd better go into reverse immediately and do a quick turnaround. It's not so easy, Bob. It's a habit. Like just now. We needed coolers, so I went over to the store. I pulled out my credit card and I bought whatever I wanted. Look at these coolers—aren't they neat? You can put cold or hot water in them. Great, huh?"

"Great, Dan, but do you really need them? Did you really need to spend that money? How much did they cost you?"

"Well, about $150."

"$150." Bob shook is head. "That was $150 that you didn't need to spend. Don't you already have a cooler at home?"

"Yes, but I didn't want to drive all the way home to get it. Besides, these are brand-new."

"Dan and Denise, you have to change this attitude of wanting everything today, rather than waiting until tomorrow to buy only those things you really need with cash. Remember, buy only the things you need, not what you want. Avoid instant gratification."

"Okay, Bob," Dan acquiesed. "This has gone too far. Denise and I'll talk about this when we get home. What we're going to do about our money and debt is going to take some serious personal deliberations! I'm here for the picnic. I want to have a good time. I like you. I might even play horseshoes with you today . . . *if* you promise not to hit me with the horseshoe. Let's face it. What we're doing with our money is our business."

"I don't mean to pry. All I want to do is help."

"Bob, you know we're not saving anything," said Denise. "How can we save anything? We're spending everything."

"Okay, okay, Denise, I know Bob might be right," Dan added. "Bob's made his point, but now let's have fun at the picnic. Okay? We'll turn things around."

"Yes." Denise smiled at Bob. "We'll turn things around. You'll be very happy with us."

But Bob wasn't through. He needed to make sure not only that they knew they were in trouble financially, but that they immediately started to get out of debt.

$$\$ \$ \$ \$ \$ \$$

Saving for the future was another subject that Bob wanted to cover with them.

Before they could stand, Bob continued. "Isn't your daughter going to start college in a couple of years?"

With that question, Dan and Denise sat back down on the bench. "Yes. We have jobs. We'll pay for it."

"Why not save some money now? Don't put such a heavy burden on yourselves in a couple of years. What about your son?"

"We have to think of Darin, too," Denise agreed.

"Wouldn't it be nice to start saving money for his college education? Why put it off until tomorrow? That's what you've been doing, you know. You've been having fun today and putting off saving until tomorrow. Now, you've just awakened to find that today is tomorrow. You're in financial trouble. You don't want to still be in financial trouble down the line when your kids go to college or when you retire, do you?"

"No, we don't," Denise admitted. "But retirement is a long time from now. College is still a couple of years away. We'll get our debt cleared by then."

"Don't be so sure that retirement is a long way off. Ask anyone who has retired. Talk to George and Gail. They're here at the picnic. Ask them if they felt retirement didn't sneak up on them a lot sooner than they had anticipated."

Dan said, "We do have a problem with our daughter's college. But our son isn't going to start college for another seven or eight years."

"Dan, do you know what a college education costs today?" asked Bob. "It costs $5,000 to $10,000 a year in a state school, and some private schools are above $25,000. That's a lot of money."

"That's terrible, Bob. When we went to school, the cost was a lot less."

"And remember, with education costs going up each year because of inflation, just think what your son's tuition, books, and fees are going to cost eight or nine years from now. It could easily be $10,000 or $15,000 a year for a state school. That's over $40,000 for the four years."

Dan seemed very concerned. "I don't know, Bob. I hope we can turn this thing around. So far we haven't saved any money. I see better now how important it is for us to get out of debt."

"That's good thinking, Dan. You're on the right path now. Just keep it up."

Bob paused for a moment, then turned to another subject. "What about your retirement funds at your job?"

"Yes, there's a retirement fund. It's a good one, but we're not in it."

Denise added, "Someday we're going to get old, you know. Do you still want to be working when you're 75?"

"No, of course not. I'm trying to get through this mind game that we're playing here. I'm worried, Bob."

"That's good, Dan."

"Okay. So we're going to restart the health insurance and life insurance. I'll look into the retirement plan. And, even though retirement and college may seem a long way off, we're going to start saving now so we can be assured that our kids get a good education and we have a good retirement."

"Now you're talking, Dan. You're rolling now."

"We're certainly rolling now, Dan." Denise was finally smiling. "I feel better already."

She turned to Bob. "There are some good benefits programs at my company. We have retirement and life insurance. I can even buy stock in the company."

"Sounds pretty good. Why aren't you in it?"

"Because to do it, I would have had to have money deducted from my paycheck."

"What's wrong with that?" asked Bob.

"I didn't want to reduce my paycheck," Denise explained. "I wanted to bring home as much as possible, so I could spend it."

"Denise, those savings plans won't eat into your check as much as you may think. The money that goes into your pension plan will probably be vested income-tax-free. It will probably accumulate on an income-tax-deferred basis. So, your deductions come right off the top, saving tax dollars and putting that money to work by accumulating for you on a tax-deferred basis. It'll be worth it, Denise."

"I know, Bob, now that my tears are gone and I'm happy about what we're planning to do. I'm so glad we have an Uncle Bob."

Bob continued. "Let me share one more thing with you."

"You mean, there are more secrets, Bob?" Dan asked, smiling.

"There's always more to talk about when you're talking about saving money, Dan. A lot of people run into a situation where everything is fine until their kids go to college, or everything is fine until they retire. In your case, the debt has already hit you. You've got to be thinking about retirement now, so that when retirement comes you're ready for it.

"When most people retire, they can live very well for a year or two. They find that even though they may have some bills and debt, they have Social Security coming in and maybe some other income from their company benefits package. So, for a couple of years everything is fine.

"Then, all of a sudden they have to start using up their principal, and before they know it, their money is gone. Would you want to be in that situation?"

"Heavens, no, Bob. That would be terrible."

"Let me tell you a story. I've got a good friend who lived much the way you two live. He had all kinds of great things. Five television sets in his house, stereos, CD players, and expensive cars. He and his family went on vacations every year, and they borrowed just like you. And when they retired, they still had all those debts to pay off. Social Security and the company benefits package weren't enough to pay their expenses and debts."

"Both weren't enough?"

"That's right. Let me explain Social Security. For a person making about $21,000 a year, Social Security will give the average retiree about $1,000 a month. That's $12,000 a year."

"What do you mean, $12,000 a year? I thought that when I retired, Social Security was going to take care of everything."

Bob responded, "Social Security is not going to take care of everything. It's going to pay you something, which is great, but in no way will it pay all your expenses. Just figure that Social Security is a supplement to all of your other savings, which you *don't* have right now."

"Okay, Bob, stop rubbing it in."

"Well, I just want to make sure that you're aware of where you are right now financially. If you don't take care of things immediately, you'll be sitting there someday with nothing."

"Bob, that would just be terrible, but it sounds like we're sitting here with nothing now."

Bob continued, "In fact, when you're talking about Social Security, I wouldn't be surprised if someday retirees couldn't start collecting Social Security benefits until some time after age 65."

"Wow," said Dan. "If I plan to retire at 55, I might not get Social Security benefits for another 10 to 15 years."

"That's right. That's why it's so important to save in other ways. Like your company benefits package and your own systematic savings program. So, back to my friend. His problem was debt. He carried his debts into retirement."

"Okay, Bob, we understand. We get your point."

"Yes, it's not a good idea to spend more than you make. But many people do it, since it's so easy to get a loan or pay with a charge card. You two are riding a roller coaster up and down a mountain of debt.

"As a matter of fact," Bob continued, "my friend had to go back to work during retirement to pay off his debts. He had to work another seven years, and that took him into his 70s."

"That's a shame," said Denise. "Of course, his problem was a lot worse than the one Dan and I have. We'll have our debts under control in another year or two. We'll stop buying things we don't need. We'll buy only what we do need, and we'll buy it only if we can pay for it in cash."

"That's right, Bob," Dan jumped in. "We thought we had lots of needs. But they weren't really needs, just wants and desires. We're not going to be in this situation next year at the family picnic. You wait and see."

"Good! Say, Dan, do you know how many people reach 100 years of age every day?"

"Yes, I watch TV; there are one or two."

"No, the latest Census report stated that in 1990 there were some 36,000 people over 100, and by the year 2030 there will be a projected 435,000 people over 100 years of age. We are living longer and longer. With the emphasis on wellness these days, that number by 2030 seems reachable. By that date your children will be only some 40 and 50 years old . . . with a longer future to come. As there's better research down the line, there will be more and more people living longer."

Dan said, "Heck, probably in 10 years people in the media won't be talking about someone being 100 and wishing them a happy birthday; they'll probably be singing 'Happy Birthday' only to those people who are 110 or older."

"You're right. The point I'm making is that, hopefully, you'll be retired for a long time. This means you'll need to save a lot of money and make it grow over your lifetime so that you'll have the kind of income that you're going to need for a good retirement. If all your bills were paid right now, would you say you were living a good life? Wouldn't you like to live a good life during retirement?"

"You betcha, Bob," said Denise.

"Well, by turning your finances around today, you're going to be able to take care of your debt, pay your bills, give your kids a good college education, and ensure yourselves a great retirement—a retirement that allows you to live the life that you've grown accustomed to."

"That sounds great, Bob."

"Now," Bob added, "one more thing."

"Oh, no. I thought we'd covered everything."

"We've covered a lot of things, but not everything. One more item today is life insurance."

"Okay, Bob. I did say I would reinstate my hospitalization and life policies at work, right away. But life insurance salespeople? I can't stand them. I don't need any of that stuff anyway."

Denise asked, "Bob, why do we need it?"

"Well, if Dan died right now, you would be left with hundreds of thousands of dollars worth of bills. You don't have any way of paying them, Denise, which means you would have to sell everything and move."

"Where would I move, Bob?"

"I'm going to ask you that question, Denise. Where could you move? What could you afford?"

"Oh my gosh, that's terrible."

"Dan, if Denise were to die, what would you do?"

"Well, I'd keep working."

"Yes, but who'd take care of the kids? Who'd take care of the house? Who'd cook? Who'd be spending time with the children?"

"Golly, I never thought about that."

"See, Dan and Denise, you do need life insurance, if for no other reason than just to replace your earning power. It would enable the surviving spouse to keep paying down all the debt and reach the financial goals we've discussed today."

"Anything else, Bob?"

"I think that's enough for now."

Dan leaped into the air and stretched out his arms. And he and Denise gave each other a great big hug, and then they turned to Bob and hugged him. "Bob, Denise and I really appreciate your help. You've opened our eyes. But, Bob, why didn't you explain all of this to us last year when we talked together at the picnic?"

"Well, I really did, Dan. You and Denise listened and said you understood. But sometimes it has to be talked about at just the right moment, and often it takes time for it to begin to sink in. You just have to be ready to hear it."

"Yep," Dan announced, "this is just the beginning. We're going to get rid of our debt, buy only what we need, save the rest, and become millionaires."

And the three of them broke into raucous laughter that made several others outside the pavilion look over at them.

Dan was still laughing as he spoke. "Well, isn't that something! Denise and I are on the brink of total financial disaster and talking about becoming millionaires. But, in some strange way, I guess I really feel that it is possible."

"I'm pleased about what you're saying, but you realize that the tough work is just starting. At least you have a handle on what to do."

"We know, Bob: buy only what we need, pay for it in cash, pay off our debt, and save everything that is left."

"You've got it."

$$\$\,\$\,\$\,\$\,\$\,\$$

Just then, Darin ran back to his mom and dad.

"Mom, can you hold my SuperFAST? We're going to play ball."

Then Darin stopped, turned around, looked up at his parents, and said, "Do we have a savings account that pays interest like Sarah's?"

"We do," said his father.

"Oh, great!"

Denise looked over at Bob and Dan, and then knelt down beside Darin. She said, "You know, Darin, I've been thinking. Bob's been talking to us today. We think it'd be a good idea for you to have your own savings account like Sarah."

"Whoopee!" said Darin. "When are we going to start saving?"

"That's what we're talking to Uncle Bob about right now," said Denise.

"I want to start saving now!" yelled Darin.

"Yes, we're going to start our savings program with you," said Dan.

"So we're going to be millionaires?" asked Darin.

"Well, we're not millionaires yet," said Denise, as she looked over at Dan and Bob, then back at Darin. "But we will be millionaires, and so will you."

4

Scott Youth:
The Jumpstart Road
to Nowhere

THE LOUD RUMBLING OF A MOTORCYCLE interrupted the serenity of Prosperity Park.

A Harley-Davidson with two riders cruised by the picnic shelter into the back end of the park. Uncle Bob stood at the shelter as he watched Scott take Darlene (16 years old) for a ride. As they went down a hill and into an open stretch, Bob could hear the cycle give a light roar as Scott accelerated on the straightaway. The machine's power was evident. It was designed for high speeds on the open road. It seemed rather out of place in Prosperity Park.

Scott turned around at the end of the soccer field. He sped down the straightaway and up the hill, just missing Sarah and Darin's soccer ball as it bounced across the road. The bike roared up to the picnic shelter.

Bob watched Darlene McNally and Scott get off the bike. As they took off their helmets, she said, "Wow, that's awesome. Thanks. See you later!" Scott turned off the engine, temporarily restoring quiet to the environment. Then he noticed Bob watching him.

"Uncle Bob!"

"Hello, Scott," Bob greeted him as he walked over to look at Scott's stunning cycle. "What's this?"

"These are my new custom cruisin' wheels."

"Very nice."

"Muscle power. Harley-Davidson. Top of the line."

Scott was a lanky six-footer. At almost 19 years old, he was somewhere between being a teenager and an adult. He wore baggy khaki shorts and an oversize black T-shirt with some jagged abstract artwork that was the emblem of a rock group. His hair stuck up in a punk style, and a small earring shone in his left earlobe.

Bob looked over the bike as Scott pointed out its features.

"1300-cc engine. Five speeds. Will do over 110 miles per hour. Zero to 60 in nothing flat. And it will stop on a dime."

Bob admired all the chrome on the bike—wire wheels, chrome fenders, chrome handlebars, chrome parts on the engine, and that long chrome fork for the front wheel.

"Why don't you get on? Check out the driver's seat."

Bob grabbed the handlebar, threw his right leg over the cycle, and plopped onto the bike.

"Wanna start it up? Just push this button to start it. All automated!"

Bob was content just to look. From the driver's vantage point, there was an impressive array of gauges and switches. And more chrome. Even a functional windshield to block the wind.

Scott handed Bob a helmet. It was black with an abstract color design on both sides. "Here. Put this on. Get the feel."

"Okay," Bob said. He put on the helmet. He was a strange sight. Uncle Bob, in his white Cardinals T-shirt and worn sneakers, looked overweight, pale, aged, and totally out of place sitting on a Harley-Davidson wearing a black helmet.

"Lookin' good," said Scott. "You've definitely got some biker in you."

In a bland tone of voice, Bob said, "Yeah, right. Born to be wild. Me on this bike is about like making George Burns the star of *Easy Rider*."

"Hey, I'm tryin' to polish up your image. We're gettin' a start. Hey, how 'bout a ride?"

"Oh, no," Bob said.

Scott threw on his helmet. He jumped on the bike in front of Bob and pushed him back. Bob tried to get his leg up to get off, but he couldn't move fast enough.

"Hang on tight!" Scott fired up the bike and off they went.

"There are no seat belts on this thing," Bob yelled over the rumbling of the engine.

"What?" Scott couldn't hear Bob over the noise.

"No seat belts," Bob screamed.

"Hang on." Bob put his arms around Scott's waist and held on as if his life depended on it.

Scott whizzed Bob over the back park road, down the hill, and up the straightaway. Bob could see squirrels and rabbits scamper away as the Harley's roar declared this machine king of the park.

They turned around at the back end of the field. Scott opened the throttle, and they sped down the straight road. Bob felt the fierce wind on his arms and legs.

"Whoaaa," Bob screamed as they accelerated up the steep hill and the bike leaped off the ground at the top.

Now Scott slowed down, and they turned back toward the picnic shelter. This two-minute ride had seemed like eternity for Bob. Ending it was like the end of a roller coaster ride at the amusement park.

Scott stopped the bike and helped Bob take off his helmet. Bob was still frozen to the bike from the ride.

All he could say was, "Scott! You could have killed us."

"Uncle Bob, relax. It's over."

"I'm so tense, I'm welded to your bike."

"Hey, Uncle Bob! Lighten up. You'll get used to it." He helped Bob off the bike. "I'll take you out again in a while. You do look like biker material."

"No, not me. I have only one life to live. No thanks, Scott."

"Uncle Bob, where's your cool? Your image?"

"My image is just fine."

"You'd look really cool on a Harley. We could ride together." Scott parked the bike.

"Scott, do you want to sit down for a few minutes?"

"Sure." They walked to a nearby picnic table and sat down. They set their helmets on top of the table. Scott made himself comfortable sitting on top of the table next to his helmet.

Bob took a deep breath. "So what's with this new image? The bike, new clothes? What happened to engineering school?"

"Uncle Bob, I'm working."

"You are?"

"Yeah."

"That's great. But with all of your school hours and studies, how do you find time to work?"

"Oh, I quit school."

"You what?"

"Yep. Sure did. Six months ago."

"I'm sorry to hear that."

"Well, it's a great deal. See, I'm working at Fast Freddie's Restaurant. I'm a shift leader in the kitchen. In a year or two, I'll be into management training. Before long, I'll be managing the place. Is that a deal or what?"

"I don't know," said Bob. "You're sure giving up a lot by quitting college."

"Hey, look at all these people who graduate from college and can't get jobs. Why get a job in a warehouse paying $15,000 a year? I'm ahead of them. I've got a job that pays $23,000 a year. I'm out earning a living instead of wasting time in school."

"Engineering graduates easily make $30,000 or more in their first jobs."

"Yeah, but my grades weren't that good."

"You're really sacrificing the future."

"The future? In no time, I'll be making $40,000, $50,000, or $60,000. I've got a great future at Fast Freddie's."

"So, what's it like being a working man?"

"It's great. It's the life."

"And what's your life like?"

"Got my own apartment. In Westfield Gardens."

"The singles' place?"

"Yeah. It's great. I share it with another guy. We have a good time. There's always lots to do. There's always a party."

"Beats staying up at night studying?"

"Yeah." Scott paused and swallowed hard for a moment. "Uncle Bob, I do miss school. I don't know if what I'm doing is right. But I'm having a good time. And I like supporting myself. I've got my own job, my own apartment, my own credit cards."

"Do you use the credit cards?" Bob asked.

"Yeah. I buy clothes with them. Got lots of nice threads now. Silk shirts. Designer jeans. You know, it's a blast."

"Sprucing up the image."

"Yeah. Got a good image. I buy my clothes at the mall. You know, these shorts I've got on are a special edition. Cost $35. My shirt is Snipers & Vipers, the hottest heavy metal band. It was $40."

"$40 for a T-shirt?"

"Hey, man, these are hard to come by." He saw Darlene walking toward the baseball field. "Hey, Darlene! Aren't Snipers & Vipers the hottest rock band?"

"Oh, yeah. They're rad, outrageous!" she yelled across the field.

Scott said, "See, Bob. You don't know what it's like today. In your day, the hottest thing was Hush Puppies."

"Well, at least they're comfortable. Scott, with the apartment, the bike, the clothes, how are you doing it? It seems as though you're spending a lot of money."

"Not true, Uncle Bob. I've got money left over each month."

"Let me ask you this, Scott. When you get to the end of each month, what do you do with the money you have left over?"

"I get together with all of my buddies, and we have a big party at the apartment. We spend whatever's left at the end of the month."

"Don't you save anything?"

"No. There's always enough there. Remember, Uncle Bob, I'm just an 18-year-old kid. I'm Mr. Youth of America. I'm having a great time today, and today is all that matters."

"What about the future?"

"I've got the rest of my life to make plans and save money. I'm having a great time today. You know, Uncle Bob, I've already gone to school for 13 of my 18 years. I'm really cool now. I've got a job. I've got my cycle. I've got all the money in the world. I've got my girlfriends and my buddies, and I go out and have a ball. Every week we bomb ourselves silly. We go all night long. That's what I call having fun."

"That may be true, Scott. You may indeed be Mr. Youth of America. But by having so much fun today, you may be throwing away your tomorrows."

"What do you mean, Uncle Bob?"

$$\$\,\$\,\$\,\$\,\$\,\$$

"Scott, let's take a few minutes and let your rocket ship cool down. I want to explain to you some things that might let you have even more fun than you're already having today."

"Hey, Bob, I'm all ears," said Scott as he patted the sides of his sparkling red metallic helmet. "I've always thought you were a real neat guy."

"I've got to tell you, Scott, I'm surprised that you quit college. Do you know that by doing that you're sacrificing your future? Do you want to work in the kitchen the rest of your life?"

"No, but they promised me I could get into management."

"Don't the managers have college degrees?"

"Well, some of them do."

"So that means you'll have to go to college if you're going to go into management. Isn't that correct?"

"Well, yes."

"And don't you want to get into management?"

"Yeah."

"So what are you quitting school for?"

"So I'd have time to work."

"Can't you move your hours around so you can go to school and work?"

"Well, I guess I could."

"Let's look at where you are right now. You have about $1,500 a month coming in after taxes, and all kinds of money going out. How will you ever get ahead of where you are now by just working at the same job? Do you want to stay in your apartment and party on the weekends for the rest of your life?"

"No, but don't you think I'm doing well now?"

"Scott, I already told you, I think you're doing great. You've gone out on your own. You've gotten a job. You're working hard. That's great. However, you'll have to look at the future, too. Don't just look at today. Today is only important for a short period of time. You've got a lot more tomorrows ahead of you."

"But my future is good. I'll get promoted in a year or two. It sure beats standing in line for a low-paying job with all the other new graduates."

"But, Scott, there's no guarantee you'll get promoted. And there's no assurance you'll keep that job forever. What would happen if your boss got transferred, or got fired, or left to take another job?"

"Nothing's going to happen to my boss."

"How do you know? What happens if he moves out of the city? What happens if he gets sick? What if the restaurant closes?"

"The restaurant's not going to close. It's doing great."

"Remember Jerry's Jelly Bellies?"

"Oh, yeah. That was a hot place in high school."

"Do you know how Jelly Bellies is doing now?"

"It's closed."

"That's right. Went out of business," Bob agreed.

"Yes, but Fast Freddie's is doing better than Jelly Bellies ever did."

"Here's my point," Bob explained. "Most jobs in business today require a college degree. Without that degree, you're cutting yourself off from a lot of opportunities. There's no guarantee that Fast Freddie's will be here tomorrow or next week. You need to equip yourself with skills and credentials that are marketable."

"What do you mean, marketable?"

"Just like you've sold yourself to your current boss, you need to be able to sell yourself to any boss. One of your credentials is going to have to be a college degree."

"Oh, I see what you mean, Uncle Bob. If I have a college degree, it doesn't make any difference if Fast Freddie's closes up tomorrow."

Scott thought for a moment and said, "Maybe I could try to find out about night school or weekend classes. I could go back to school while I work."

"Right on, Scott. You get your college degree and you'll have real muscle power."

"Well, I'm not going to be a short-order cook for the rest of my life, Uncle Bob. Just call me chef Scott."

$$\$ \$ \$ \$ \$ \$$$

"Many young adults today live a carefree lifestyle, but do so by creating debt."

"Debt? What do you mean?"

"Do you buy with cash?"

"Heck, no, Uncle Bob. I've got a bunch of credit cards. When I go to the store, I just flip out that credit card and sign my name. I feel like a bigtimer. I buy something I like and I'm on my way."

"So, you buy $40 T-shirts with your credit cards?"

"Yeah. This credit card offer came in the mail. They gave me a $5,000 credit limit. I was preapproved. All I had to do was send in the application."

"So you've been using the card?"

"Oh, yes, a lot."

"Do you pay off the balance?"

"Well, I'm paying what they ask for. It's like a $25 minimum payment. That's what I send. Isn't that good? For a small payment, I get to use all this money, for free."

"Well, not really. Scott, you and most young people don't realize that there's a large interest charge tacked onto your unpaid balance."

"Oh, I know there's an interest charge, Uncle Bob."

"Yes, but did you know it was 18% to 21%? Did you know that at just 15% compounded annually, your bill doubles in about five years?"

"It doubles?"

"Yes, that's right. If you don't pay down that balance, it just snowballs. So, you've got to pay off your bill now. Today, right away. And stop just buying things that you like, on a whim."

"What do you mean, stop buying things that I like?"

"Just buy those things that you need. Buy only what you can afford to pay cash for."

"Cash? That'd put a real crimp in my lifestyle. I won't be able to have fun."

"I disagree. You'll have fun today—and tomorrow. Definitely more fun tomorrow. If you let those credit card balances run higher, it could take you years to pay them off. And, you'll be paying hundreds of dollars a year in finance charges. That is throwing away money."

"I see what you mean. That's why they write me and call me a valued customer. I don't pay my balance. They make lots of money off me from all the interest charges."

Bob and Scott watched a squirrel on the ground in front of them. It picked up an acorn and scampered up a tree.

"You see that squirrel?" asked Bob. "There's a good lesson. In nature, many animals collect food and save for times when food is less abundant. They gather it in summer and store it for winter. That squirrel is storing his food for winter.

"We humans need to be the same way about money. There are times in our lives, like when we retire or when emergencies arise, that we need to draw on the resources we've stored. That's why it's important to save money." The squirrel took the acorn into its nest in the tree.

"That's why they call it squirrelling away money!" Scott said, seemingly pleased with his insight.

"Right." Bob smiled. "Let's talk about your debts some more. What about the Harley?"

"Oh, that was the greatest deal. It only cost $8,000. All I had to put down was $800. I'm paying a little over $160 a month for the next five years."

"Scott, that's over $9,600 plus your down payment. So it's $10,400 that you're paying for the motorcycle with 12% interest on the loan!"

"Oh, really? I never thought about that. So my $8,000 motorcycle actually is going to cost over $10,000 with interest payments?"

"Yes. You're paying over 20% more for the motorcycle."

"But, Uncle Bob, I couldn't buy it all now. You know I had to have this motorcycle. This is cool. Don't you think it's cool?"

"Yeah. It looks great. Looks like you have a lot of fun with it. We need to have fun."

"I just want to enjoy life," Scott explained.

"Say, Scott. Would you like to make so much money that you become a millionaire?"

"Oh, you bet, Uncle Bob. If I could be a millionaire, I'd do anything."

"Anything, Scott?"

"You bet, Uncle Bob. If I was a millionaire, I could do anything I wanted to do. I could go anyplace. I could buy anything.
I could have anything. It would be great. Yeah! I want to be a
millionaire."

"Okay, I'm going to explain to you how you can become a
millionaire, but don't forget you said you'd do anything."

"Right on, Uncle Bob. Let's go. The sooner I find out how to
become a millionaire, the quicker I'm going to be one."

"Let's talk about it then, Scott."

$$\$\,\$\,\$\,\$\,\$\,\$$

"Let me tell you how you can become a millionaire by saving
a total of—are you ready?"

"Yeah, I'm ready. How much am I going to have to save?"

"You're going to have to save a total of—"

"Well, Uncle Bob, tell me. How much am I going to have to
save to become a millionaire? It takes a long time to save a million,
I bet."

"You don't have to save a million dollars to become a millionaire. Right now, Scott, all you have to do is save $16,000."

"And I will end up with a million?"

"Yes."

"Where does the other $984,000 come from? Federal match-
ing funds?"

Bob laughed. "No. Just by the Magic of Compounding. By
the way, I'm pleased to see your math skills are still good."

"So, if I saved $16,000 right now, I'd have a million by the
time I turned 65. By magic."

"The Magic of Compounding. Just by investing the money,
adding your earnings to the investment, and letting it grow."

"That's great. Now, where do I find $16,000? That's over two-
thirds of my salary."

"You don't have to save it all right now. Listen up. Uncle Bob
has a secret plan."

"The man has a plan," Scott announced in a loud voice, but no one was near enough to hear him except Bob.

"Do you think you can save about $200 a month right now?"

"Maybe. I'd probably have to stop some of my parties. Maybe I'd have to stop buying clothes—I guess I've got enough already. Maybe I'd have to stop going out on so many dates."

"So maybe you could save $150 to $200 a month?"

"I think so."

"Well, that's good enough for now. I'm going to show you my secret on how that $150 to $200 a month is going to make you a millionaire."

"$200 a month? A millionaire? Is this Uncle Bob amazing or what?"

"Here's how it works. If you save $200 a month, how much would you have in a year?"

"Over $2,000."

"Okay. Let's say there are two months where you are not able to save that much, so that leaves you with an even $2,000 saved for the year. Does that seem realistic?"

"Sure."

"Let's save $2,000 for the next eight years. From now until you're 26. If you do that, Scott, how much will you have saved over the next eight years?"

"$16,000. That's how much I need to become a millionaire?"

"Not exactly, but pretty close, Scott. Now I'll show you how to get that million dollars. It's by investing it. Let's find an investment that makes 10% a year. Now, that's not easy to do, Scott. You're going to have to work with some kind of adviser, or financial planner, or investment broker to find that investment."

"Well, where do I find these people? None of my friends know anything about this stuff. They blow their money the same way I do."

"Just ask around. Ask your parents. Ask your boss. You can also look in the newspaper and see when there are financial meetings or investment seminars. You can find them if you really try."

"So I'll ask people. I'll get a financial adviser. But I think I'll put this off a year or so. I still need to buy some things to get myself established."

"Putting it off is a bad idea. Putting it off means you're going to do it when you get around to it."

"What do you mean, around to it?"

"Putting it off until you get around to it means simply that tomorrow you're going to wish you had saved today."

"Uncle Bob, are you going zingy on me?"

"No, I'm not, Scott. In fact, here's an example of how putting it off and getting around to it later can keep you from becoming a millionaire. Let's say you save your $2,000 a year from today for the next eight years. Not only have you saved $16,000, but your money has earned 10% each year. So actually at the end of eight years you will have saved $16,000, but you will have a total of $25,158. If you didn't add any more earnings, your money would still continue to earn 10% compounded each year."

"So, Scott, by the time you reach 65 years old, how much money would you have?"

"Let me guess. $200,000, $300,000?"

"More."

"$500,000?"

"More."

"$800,000?"

"More."

"A million?"

"Right. You'd have over $1 million that had grown from saving only $16,000."

"On just $16,000? Amazing!"

"That's the Magic of Compounding. You see, you've invested this money and compounded it for 46 years. It just grows and grows. It doubles every seven and one-half years."

"I am in awe. Uncle Bob, you have made magic."

"Thanks, Scott. That's why I keep saying over and over, to

everyone I meet, don't wait until tomorrow. Don't keep living for today. If you want to be a millionaire, start saving today. Buy only those things that you need, and buy only with cash."

"Wow, Uncle Bob! That's great! It's like magic. That's real muscle power."

"Becoming a millionaire, Scott, *is* like magic. We call it the Magic of Compounding. Let me tell you about it. Scott, if I had a machine that you could place a dollar into, and at the end of a certain period of time two dollars, or four dollars, or five dollars would come out, would you buy the machine?"

"You bet I would. Muscle power!"

"How much would you pay for the machine?"

"A lot!"

"You probably would. What if you could buy a machine that, for every dollar you put in, ten or twenty dollars would come out?"

"Sure, I'd buy it!"

"What if I told you, Scott, that you could buy that machine for nothing?"

"What's the catch?"

"The Magic of Compounding is free. All you have to do is save money. And, the younger you start saving, the more money you'll have down the line. The Magic of Compounding will work that much more for you when you're young. You have more time for your money to grow."

"This is really fantastic, Uncle Bob!"

"Scott, you're good in math. Let me show you some simple ways to calculate how fast your money will grow. One is called the Rule of 72. According to the Rule of 72, the amount of your investment will double every 7.2 years, at a 10% rate of return."

"So after the first seven years, my $2,000 would become $4,000. Then in another seven years, $4,000 becomes $8,000."

"Right. But don't forget all the other $2,000 each year that you're saving. That money will compound also."

"Uncle Bob, this is exciting. Gee, I can be a millionaire. With all that money, I'll probably own my own restaurant! I could work whenever I want to, do whatever I want, and live a really neat life. Muscle power!"

"That's right, Scott, and all you have to do is start saving your money now. But first, do you know what you have to start doing immediately?"

"What, my money master?"

"Before you can start saving, you have to get rid of your debt."

Scott stepped off the picnic table and sat in the grass. He picked some daisies and began pulling off the petals one by one. Bob sat down next to him.

$ $ $ $ $ $

"We need to get you out of debt."

"How do I do that?"

"First, slow down on spending. Don't buy things just because they look good; buy only those things you need. Don't add to your debt."

"I know, Uncle Bob. Don't buy anything I don't really need, and when I do buy, pay for it in cash."

"That's right. You've got it now, Scott. The next thing you need to do is start paying off your debt. In other words, pay your bills."

"What about the credit cards? If I just make the minimum payment, they'll take years to pay off."

"Look at your budget. Pay off as much as you can each month. That'll knock out those balances quickly. Ignore the minimum payment. Pay as much as you can. Your goal is to pay your balance in full each month, so that you have no finance charge."

"I'm already paying a hefty sum in finance charges."

"Make it a priority to pay off every bill. You might have to stop some of the parties you're having. You might even have to stop some of the great fun you're having."

"I can still have fun without spending so much money."

"Here's another idea, Scott. Add to your monthly payments on the motorcycle. Try to pay that off early."

"You said earlier that when I consider interest charges, I am paying over $10,000 for an $8,000 motorcycle. I want to get my wheels paid off A-S-A-P."

"How much is your rent?"

"$500 a month."

"Scott, have you ever thought about owning your own home?"

"Awesome, Uncle Bob. That sounds great, my own home. Wow! I guess every millionaire owns his own home."

"Most of them do, Scott. After you get your other debts cleared, you could buy a home. Instead of paying rent, find a home that would have a $500 monthly payment. You'll start building equity in your home, instead of getting nothing back as you do renting. There are some tax advantages to owning a home, too."

$ $ $ $ $ $

Scott and Bob both lay back in the grass. They were chewing the ends of daisy stems. Scott visualized his future. He would go back to school to get his degree. He would start immediately to pay down his debt. Then, he would save as much money as possible for the future.

"What could I do with this million?" he thought to himself. "Buy a million-dollar home. Or, own my own restaurant!"

Just then, Uncle Bob spoke up. "Scott, did you ever think of owning your own restaurant?"

"Amazing! That's just what I was daydreaming about."

"With the right amount of savings, you could probably open your own restaurant."

"Yeah. Know what I'd call it? Scott's Skillet."

"Hey, that sounds impressive."

"Scott's Skillet. Muscle power."

"Scott, now you're on the right path for financial success and becoming a millionaire. By the time you're 40 years old, you'll look around and see that you have no bills, you own your own home, and you own your own restaurant. You'll have only one problem."

"What's that?"

"Your problem, Scott, will be that most of your friends will not have saved their money. They will not have stayed out of debt, and they just won't understand how and why you've become so successful."

"Friends can be kind of geeky sometimes."

"Now they're going to say that you're nuts for saving money. 'Why should you save money?' they'll ask. 'Let's spend it,' they'll tell you. 'Let's have a good time.' 'Don't worry about tomorrow.' "

Scott replied, "I can have fun now, Uncle Bob, but I'm going to save money and enjoy myself also. Don't worry, I'll take care of my friends. I'll help them, but I'm going to help myself first. If my friends don't like me the new way, then I guess, Uncle Bob, they really aren't my friends anyway."

"You're right there, Scott. Remember, you can work very hard and throw away your money, or you can work hard and save your money and make it grow. It's somewhat like a golf game. You play golf, don't you?"

"Sure. Great sport."

"You play each round one hole at a time. If you make par on each of the 18 holes, then you have par for the game. If you save money every day or every month, your total score over the long haul will be very good, too."

"Wow, Uncle Bob, we're really rolling today. Anything more?"

"Not right now," answered Bob. He thought he had thrown enough at Scott already. Scott seemed to be headed toward the path of financial success.

"Hey, Bob, how about another ride?" said Scott as he tossed a helmet to Bob.

"Okay," said Bob. "I'll trust your ability as a motorcycle jock. That's because I believe that you are going to drive your financial life on the highway to success."

"Thanks, Bob. I'll do it. I won't give you such a wild ride this time."

They strapped on their helmets. Scott swung his leg over the cycle and sat on the seat. Bob got on behind him and held the bottom of his seat with his hands.

Scott pulled the machine off its center stand and pushed the starter button. The big Harley motor rumbled. Scott punched the throttle, and the machine roared. Off went the two easy riders out the park entrance and onto the main highway. They enjoyed a delightful ride cruising in the wind. Bob held on tight, and felt good that Scott was on his way to becoming a millionaire.

5

Larry Lost:
Don't Let Crisis
Uproot Your Finances

A BRIGHT AFTERNOON SUN shone over Prosperity Park's baseball field. It was a field of dreams for these Sunday afternoon players, who left behind their everyday lives to test their hitting and fielding skills. The game was the major event of the annual picnics.

A large backstop identified home plate. The finely graded infield was marked with fresh white bases, and on each side there were benches for the teams. Behind the backstop, Darin, Sarah, and other young children kicked a soccer ball and drank lemonade. Uncle Bob, along with several senior citizens and a mother with a baby, sat in lawn chairs to watch the action.

The players on the field were a mix of men and women, boys and girls, dressed in picnic attire. Several of the adults and youths were experienced players who regularly competed on teams. The others were just out for a good time. The players had divided themselves into two teams with approximately the same number of players on each team.

As each batter swung at the ball, there were swirls of activity and cheering. Fielders chased balls and threw them back while runners kicked up clouds of dust around the base paths.

Excitement peaked as Ben rounded third as a bullet throw rocketed from the outfield to home plate. Ben and the ball simultaneously converged on home plate, where the other team's catcher, Larry, positioned himself to receive the throw and tag the runner.

At the last minute, Ben dropped his shoulder and barreled into Larry at the plate. The smacking sound could be heard across the field as Bigtimer, who was about 50 pounds heavier, collided with Larry. Ben sent Larry in a backward tumble, head over heels, and Larry ended up flat on his back. The stunning impact jarred the ball loose from Larry's glove, and Ben was safe.

Ben jumped up and dusted off his pants. He ran to his cheering teammates. At the same time, players from the other team rushed to check on Larry. He was lying on the ground on his side, with his knees bent.

Scott was the first to arrive. "Larry! Are you okay?" he asked.

Denise was next. "Are you okay?"

Larry groaned for a moment. Then he nodded his head. Gasping for air, he said, "I'm okay. Just got the wind knocked out of me. My head hurts, too. He hit me in the head."

Denise said, "That Ben!" as she looked toward the other team's bench. "Why does he have to play that way? This is supposed to be fun, you know!" Larry was sprawled out on the ground with his hands over his head. His catcher's mitt had been knocked about five feet away from him and lay upside down. Denise and Dan helped Larry to his feet.

"You sit out for a while," Dan suggested. "Put your arm around my shoulder and let's walk over to the bench together. How you doin'? Are you okay?"

"Yeah, just a little sore. I think he hit every place on my body."

A voice from the other side of the field shouted, "Come on, let's play."

Larry stopped walking and looked for his mitt. He said, "Who's gonna play catcher? I can't sit out."

"Larry! You've got to sit out at least the rest of this inning," said Denise. "We need to get some ice for your head." She reached for the first aid kit and pulled out a dry ice pack. Looking over at Uncle Bob, she shouted, "Bob, we could use your help over here!"

Bob got up from his lawn chair and joined Dan. They supported Larry between them and headed for the bench. Denise went over to get some ice to put in the ice pack for Larry's head.

Dan and Bob eased Larry down on the bench. "Bob," Dan announced, "you're now Team Trainer and Doc, in charge of helping injured players."

Dan went running back to the game with Scott. Scott yelled to everyone, "Trainer Bob is on the job taking care of Larry. Let's play ball!"

Play resumed. Larry's team took the field with eight players. George agreed to serve as catcher until Larry could come back into the game. Sam took the mound to pitch.

In the meantime, Bob sat next to Larry on the bench, helping him hold an ice pack to his head.

"Come on, let's hold 'em," yelled Larry, who then moaned, "Oh, my head hurts."

Larry "Lost" (as Bob calls him) had a knack for being in the wrong place at the wrong time. Three years ago, he had got his dream job of being personnel manager for a large manufacturing company. Six months after he started, the company was bought by a conglomerate and his job was cut.

Once, an errant motorist had driven his car into the front of Larry's house and knocked out the living room window. Another time, Larry had broken his ankle when a display of two-liter soda bottles fell on him in the grocery store. As a youth, he had always been the one who got caught pulling pranks and was sent to the principal's office while his friends went unnoticed. And it had rained on Larry's wedding day 14 years ago.

Now, Larry was involved in one of life's biggest jolts—much bigger than Bigtimer's full-speed assault at home plate. Larry and his wife, Linda, were planning on a divorce. A few years earlier, Larry and Linda had watched friends go through divorces. They had both felt sorry for their friends, but they couldn't understand why they would divorce. They also couldn't understand the trauma of a divorce. Now they both felt the pain for themselves.

Bob knew what major financial changes can be brought on by a divorce. The expense of running two households instead of one forces a reduction in lifestyle. Costs for attorneys can wipe out savings or, worse, put people deeply into debt. Often, high costs are incurred for extended treatment by psychologists and therapists who help the family adjust.

The myriad emotions in a divorce can make financial matters difficult to handle. People during this time can carry tremendous anger and hurt, and managing finances may seem unimportant. Higher priorities may be handling problems with the children or adjusting to a new lifestyle as a single person. With all these emotions running high, people can go on spending sprees for clothes, cars, and vacations and not care at all about tomorrow. The only thing they are interested in is getting rid of the pain today. Many times they feel as if they tried hard enough, but things just wouldn't work out. There is a sense of failure, that they couldn't sustain the marriage relationship. Others feel that they were victimized by the system, that they were given a bad deal.

There are high costs, both emotionally and financially, to the legal battles that occur over child custody, division of assets, alimony, and child support. Because of clogged court dockets, divorces can take one to two years to settle. Throughout that time, there are constant meetings with the attorney, court appearances, and depositions. Legal costs in some divorces, particularly those involving child custody issues, can run $10,000 per person or higher.

$$\$ \, \$ \, \$ \, \$ \, \$ \, \$$

"Larry, I'm sorry to hear about you and Linda," Bob said sympathetically.

"Yeah, it's too bad," Larry admitted.

"How are the kids?" asked Bob. There were Jennifer, a shy but academically gifted 12-year-old, and Jason, a fun-loving but nonathletic boy of nine.

"They're doing all right," Larry said. "They're seeing a therapist once a week. It's been helpful. They get a chance to talk some things out. And they find out that there are other kids going through the same thing. Jason told me, 'Dad, it's okay. All my buddies are in the same situation. Their parents are divorced, too.' But, Bob, that doesn't make it right, and it doesn't make me feel any better. I'm just really down about this whole situation."

Bob was very supportive. "I'm sorry to hear that. But it's good you are taking care of the kids. They need to adjust and remain healthy. Both you and Linda are helping in this, I presume?"

"Yes. She takes them to counseling one week; I take them the next."

"So you're still working together okay when it comes to the kids?"

"Yeah, although something she did recently bugged me. A couple of weeks ago, she decided to go to her mother's for a week. Now I'm supposed to see the kids on Wednesdays and every weekend. But she just packed up and took them with her. Never talked to me about it."

"So you missed some time with the kids."

"Yeah. She did it just because she felt like doing it. And probably to spite me."

"I'm not sure she was trying to spite you or hurt you. Maybe she just needed to get away for a week. What you're going through isn't easy."

Larry nodded his head.

Bob said, "Here's an idea. Why don't you just try to make up the time? Ask her if she could give you the kids for a week?"

"I suppose I could. Let's see, I would have to rearrange my tennis on Tuesday. And I go bowling on Thursday night. Our bowling team is in third place."

"Larry, you're talking out of both sides of your mouth. You complain about her taking the kids. But then you say that for you to take them is inconvenient given your schedule."

"Well . . . not really, Bob. Okay. I can miss a week of tennis and bowling for my kids. They're more important. After all, they're all I have now."

"Larry, I understand something of what you're going through. It's a hard adjustment, and it just takes time to work things out. And it could take a long time before you really feel comfortable with the situation. There are a lot of bad feelings. You need to work through it and talk it out. But whatever you do, stay close to your kids."

"I'm doing okay with that. They're here at the picnic today, you know. They're over at the volleyball court now."

"I thought this might be Linda's weekend."

"She let them come because they've been coming to these family picnics since they were born. They look forward to it."

"Good! There's a start on how you can share the kids. Put their needs first."

$ $ $ $ $ $

"It's true we both love the kids and want the best for them. But we still have to divide the property and set up a schedule for the kids. Dealing with these lawyers is a real pain. Her lawyer is a jerk. He tries to make an issue of everything."

"When you get the lawyers involved in every little issue, it can get expensive real fast," said Bob.

"I just found that out," said Larry. "I just got a bill for $500 from my lawyer. Do you know what it was for?"

"I don't know, what?"

"For negotiating who gets the patio furniture."

"Oh, my gosh."

"I wanted the patio furniture for my apartment. I've got a nice patio, and I thought the furniture would look good on it. The stuff is nothing special—a wrought iron table and chairs that might draw $50 at a garage sale. She didn't want to give it up; she says she needs to furnish her patio. Now keep in mind that I haven't taken one piece of furniture from that house. I rented a furnished apartment. I want a couple of lousy pieces of patio furniture, and she won't give it up.

"So to get this patio furniture, it cost me *more* in attorney's fees than it would have cost to buy a brand-new set! Is that ludicrous or what?"

Larry slammed the icebag down on the bench. He didn't realize it, but as he talked he was getting louder and louder.

Bob said, "Larry, calm down. Just relax. Keep that icebag on your head. Let's just talk it out. See what happens, Larry—you start talking about the divorce and you get upset. You lose track of the primary concerns. Those should be you and your children and Linda. Not patio furniture."

"Yeah, you're right, Uncle Bob, it's all out of sync. Everything has gone tilt. Like when I was a kid and used to play the pinball machine all the time. Uncle Bob, I was the best. I had complete control of that machine. I could nudge it, move it, shake it, and that pinball would go wherever I wanted. And a flipper master. I was the best. I was king of the flippers. I could wait until the very last split second and flip those flippers and make that ball fly to the top of the board and score. My machine never went tilt. I was in complete control.

"Now, my whole world has gone tilt. I'm upside down, and I don't know how to get back right side up. It was easy when it was a game, Uncle Bob. If I ever did go tilt, all I did was take another quarter out and start the game all over."

"Well, Larry, you can take another quarter out."

"What do you mean, Uncle Bob?"

"You don't have to keep going down this path of antagonizing yourself or each other. You could sit down and try to work these things out."

"No, Uncle Bob, it's never going to work. But let's talk about that later."

"Larry, let's talk about it now."

Larry yelled, "Get in the game, guys."

"Now, Larry, back to the attorney's fees. $150 an hour sure

adds up fast. That's when a lawyer can laugh all the way to the bank—when the couple skirmishes over silly issues like patio furniture."

"God help us when we get to the big stuff, Bob."

"That's why it pays to communicate with Linda on everything. That's probably where your marriage fell apart."

"What do you mean, Bob?"

"Your marriage probably fell apart because the two of you were so busy doing everything that you just forgot to do one thing."

"What's that?"

"Communicate. You forgot to talk to each other. You forgot to listen to each other. You forgot to just sit down and find out what was going on. You were both too busy to really see what was happening to you. You probably just pulled farther and farther apart."

"You're right, Bob. There at the end, we never talked to each other."

"See what I mean, Larry? You need to communicate. Try to maintain some communication with Linda all the time. Maybe even every day. It will help both of you. It will at least help the divorce go smoothly, and it might help in other ways."

"What do you mean?"

"Well, it will help with the kids. They'll see that the two of you are getting along better. It might make both of you see that you weren't communicating before, and maybe now if you did communicate you just might be able to get along again."

"I don't think so, Bob. But do you really think so?"

"I sure do, Larry."

"Boy, wouldn't that be great? We could be together again with the kids. As it's going right now, we're going to be raising the kids on our own separately.

"The lawyer always wants to speak for me; he wants to take everything to her lawyer. I bet they go into a room and laugh.

They're probably golfing buddies. You're right, Bob. Linda and I should figure things out."

"Sometimes there's a place for attorneys. I'm not saying you should ignore your attorney's advice. Just keep the communication with Linda open. Try to work things out on your own.

"Larry, here's something else to consider. Have you ever heard of mediation?"

"No."

"For some people, it's a good alternative to going to court. It can save thousands in attorney's fees."

"Well, that's for me for sure."

"And you would have a settlement you created on your own, Larry. Not something imposed by a judge. But the parties have to come to the table ready to talk and be reasonable. Sometimes people aren't reasonable, and the only choice is to go to court."

"It would save a lot of money and heartache if we could work some of this out ourselves." They both sat and watched the softball game for a few minutes without saying a word. Larry sat on the bench holding the ice pack with his left hand, his right hand resting on the bench at his side. Bob leaned forward with his elbows on his knees and his hands on his chin. The two watched the action on the field.

With the help of Sam's friendly, high-arching pitching, the other team had gotten three more hits and scored another run. There were runners on second and third with two outs. Everybody was yelling now. It was like a big-league ballgame. Larry looked at Bob. "Hey, this is fun. You know, this is the first time I've smiled for quite a while. I can't wait to get back in there."

"Larry, a couple more minutes and you'll be back in there."

$ $ $ $ $ $

"So, Larry, you moved into an apartment?"

"Yeah. Someone had to move out, and I wasn't even thinking at the beginning. I just had to get out of there. So I just picked up and left. I walked out. I guess I figured she'd be taking care of the kids; I didn't even think. I didn't know what to expect. We've had friends who got divorced, and we tried to console them and tried to help them keep it together. We never thought it was going to happen to us. Then all of a sudden, boom, it happened."

"So, how do you like the apartment?"

"It's great. It's got a swimming pool and a health club—and lots of great-looking single women. It's great going to the pool."

"Do you miss seeing the kids every night when you come home?"

"Yes. Of course I do. It was old hat to me then. I didn't realize how much the kids meant to me. How much I would miss them. They were just always there. Now it's different. This kind of life, Bob, is the pits. There has to be something better."

"Well, you had a better situation when you and Linda were together. Are you dating yet?"

"Bob, the first couple of months after I knew it was over, I went out and hit the bars and nightclubs every night. After about five weeks of that, I was wiped out. I really haven't done any dating since then."

"Not any?"

"Not any. It's been six months since we separated now, and I don't have much free time, between my job and the kids. I'm really not looking forward to starting all over again."

"It must be awkward going back to dating again."

"I hadn't done it for years. It's like high school all over again."

"Larry, you're looking sharp. Designer shirt and a gold neck chain. That's a new haircut, too, isn't it?"

"Yeah. I'm a brand-new man. I'm single, I'm on my own. I'm young again. I'm not very happy, Bob, but again, I guess, I'm on my own."

"Well, isn't that what you wanted, Larry?"

"It's what I thought I wanted."

"Well, remember the communication. You never think things

will wind up as they do sometimes. But if you communicate and plan ahead, there won't be any surprises."

"Bob, this was the biggest and ugliest surprise of my life."

"Well, if you want to be single, congratulations. You're basically an unmarried man. Suddenly single. Starting your second life."

"I'm trying to have a good time. I'm trying to have more fun than I've had in years, but you know, Bob, it's kind of shallow. I come home to an empty apartment. So I decided to take care of myself. I need to have fun. Do you know what I bought?"

"What?"

"A new car. I finally got rid of that old Ford LTD sedan. I bought myself a Chrysler LeBaron convertible. Lots of fun. Looks great."

Bob was not impressed. He shook his head, then looked out to the field as another hitter drove home a run. Larry could tell that Bob had something on his mind.

"Okay, Bob, what's the problem?"

"Larry, you're spending money too freely. I know you can't afford all this. New clothes, new hairstyle, new car, and apartment. You can't possibly have the money to be buying all these things."

"Maybe I can, maybe I can't."

"Larry, remember what I've always said to you and Linda about buying only what you need and not whatever you want."

"Yes, I remember. But, Bob, you've never been divorced. You don't know what it's like. It's crazy. Linda says I'm boring. Well, you know what? I'm not boring. So, Bob, there are some things that I just needed to do. I've gotta stay on my feet. I have to keep myself happy. No one else will."

"I understand that you have to take care of yourself. And, sometimes, if you're going through tough times, you have to buy things to make yourself feel better. That's fine. But not at the rate you're doing it. It seems as if you're trying to get back at her and prove something."

"Bob, you're right. That's part of it. I spend money because I figure, what the heck? She's going after it all anyway. You can divide a bank account in half. But you can't divide a car in half. And she can't take away my Florida vacation."

"You went to Florida, too?"

"For a week this spring. I lay on the beach for a week. Surrounded by college students. Lots of good-looking college girls in their bikinis."

"Larry, it sounds as if you aren't thinking about your finances. You're just doing what you feel like doing at the moment. You haven't started planning ahead. That's when you'll really begin to look out for yourself—when you start planning ahead."

"Bob, I'm fine. It's all her problem. She's the one who's being unreasonable."

"Larry, you're just as hard-headed as she is."

Wilma's son Warren was up to bat. He corked a deep shot to left center, over the outfielders. Both runners scored, plus Warren, putting the team up by three runs.

"Come on, let's hold 'em," shouted Larry.

$$\$ \$ \$ \$ \$ \$$$

Larry adjusted the ice pack on his head.

Bob looked at Larry. "You feeling good enough to go back in?"

"No, Bob. I think I would rather sit here quietly and talk out some of these problems."

"Okay," agreed Bob. "Larry, the first step is to have some kind of financial plan. You have to know where you are today financially. Do you know how much money you have coming in?"

"Of course I know how much money I have coming in."

"Do you know what your expenses are?"

"Well, probably. I mean, sure, I know what my expenses are."

"What are they?"

"Bob, I don't know. We're playing a softball game. I don't take my expenses around with me."

"Yeah, I understand that, Larry, but you need to know what your expenses are and what the difference is between your income and your expenses. This is so you know what you have left over to save."

"Well, all I can tell you, Bob, is that it seems that everything that comes in is gone before it hits my checkbook. So what I do is go out and buy whatever I need to buy."

"Yeah, but Larry, are you buying what you need or are you buying what you want?"

"Is there a difference, Bob?"

"Of course there's a difference. You don't go out and buy a shiny new car just because it looks good. You go out and buy something only if you really need it, and then you only buy it if you can afford it. And then you buy it only if you have cash."

"I can afford it."

"Yeah, but how did you buy it? Did you pay for all those things with cash, or did you put them on credit cards?"

"Well, I didn't have the cash."

"But you bought them anyhow."

"Everyone else buys on credit. Why shouldn't I? It's the American way."

"Well, Larry, when everyone else gets into their 40s, 50s, and 60s, they're not going to have anything to retire on because they built up an enormous amount of debt. They got instant gratification in their early years, but they are left with no emergency funds or retirement dollars.

"Larry, you're in a worse situation than a lot of people now. When you're divorced, your expenses will be higher. You'll be taking care of two households. Plus, you'll still need to save money for yourself and your kids' college education down the line."

"Bob, I don't have time to think about that right now. I'm trying to put my life together."

"You've got a responsibility to those two kids. If you and Linda don't see that, then there's a big problem. You can't just think about numero uno, Larry; you've got to think about Jennifer and Jason. They're good kids, but they're going to need two good parents, and they're going to need a good education to become successful in life later. You know how important that is."

"I know, Bob, you're right, you're right. But what can I do? I don't have time to figure out what my expenses are."

"Sure you do."

"Besides, Bob, when we were married, Linda handled all the finances."

"Larry, both spouses should work together, not only in handling the finances but in making all the decisions. Remember, I told you that your problem may be that you stopped communicating. When you two stopped communicating, I bet that's when your problems started."

"You're right, Bob. Everything was going well, and then we got kind of carried away. I started doing my thing. I started going out with the guys on the bowling team, and then I was playing tennis, and Linda didn't want to play tennis. She started doing her own thing, and before I knew it we didn't see each other anymore. We never talked to each other. We didn't know each other anymore. We just kind of went our separate ways."

$$\$ \$ \$ \$ \$ \$$$

"Larry, while this innings is still going on, let's get a quick handle on your budget. You will want to find out your income and expenses, along with your assets and liabilities. Let's see where you are."

"Okay. Let's do it."

"Let's start with your assets. How much is your house worth?"

"About $120,000."

"How much do you owe on it?"

"About $50,000."

"So your equity is $70,000. Savings accounts?"

"We have about $20,000."

"Any IRAs?"

"Yest, about $6,000."

"How about cars?"

"My convertible is worth $17,000. Her van is worth $12,000."

"Any other assets?"

"Yes, Bob. You know, I had to go through this for the attorney. The court wants a statement of assets, income, and expenses from each of us."

"Any other assets?"

"She has jewelry worth about $2,000. Then it's just household furnishings and clothes."

"Any antiques or art, or any unusual item that may be worth some money?"

"No, that's it."

"Now, how about debts? Besides the mortgage on the house, what else do you owe?"

"We owe $5,000 on a home equity loan. I owe $10,000 on the convertible. We owe $8,000 on the van. Linda and I both have balances on our credit cards. Mine is about $2,000. Hers was $1,000 a couple of months ago. I don't know what she's run it up to now."

"Anything else?"

"No other debts."

"So, Larry, if we list your and Linda's major assets and liabilities, this is what it would look like."

Bob showed Larry his handwritten list (see top of page 105).

"That's not bad, Larry. That's a lot better than it could have been. A lot of people have a lot more debt than you and Linda have right now."

"Well, we've got enough, don't we?"

"You have enough, but at least there's light at the end of the

Assets		Liabilities	
House	$120,000	Mortgage	$50,000
Savings	20,000	Home equity loan	5,000
Car	17,000	Car	10,000
Van	12,000	Van	8,000
IRA	6,000	Cards	3,000
Total	$175,000	Total	−$76,000
Net Worth			$99,000

tunnel. When you get divorced, keep in mind that the court will probably want to divide the assets and liabilities equally. That's so that each of you ends up with the same net worth. One of you may have the house, the other cash or vehicles.

"So, you'll be starting over with almost $50,000. That's less whatever you spend on attorneys."

"I had no idea we were worth that much. It's amazing when you add it up."

"So you've got something worth preserving. Don't blow it on any more cars and vacations. Now, how about income and expenses?"

"Okay."

"What's your salary?"

"$50,000 a year. Plus, I make $7 an hour at the hardware store. I work 10 hours a week; that makes $70. Multiply that times 52 weeks, let's see—"

"I've got a calculator," said Bob. He pulled out his wallet, which had a built-in calculator. "Let's see, that makes $3,640 a year. Figuring your taxes at roughly $15,000 on gross income of $53,000, that leaves $38,000 of take-home pay. That would be about $3,100 a month take-home pay. Is that about right?"

"No. I thought I was bringing home more than that, maybe about $3,500 to $4,000."

"Are you taking your withholding as married or single?"

"Married."

"As long as you're married at the end of the year, you can

file a joint return. But by next year, you'll be filing as single. Have you noticed what your taxes would be as a single person?"

"No. Linda always did the taxes."

"Well, the taxes are much higher on singles. You may be paying several thousand dollars more. It would be wise for you to sit down with your tax professional and estimate what your taxes will be next year."

"So my taxes are going to go up?"

"Yes. Way up."

"Will Linda's go up, too?"

"Yes, but not much. If the children reside primarily with her, she can file as a single head of household. Those rates are just a little higher than married filing jointly."

"What if we have a joint physical custody arrangement, where the kids live half the time at each home?"

"You'd have to work that out. Your tax professional could help."

Larry asked, "I have another question. If I'm paying alimony and child support, can't I deduct that?

"Alimony, yes. Child support, no. For alimony, you can deduct any amount you pay on the front of Form 1040 as an adjustment to income. Linda has to add it to her income, and pay tax on it.

"Child support is just the opposite," Bob continued. "You cannot deduct it. Linda does not add it to her income. In other words, you pay child support in after-tax dollars.

"In working out your settlement, something that you and Linda should consider is who receives the dependency deductions for the children. I can't advise you one way or the other, only that you two should come up with a fair and equitable solution."

Larry thought a moment and said, "I hadn't thought of all these things. How we do this settlement will really affect my future."

"That's my point," said Bob. "Take a thorough look at your

situation. You're going to have to live with this for a long time—the rest of your life. You've got to communicate with Linda. If the two of you can work this out together, it's going to work out better for both of you financially. It's going to work out better for all of you, including the children. They'll see that you're working together. Believe me, Larry, it will make them feel a lot better."

"I see what you mean, Bob. I'll talk to Linda. I'll see if we can start communicating again."

"Who knows, Larry, you might be able to communicate to the point where you both feel better about each other. Possibly, you may even realize that you might be able to communicate in a way that would allow you to get back together again."

"I doubt it, Bob."

"Yes, but there's always a chance, Larry."

"Well, I haven't thought about that lately, but maybe you're right."

"Now, let's get back to your budget. How much does it cost Larry to live?"

Bob got out his pencil and paper again. He turned over the paper with the list of assets and liabilities, and wrote the word "Budget" at the top. He said, "Let's make a list of your income and expenses."

"Okay."

"First of all, are you paying Linda anything now?"

"Yes. There's a temporary order, $500 in alimony, $900 in child support per month."

"Okay. What's your rent?"

"$600."

"And the utilities would run about $100?"

"Yes."

"How about the car? How much is that costing?"

"The payment is $300 a month."

"There are more expenses to a car. How much is gasoline?"

"Well, let's see. I fill it up about two or three times a week. It costs about $10 each time."

"So maybe $100 a month for gas. Then, let's add on taxes, insurance, license, and maintenance. That would be another $150 a month. So we have about $250 per month in costs to own and operate your car."

"This is starting to add up fast."

"How much are you paying on the home equity loan and the credit cards?"

"Just the minimum. I put in maybe $100 a month on both."

"Okay. What other expenses do you have?"

"Well, I have a health club membership. That's $50 a month. Then there's $200 a month for health insurance for the family."

"Life insurance?"

"Yes, I have a life insurance policy that runs about $600 a year."

"So that's $50 a month." Bob wrote as he spoke. "What else is there? Food?"

"Maybe $50 a month."

"$50 a month? Larry, you've got to be spending more than $50 a month on food."

"Bob, I don't know. I'm telling you these figures are just rough. I don't know exactly what I spend."

"Well, you've got to find out now if you're really going to figure out what your expenses are."

"Okay, but how?"

"Let's put that aside for right now. Let's stick with the expenses that you know of. That $50 a month sounds awfully low. Think about it a minute. Groceries, and meals out for you and the kids?"

"Okay, let's say $150 a month."

"All right. How about the attorney? Are you paying him?"

"Yes. About $100 a month."

"And didn't you say the kids were in therapy?"

"Yes. I'm paying about $50 a month on that. Insurance also covers some, but we're not paying all of it. We're running up a balance."

"That you'll have to pay off some time."

"That's true. But maybe she'll have to pay it in the settlement. Right now, who cares?"

"The bill won't go away," said Bob. "They'll come after you until you pay it.

"What else? Clothes? You've been buying clothes. And it looks as if you're going to a new hair stylist. How much would you guess for those?"

"Let's say $75 a month for clothes and hair," said Larry.

"I bet it's a lot more, Larry." Bob wrote down the figures. "I'm also going to add another $50 for miscellaneous expenses. That would include things like entertainment—going to a show, buying popcorn, grabbing those quick lunches."

"When I bowl on Thursdays, we always get a few pitchers of beer, and we go out to eat afterward."

"So that $50 miscellaneous is probably low. At least it gives us a starting place. You know, Larry, we spend a lot of money without realizing it. That's why it's so important to keep track of expenses. You can't control your expenses unless you know where you're spending money."

"The paycheck comes, then it's gone. I have $100 in my pocket, and it disappears before I know it."

"Here's a suggestion. Every time you buy something, save the receipt. Mark on it what you bought, bring it home, and put it in a cookie jar."

"What if they don't give you a receipt?"

"Then just make a note on a slip of paper."

"So I end up with a jar full of receipts."

"Right. That's what I call my Cookie Jar Expense Checklist system. At the end of the month, pull all your receipts out of the jar. Sort them out and add them up. You'll be surprised at what you find out."

"That I'm spending more than I thought."

"Right. And maybe not exactly where you thought you were spending it."

"And maybe I can find ways to cut expenses and still have a good time."

"Good idea."

"On Thursday bowling night, there are a couple of things I could cut. One would be that second pitcher of beer. When we go out afterward, I could skip getting a full meal, and instead just order a drink or dessert."

"You're on the right track, Larry."

"So, Bob, let's add this all up."

Bob hit the buttons on the calculator. He looked at it for a moment, then wrote down a figure. "Your expenses total $3,675 each month."

"That's more than I have coming in!"

"That's why you have to get a handle on your expenses."

"So I need to start saving receipts, and tracking what I spend."

"Yes, and don't use credit cards. Buy only what you need, and just pay cash. If you don't have enough money, then don't buy it."

Bob handed Larry his written list of expenses (see top of page 111).

Two infield hits had put two more runners on base. But Denise grounded to shortstop Scott Youth. He scooped up the ball and flipped it to second base for the force-out. The long inning ended. Larry's team was down by three runs.

$ $ $ $ $ $

Larry yelled to his returning teammates, "It's about time. Let's get some runs!"

Scott, Denise, and the others asked Larry how he was doing.

"I'm doing better. I'll be ready to go back in soon."

Alimony	$500
Child support	900
Rent	600
Utilities	100
Automobile - gasoline, tax, insurance, maintenance	250
Automobile - payment	300
Debt payments - home equity loan	100
credit cards	100
Attorney payment	100
Therapist	50
Health club	50
Health insurance	200
Life insurance	50
Food	150
Entertainment	100
Clothes, hair care	75
Miscellaneous	50
Total	$3,675

"Who made the last out?" yelled Scott.

Dan said, "I did. Denise is up first."

Scott walked over to Uncle Bob. "Hey, you takin' good care of our catcher? Gettin' him well?"

"Sure am," replied Bob.

Two players jumped up. Each ran to a different coaching area, one down the third-base line and the other down the first-base line. A couple of teammates grabbed bats and started swinging them near the warm-up circle. Everyone else was at the water cooler. It had been a long, long inning for those out in the field. They had taken a lot of abuse and were now ready to return the favor. It had been a long inning for Larry, also. Bob had come down on him pretty hard, but he realized he needed it. Bob and Larry resumed their conversation.

"Larry, here's why this budget is so important. In the next year, you'll be settling the divorce or maybe getting back together.

You want to make sure you've set up a budget that you can live with."

"I'm going to get taken to the cleaners, I just know it. Everything always happens to me. That's what's going to happen; I'm going to get taken to the cleaners."

"Larry, you can't look at it that way. You're making yourself a victim."

"It's hard knocks. Everybody's had their share of hard knocks in life. I just get handed more."

"But you've made it so far. You're a survivor; you'll make it," Bob assured him. "Sometimes people create their own luck. Stop looking at this negatively. If you see yourself losing everything, that just may happen. Emerson said, 'A man is what he thinks about all day long.' "

"People say I've had a knack for being in the wrong place at the wrong time ever since I was a kid."

"Larry, it's up to you. It's all in your attitude. Start each day fresh, and make it the best you can."

"So I need to stop blaming other people. I need to take responsibility for myself. I've heard that. I know I need to do it."

"Right. Start taking responsibility for your own life."

"Getting the car was fun. I did that on my own. But, yes, I need to move my life in positive directions. And that's up to me."

"And one way to move your life ahead is to get control of your money. Stop wasting money. Will you do that?"

"Okay."

"Larry, here's what I want you to do with that budget. Figure out some ways you can cut expenses, so you can start saving.

"You'll need to be able to provide for emergencies, for your needs, and for your retirement. And you still want your children to go to college, don't you?"

"Yes. But why should I start saving now, when she'll want half of everything I save?"

"I don't know if it will work that way," said Bob. "Besides, you're better off with half of something than 100% of nothing. There's one other problem, Larry, that you need to deal with."

"What's that?"

"Debt. You started with debt on your house, the home equity loan, and credit cards. You've added the car loan. And it sounds as if your credit card balance is increasing. Plus, you said you aren't paying the therapist in full."

"It's a crazy time. I'm just trying to stay afloat. I don't want to drown, Bob. All of this is swirling around in my head like Ben just unloaded on me again."

"Don't dig yourself too deep a hole," said Bob. "You could be in much better shape than Ben."

"Me in better shape than Ben? He's a millionaire. He's got no problems."

"Believe me, Larry, everybody has problems of some sort. Don't let those debts run up. It could take years to pay them off. Or you might never pay them off, and then things would even be worse than they are right now."

"You know, Bob, that convertible's really fun. But it's not what I really need. There's no room in the backseat for my kids, especially if they have friends along. Maybe I'll sell it, and get something less expensive. That'd be one debt I'd be out from under."

A voice from the other end of the bench shouted, "Hey, Larry, you're next on deck."

$ $ $ $ $ $

Larry put down the ice pack, which had done its duty, picked up a bat, and began warming up next to Bob. Larry was ready to get back in the game.

"Here are just a few other issues to think about," said Bob.

"Name them, Uncle Bob. I'm ready."

"One issue is your home. Will Linda stay in the house and buy out your half? Will you buy her out? Or will you sell the house?"

"Haven't thought much about that yet." He held two bats and took practice swings.

"What's the other issue?"

"Your will. Do you have one?"

"Of course. We had it written several years ago."

"But Larry, that's a will for both you and your wife. If you get a divorce, it's no good anymore. Once you're divorced, you need to rewrite it."

"Back to the lawyer again. Those guys never stop making money."

"A will is something you can't do without."

There were now two runners on base and one out. The batter ahead of Larry hit a ground ball to third. The third baseman bobbled the ball, and everyone was safe.

Now, the bases were loaded for Larry. His team was three runs behind, and a home run would put them ahead.

As he stepped to the plate, he noticed Ben playing shallow in left field. Larry's head still throbbed from the crash he had received. He was ready to get even.

On the second pitch, Larry swung with all his might and sent a towering shot into left field. Ben chased the ball, but by the time he got it, whirled, and threw it back to the infield, the three base runners and Larry had all crossed the plate. The crowd cheered Larry's grand slam home run, and everyone was going crazy. People were jumping up in the air.

Scott ran over to Uncle Bob and said, "Uncle Bob, I don't know what you did, but you sure cured Larry. The master does it again!"

Larry came running back to the bench and saw Scott and Bob.

Larry greeted Bob with a high-five, then a hug and a pat on the back. "What a hit! Did you see the look on Ben's face? Hey, Bob, thanks for all the encouragement. I'm going to pick myself up and get my life together, too. I'll start managing my money.

And I'll hit lots more home runs—with my money, my family, and my career. Thanks, Bob."

"Keep up the good work. Keep hitting those homers. You're a winner. Don't let anything stop you."

6

Wilma Widow: Planning Pays Off

UNCLE BOB WALKED CAREFULLY as he held a paper plate heaping with food. The plate overflowed with barbecued ribs, potato salad, baked beans, creamed spinach, orange jello salad, green bean salad, chips, and three pieces of hot bread with melted garlic butter from the grill.

Most of the picnic benches were filled. He was looking for a place to sit when he heard his name called.

"Bob, come join us. We have an extra seat."

It was Wilma. She was a 50-year-old woman who exhibited poise and class. She wore a red, white, and blue flowered blouse with white pants. A gold chain with a cross hung around her neck. Her hair was short and neatly trimmed, a mix of blonde and gray.

Wilma was average height and not a pound overweight. She was tanned and looked as if she had just come off the golf course.

She had followed Bob's advice for a long time. Years ago, she and her late husband, Jerry, had talked to Bob about estate planning.

That advice had worked. Five years ago, without warning, Jerry had had a massive heart attack and died. Because of proper planning, the house was paid off, the kids' college education was paid for, and Wilma had enough money to live very comfortably.

In fact, it had been at one of these picnics that Bob, Jerry, and Wilma had first talked about saving money.

As he walked toward Wilma, Bob gave a wide smile. He spotted Wilma's two children, Warren, 17, and Wendy, 15. Both were outstanding students at their high school. Like their mother, they too had short, well-groomed hair. Wendy's was thick and blonde; Warren's was brown and parted on the left.

Warren wore a black T-shirt with GEORGETOWN UNIVERSITY written on it; Wendy's white T-shirt had a multicolor abstract design of a swimmer.

Wendy noticed that Uncle Bob had his hands full with that huge plate of food and hadn't been able to carry a drink. "Want something to drink, Uncle Bob?"

"Well, yes. A lemonade would be great, Wendy! Thanks."

As Wendy left, Bob said, "Wendy looks just great. Wilma, you sure have a wonderful daughter."

"Yes, I agree. Did you know that she got two medals at the state swim meet?"

"Hey, that's wonderful!"

"She placed first in the 100-meter freestyle and second in the 200-meter backstroke."

"Good for her."

"Wendy also sings in the choir at church. And she's been using computers since she was 12. She helps me with my computer work."

"That's terrific. What about Warren?"

"He's a National Merit Scholar. We are so proud. He has been accepted at Stanford and Georgetown. And that's not all."

"Mom, come on. Uncle Bob doesn't want to hear all this."

"Oh, yes, I do, Warren. This is great."

"Well, okay. Our debate team took first place at state."

"This is good training for Warren. He wants to go to law school."

Warren responded, "And we're proud of Mom, too. Bob, did you hear about Mom's new business?"

"No. Wilma, what business is this?"

"Well, I always liked to decorate around the house. Now that the kids are going to be leaving pretty soon, I thought I would start my own interior decorating company. Last fall, I took the plunge."

"That's great. How are you doing?"

"Well, I'm doing pretty well. I'm off to a good start. I'm making money."

Wendy returned with a lemonade for Bob and one each for her mom, her brother, and herself.

Wendy said, "Hey, Bob, when I was at the serving table, I noticed that the horseshoe pit is free. Do you want to play when you're done eating?"

"Sure. Thanks for asking. I've been wanting to play a game of horseshoes all day."

Warren suggested, "Wendy, let's go practice. We'll keep the pit reserved so no one else takes it."

"I'll join you as soon as I'm done eating. See you in a few minutes."

Bob and Wilma watched the two young adults run to the horseshoe pit. The last five years had been very difficult with Jerry gone, but because of proper estate planning the bills were paid, the children's education was assured, and Wilma could continue to spend as much time as she wanted with her children.

"Wilma, those kids are great. You've really done an excellent job of raising them. As you know, it's tough for a single parent to bring up kids."

"You're right, Bob, it's tough. But we planned for emergencies, and we certainly had one when Jerry died. Bob, you know Jerry and I were fortunate to talk with you so often after we first got married. You sat us down and had us do a financial profile. We had a lot of money coming in, but we just didn't know what to do with it. Remember when you started us off with our Cookie Jar Expense Checklist?"

"Yes. That seems like a long time ago."

"Well, the kids and I do it every month. Every time we spend money, we write it down on a piece of paper. We write the amount we spent and what it was for. We put that piece of paper into a pocket until the end of the day. Every dollar we spend, we write down. Then when we get home, we lift the lid off the cookie jar, take the slips of paper from our pockets, and put them inside. We do it every day, Bob, just as you suggested.

"At the end of each month we gather around the kitchen table with the cookie jar. We pull out all the slips of paper and sort them out. We add up all the categories. Entertainment, education, utility bills, transportation, or whatever. We go over everyone's expenses. Then we discuss where we could cut down."

"So the next month, you spend money more wisely," chimed in Bob.

"The kids are really into saving, Bob. They put away 10% of everything they make."

"That's good. Do they do the pay-yourself plan also?"

"Yes. They pay themselves first on each paycheck. Every time they get a paycheck, or they get any money at all, the first thing they do is write a check for 10% of the total amount of money they have just received. They deposit that amount into their second checking account. It grows every year. Remember the Magic Money Machine?"

"I remember, Wilma."

"Well, the kids think that's really neat. Their Magic Money Machine is at work for them already. They are way ahead of most kids their ages."

"That money-making account is really worthwhile," agreed Bob. "Wilma, they'll be financially ahead of most of their friends for the rest of their lives. They'll have more fun than all the other kids, too."

"Bob, a lot of their friends tell them that they're nuts to save money. They say they should spend it all right now and have a good time. 'Don't worry about the future. Retirement is for old people.' "

"That's too bad."

"Bob, when Jerry and I made plans for the future, I never expected to lose him. We talked about the what-ifs. What if something happened to one of us? What if we got sick, if we lost our job, if one of us died? That seems so long ago now. But those what-ifs can really come true. So it's good we prepared."

She continued.

"You helped us set goals. Did we want to buy a home? How much would college education cost? What about retirement? If something happened to one of us, how much money would be needed to pay all the bills and get the kids through college? How much to make sure the living spouse wouldn't have to work and could spend time with the kids as they grew without having to worry about finances? You told us about inflation. You explained how inflation eats away at our hard-earned dollars—at a rate of about 4% a year."

"That's right, Wilma. Most people never really understand inflation. They don't know it's there."

Wilma interjected, "When we set up our estate plan, Warren was five and Wendy was three. College costs were running about $8,000 a year. We figured a 4% inflation factor would take that figure to about $13,320 by the time Warren started college. Two children at four years each equals close to $120,000 of college costs, and that's just tuition, books, and fees. You told us that if one of the kids decided to get a master's degree, we could add another two years of costs or another $30,000 to the total. If both children got advanced degrees, we'd be talking almost $60,000 more for the additional degree. That total could grow to $180,000. You know, Bob, that's about what we projected when we set up our plan years ago.

"Then we figured out how much it would cost for one of us to bring up the kids on our own if the other spouse died, regardless of which one of us it was. We figured our current expenses were about $45,000 a year. Then you told us that one person couldn't live on half of what two people can. You said to figure that one of us could live on about 75% of what we spent while both of us were living. We added that to the children's college costs. We concluded that the children would probably be dependent on us for an additional 18 years."

Bob nodded his head. "And Wilma, remember what I said about paying off your home mortgage in case of an untimely accident or death."

"Our home at that time was a nice home. It was worth about $95,000, so we took out a $100,000 decreasing term program. I didn't even know what decreasing term was; you told us that as the mortgage goes down each year, so does the amount of insurance coverage. If one of us had died the first year, the policy would have paid $100,000. If one of us died after 10 years, it would have paid only $70,000. It was really cheap coverage that paid off for us in big dividends if either of us died.

"You mentioned also that our permanent life insurance program should have a waiver of premium benefit so that if one of us became disabled, the monthly payments would be made automatically. The cash in the policy could accumulate tax-deferred, and we could use the cash tax free for emergencies, college education, or our future retirement down the line.

"It worked out great. We started one policy for $500,000 on Jerry and one for $250,000 on me. In addition to those mortgage policies and the insurance policy, you suggested getting another permanent insurance policy to cover all our other expenses. I didn't realize what you meant at that time about permanent insurance and buying it when you're in good health. But I certainly do now. I developed diabetes about three years ago. I'm not totally uninsurable, but if I had to buy insurance today, it would cost me a lot more than it would someone else my age who was in good health."

"And a lot more than when you were younger," Bob interjected.

"So we totaled up the numbers. We added living expenses, college costs, and emergencies. We counted inflation at 5% a year. We tried to cover everything. We added it up. We couldn't believe the total. It was well over $1 million. We couldn't believe it."

"I remember that, Wilma. There are always so many expenses. It's easy to see how a family can spend well over $1 million on their kids, their house, and all their other expenses from the time they get married until the time the kids finish school."

"As you told us to do, Bob, we used both life insurance policies as a kind of a savings plan. We knew that if nothing happened to us, we could use the money in the investment side of the life insurance policy for emergencies or even to take care of the kids' college education."

"That's right. Most people don't understand the savings side of life insurance," said Bob.

"Then, Jerry died and—well, you know what has happened since then. I've not had to work. I've been able to raise the kids without worrying about money. We've tried to have a normal life. We take a vacation together every year. The kids have their music lessons and their sporting events. Considering the situation, I don't know how it could have worked out any better."

"You two did a great job of planning early. You stayed out of debt. You got rid of your credit cards, and you tried to save. Although your loved one was taken away from you, at least you've been able to have a financial worry-free life of raising your family. Just as you and Jerry had planned. Look at them now," Bob said, pointing to the kids at the horseshoe pit.

"Bob, I can't thank you enough for helping us." Wilma leaned over and gave Bob a hug.

$ $ $ $ $ $

"Hey, Bob, are you going to play horseshoes with us? We're ready," called Warren as he came over with a glass of lemonade.

Bob really wanted to play horseshoes. But he also wanted to finish this conversation with Wilma. Horseshoes could wait.

"Thanks for the lemonade. In a few minutes I'll be throwing the ringers with you."

He looked back at Wilma. "Even though you've got enough money to put Warren and Wendy through school, you still might be able to get financial aid. There are a lot of scholarships available."

"You know, I never really thought about it. We've got the money, so I felt that I would just go ahead and send the kids to any school they want."

"You can still send the kids to any school. But if Warren or Wendy gets a scholarship, you will have that much more money for your retirement."

"Where do I find out about scholarships?"

"There are a lot of books written on college scholarship programs. The colleges and universities can help you, too. Many foundations, companies, and associations offer college scholarships. Some are very specific, for students from certain backgrounds or with certain majors. Warren's and Wendy's high school guidance counselors can also help."

"Bob, is it worth the trouble? I have the money."

"Sure it is. You'd be surprised how many scholarships there are at universities and colleges throughout the United States. It's just like anything else, Wilma; you've got to know what to look for, and you've got to know the questions to ask. The way to get the answer is to work with the professionals at your high school and at colleges who specialize in scholarships and financial aid. Start with your high school guidance counselor. He or she will know whom to write and what questions to ask."

"Gosh, Bob, that's terrific. I didn't even think about that."

"You know, Wilma, with Warren being a National Merit Scholar, it's possible he could get a scholarship at Stanford or Georgetown. Wendy could get an athletic scholarship. As good a swimmer as she is, there are probably a lot of colleges that would like to have her on the swim team. Remember how much college costs these days, Wilma. If you can save that money, you will have a lot more money left for other emergencies, or for weddings, grandkids, and your retirement."

"It sounds good to me, Bob."

$$\$\,\$\,\$\,\$\,\$\,\$$

"So how about the business? Are you making any investments through the business? Like a pension plan? An IRA, a SEP, or a 401(k) plan?"

"Wait a minute, Bob. I'm just getting started. I don't have any spare money yet."

"Isn't there something you can save?"

"Bob, I don't have any other employees and I'm just barely making ends meet. Although I think I'll clear somewhere about $15,000 to $20,000 this year."

"Well, then what about a self-directed IRA?"

"A self-directed IRA! What's that?"

"You can set up an IRA and put up to $2,000 a year into it. But if you have your own company, and you don't have an IRA, you can put up to 15% of your income or $30,000, whichever is less, into your own self-directed IRA. You can set aside that money and it will accumulate income-tax-deferred."

"I didn't know I could do that, Bob."

"You can put it into any investment that Uncle Sam thinks is prudent. You can invest it in mutual funds, stocks, bonds, CDs, or Treasury bills. The list of investments goes on and on. You save money for yourself that would otherwise go to the government. If you invest it properly, it will be waiting for you at retirement. You can't touch the money without a penalty until you're 59½. But after that, you can take the money out anytime you want. You don't pay tax on the money until you withdraw it."

"That's great, Bob. You know, now that I think about it, retirement is not that far away. I've been so concerned about getting the kids through school and making sure all the bills were taken care of that I haven't thought very far ahead. Jerry's death just kind of stopped everything. I want to keep making my money grow so I can continue to live a good life, not only now, but after I retire. I know my business will be successful. I'll start that special IRA this week. Each year I'll make sure I save more."

"Great," Bob exclaimed. "Just think, in a couple of years the kids are going to be on their own. They'll probably be getting married and having their own families. You're going to have grandchildren around your feet, and it seems like just a couple of years ago it was your own children that you were nurturing and raising. Isn't it amazing how quickly time goes by?"

"I can't believe the years have gone so quickly. Here I'm thinking about retirement coming up, and it seems like just the other day that Jerry and I were planning on the future together."

"The future is here, Wilma, and you've got to keep doing what you've been doing. You've got to take advantage of every opportunity to save money. The IRA plan will help. Then when your company grows and you have more employees, you might think about setting up a pension plan. There the money goes in tax free and accumulates on an income-tax-deferred basis also, and you include your employees as well."

"Gosh, Bob, there's so much to know about investing and saving and planning ahead. Time goes by quickly. Every time I think I've got a handle on everything, you remind me that there's more to do."

"That's right, Wilma. Financial planning never stops. We need to stay on top of our money and our financial goals and desires every day. The minute we stop thinking about saving money and staying out of debt, we start falling behind on meeting our financial goals. Time goes by very fast. If you don't save money toward retirement, retirement can be bleak. But by saving systematically, you will be assured of a great retirement—a retirement you can enjoy worry-free."

"Bob, it makes me want to work that much harder so I can retire that much sooner."

"You're on your way, Wilma, and before I dash off to play horseshoes, there are a couple of other matters. For example, Wilma, what have you done about your estate?"

"What do you mean, Bob?"

"Have you updated your will? Have you done a trust?"

"I reviewed my will and updated it about five years ago. But I haven't done anything with a trust. Should I?"

Bob smiled and nodded his head.

"If you were to become disabled or die, your estate would go through probate. Even though you have plenty of liquid cash right now to pay your bills, it might be difficult for the kids to get to the cash if it's tied up in probate."

"I thought that if I had a will, there wouldn't be any probate fees."

"Not necessarily so. Are all of your assets in your name only?"

"Yes. I think the kids are too young to have assets in their names."

"In that case, your money could go through probate. Because you're widowed and have a will, and own everything in your name, your estate could go through probate, and that takes time. In some cases, probate takes a year or more to finalize. Your kids might not be able to get to the money they need to take care of all their expenses and ensure their college education."

"That would be terrible. There's so much happening in the next couple of years with our family. The children will graduate from high school and go to college. I'm looking forward to my own company growing."

"Here's what to do. Ask your attorney about the importance of a trust from the standpoint of probate and federal estate taxes."

"Bob, I've heard you talk about trusts before. What are federal estate taxes?"

"They are the taxes that we are obligated to pay when our estate surpasses $600,000. If married, each spouse has a $600,000 exemption. This means there are no federal estate taxes up to $1.2 million for a married couple. However, when there's only one spouse, as in your case, federal estate taxes will start at $600,000, and probate fees might start on an estate as small as $15,000.

"Wilma, you won't believe it, but federal estate taxes are the highest taxes we pay in the United States. They start at 37% and go all the way up to 55%."

"You're kidding. 37 to 55%!"

"That's right, Wilma. Let me give you an example. What do you think your estate is worth right now?"

"Probably, it would come to somewhere around $1.5 million right now."

"If you were to die now, with your will and everything you

own in your name, your estate could go through probate court. Because your estate is larger than $600,000, your federal estate taxes and probate fees could be somewhere around $400,000."

"$400,000? How do you figure that?"

"Well, federal estate taxes won't start until $600,000 and would be about 37% of every dollar thereafter. So on a $1.5 million estate, you would pay federal estate taxes, along with probate fees and administrative expenses. That could come to somewhere around $400,000."

"Bob, that's a lot of money."

"It certainly is a lot of money."

"When is that paid?"

"It's paid upon your death. Uncle Sam might not come knocking on day one, but sometime during the first year after your death, he is going to come knocking on the door of your loved ones. They're going to have to pay it."

"Well, what else can a trust do besides help protect my estate from federal estate taxes and probate fees?"

"It sets up your estate as you want. In fact, Wilma, what a trust does is allow you to give your money, upon your death, to whom you want, when you want, and how you want. You see, without a trust, you really can't leave your loved ones the *amount* of money you would like to, and leave it to them in the *manner* in which you would really like to have them receive it. Right now, you wouldn't want Warren and Wendy to receive a lump sum of a million dollars if you died."

"My goodness, no. Even though they're smart and educated, and they're wise about investments, they're still teenagers."

Bob added, "You never know. They might see a red convertible out there someplace that they might want to buy. They're smart kids, but the lure of a pot of money and undefined financial goals could ruin all the financial plans that you and Jerry started years ago."

"You're right. They wouldn't know what to do with the money."

So you might want to set up the estate with no lump sum paid to them at the beginning."

"No lump sum."

"That's right. What you would want to do is leave the money to them in the trust, so that they could take care of their expenses, education, welfare, and health until let's say they're maybe 25 or 30. Then let them have one-third of the principal. However, continue to provide money for health, welfare, maintenance, and education. Then maybe give them another third at age 40, and maybe the final third of the estate at 45 or 50. You pick the ages."

"This really sounds good. I can set this up with my attorney?"

"That's right. Most attorneys understand the importance of a will and a trust. I'm sure your attorney will sit down with you and explain to you why a trust might be more beneficial to you and your loved ones than your current will."

Bob added, "Most people work all through life, save their money, stay out of debt, provide a great education for their children, meet all their financial emergencies, and have a tremendous retirement. But when they die, most people don't have their estate set up properly, and their money gets tied up in probate. We have to make sure that when we die, we leave our loved ones what we want, when we want, and how we want. Make sure you call your attorney this week."

"I will, Bob; I will."

Just then Sarah and Darin came running through the picnic area. Sarah saw Uncle Bob and pulled Darin by the shirt. "Let's see what Uncle Bob is doing," she suggested.

They both slowed their pace and headed toward Uncle Bob. "What are you talking about, Uncle Bob? Becoming a millionaire?" asked Darin.

"Well, we are talking about saving money and making it grow," answered Uncle Bob.

Sarah noticed that Uncle Bob had finished his meal but hadn't opened his fortune cookie.

"Uncle Bob, what's your fortune?" she yelled.

"Yeah, Uncle Bob," said Darin. "What is Uncle Bob's fortune? Read it, Uncle Bob.

Uncle Bob leaned over, grabbed his fortune cookie, and cracked it open. He pulled out the fortune and read it silently to himself.

"What's it say, Uncle Bob?" the two youngsters yelled. "What is Uncle Bob's fortune? What does it say, Uncle Bob?"

Uncle Bob looked at Sarah and Darin, and said, "Uncle Bob says, start saving today and your financial dreams will come true tomorrow."

Darin and Sarah jumped up and down several times yelling "Awesome" with each jump.

"I'm starting today, Uncle Bob. I want my airplane!" exclaimed Darin. With that statement, Darin took off running for the soccer field. "Beat you there, Sarah!"

"No you won't," she yelled to Darin. And they were both gone, happy to have spent some more time with Uncle Bob.

$$\$ \$ \$ \$ \$ \$$$

"Bob, it sounds as though when I get this done, I'll have everything taken care of."

"Wilma, you know better than that. Estate planning and financial planning never come to an end. We have to constantly update and upgrade. We have to continue to do a financial profile every year. I know you do your expenses every month, and I know you know where you are with your investments. But make sure you just keep updating with your professional advisers. Do what you've been doing.

"I want you to go into retirement and enjoy the same lifestyle you're living today. You certainly don't want to have to change your lifestyle after all these years. You'll be able to enjoy every day of retirement because you know you will be able to control your expenses and have no debt. Your dollars will continue to grow. As inflation continues to eat at your buying power, your needs for income will grow. You'll never run out of money as some people do. They wake up one morning to find out that their money is gone, but they have years to live.

"I want you to live a wonderful life in retirement. You will be able to continue to guide your children financially and help them take care of their financial needs and those of their children, just as you've helped them take care of themselves in the years gone by.

"Another thing, Wilma—you still need to have as much growth in your investments as possible. We can never have enough money for retirement. We need as much money as possible, so that money can make more money for us through proper investments. Within the next 10 to 15 years you might want to retire from your business. You might want to sell it. You might want to spend more time with your kids and their kids. You need to have your investment grow. You need to buy top quality, long-term investments. We can never have enough money generating more money for us."

"I have never bought short-term, Bob. You've always told me to stay with long-term, highly rated, highly ranked investments."

"Just build a diversified portfolio. Keep adding to your financial base. Start with guaranteed investments like Treasury bills, Treasury bonds, CDs, double E bonds, and money market accounts. Make sure you have all of your insurance, and I mean *all* of your insurance. You know life insurance, hospitalization, disability, and disability income. Then, after you have all of your insurance and your guaranteed investments secure, and only then, can you afford to take any risk with your money. Your highly rated, highly ranked investments such as mutual funds, certain stocks and bonds, and other investments that fall into this category should be able to give you the kind of return that you need."

"Bob, that really sounds terrific. That's what I've been doing. I'll keep saving and planning forever. We really appreciate all you have done over the years. We do love you!"

"Wilma, how about a game of horseshoes?"

"Not right now, Bob. By the way, look at the sky. Looks like a shower is coming. Maybe you can catch Warren and Wendy before it starts raining."

"Well, don't say I didn't ask." And with that, Bob headed toward the horseshoe pit.

7

Benjamin Bigtimer: When Success Puts You on Top of the World

"HI, BOB, HOW ARE YOU DOING?" said Ben as he walked up to the picnic shelter with his wife, Betty.

"Hi, Ben," said Bob.

Ben greeted Bob with a bone-crushing handshake. His six-foot-five frame towered over Uncle Bob, who was five-foot-nine. Ben wore a black silk shirt and black designer jeans. Two gold neck chains showed in the open collar of his shirt. He also had on a gold bracelet and three gold rings. A strong smell of cologne followed him.

Bob greeted Betty. She was a slender woman with blonde, shoulder-length hair. She wore a cream-color, buttoned blouse with deep purple slacks. She had on a gold necklace with a diamond pendant. Her wedding ring had a huge diamond—at least three carats.

Ben pulled a gold cigar case out of his pocket. He opened it and took out a cigar.

As he lit up the cigar, he said to Bob, "The gang's going to play some poker. Do you want to play?"

Bob hesitated.

He knew that when you played cards with Ben, the stakes

were high. Bob would probably lose some money. As investments went, playing poker with Ben was not a very good one. But Bob wanted to find out about Ben's finances. Betty had put a short note on her return card that read, "I need to spend some time with Bob concerning our finances. Ben is still up to his old tricks."

Bob said, "All right, Ben, I'll play with you and Betty, but only for pennies and nickels. Nothing higher."

"Aw, Bob! Okay, we'll play for pennies and nickels now. But when the guys get here, we're playing for real money. You're not gonna quit on us, are you?"

"Well, we'll see."

Ben liked to do everything big. He was president and CEO of Bigway Construction, a multimillion-dollar construction company he had started in his garage at age 30. That was 25 years ago. He and his company tackled the big jobs, the risky jobs, the jobs that his competitors wouldn't. Through the years he had built Bigway Construction by being tougher than the competition. His company was both respected and feared for its tough, demanding style. He expected 150% from his employees and his suppliers.

He had dropped out of college to go to work in construction, and he didn't have much use for management theories. He believed in one simple principle: Work hard, be demanding, and success will be yours.

Ben was big in every way. His physical presence intimidated those around him. He had a booming voice, and when he talked, he seemed to yell. His language had the rough edge of the East Side, the tough part of town where he had grown up. So far, every principle that he practiced had worked for him. He was wealthy, and he had a loyal wife and family.

But Bob wondered seriously about Ben's finances. Several times before, they'd talked about estate planning, trust programs, and having good company benefits for the employees and Ben. But as far as Bob knew, nothing had been done.

As Ben shuffled the cards, Bob asked him how business was doing.

"Better than ever. We just outbid 20 competitors to get a hospital job in Indiana."

"Still killing the competition, huh?"

"They know I'm one tough son of a gun. I bid the best prices. I give the best service. I get the best from all my people."

Suddenly, an electronic warble was heard from a nylon bag that Ben carried. It sounded like a video game.

"Excuse me, that's my office." Ben pulled out a portable cellular telephone and answered the call.

While Ben sat at the table talking on the phone, his wife, Betty, motioned Bob aside. Like Ben, Betty had grown up on the tough side of town and did not have a formal education. She knew her place with him. She had opinions, but she knew they had to be expressed carefully.

"Bob, you know it's the same old thing with Ben, work, work, work. Here it is Sunday, and he's got six people in the office working on a bid. He works hard, and he works them hard. They all work 12 to 14 hours every day."

"He always has worked hard," Bob agreed.

"I'm worried. He can't keep this up forever. He's 55 years old, you know. What if he gets sick? Bob, please help us," pleaded Betty. "Talk to Ben. Help him to see that we need financial help."

"Sure, I'll help, Betty. Let's hope Ben will listen. Don't you two take any time to relax?"

"Oh, sure. We go on vacations and trips. But he always has his phone. He's calling the office or they're calling him or he's working on plans. He never gets away from the business."

"What about the planning I talked to you about a couple of years ago? The financial planning?"

"Planning?" asked Betty.

"Planning for the future. The savings program. The benefits package at work," stated Bob.

"He hasn't done a thing," Betty answered, shaking her head. "All I know is that the last time you talked to us about saving money, Ben said he would think about it. I think that's the last time he thought about it. You know, on investments, he and I don't agree. He's always making those wild investments in grain or corn or gold."

"Commodity futures."

"Yeah. That's what they're called."

"That's a high-risk investment," said Bob.

"Then we have diamond mines and gold mines. It's fun to think we own part of a gold mine, but I don't know if it's a very good investment. Why not just some good old-fashioned CDs? When I grew up, my family were simple people. We just kept our money at the bank. When we could set something aside, we saved it. It wasn't much, but we did what we could.

"Now, we have all this money. But I don't know if we're any better off. It scares me. He doesn't hesitate to drop $50,000 into one of those risky investments."

"That's a lot of money to put at risk."

"He's always saying that when he invests, he's going to hit it big and he's going to make a million dollars," Betty stated.

"That would be great," Bob agreed. "But, Betty, it seems like you're already worth a million dollars. You've made *lots* of money through the business. Why do you need to invest in commodities? You said that when you were growing up, your family saved. You know what? That type of low-risk investing would work for you today."

"It's what I grew up with," Betty agreed.

"Since you've got so much money coming in, you could save a lot. Invest it wisely, and you'd make that million bucks fast. Probably a lot faster than you would in a diamond mine."

"That's right. Now try to tell him that." They both looked at Ben.

"What about Ben, Jr.?" asked Bob.

"He's still the same. He'll never be able to care for himself. That Down's syndrome is tough."

"Did you ever set up a trust for him?"

"Nope. We haven't done anything. Ben just keeps saying 'I'll do it later. There's no rush. There's no problem.' "

They paused for a moment and looked at Ben on his call.

"There's another problem I think you have. Debt. Where are you regarding debt?"

"Just as bad as ever. Or worse. I'd bet we have a million dollars worth of debt or more."

Bob shook his head. "That's no good."

"Yeah, Bob. We've made millions through hard work. But we spend even more. We keep buying. We keep building. We have the summer home. We have the winter cottage. We added to the house. Then we added to the office, and we bought more land for the business machinery."

"How are you paying for all this?"

"We borrow every single time. If there's a place where money grows on trees, it's at the loan company. Ben must have some good friends there. We don't pay for anything with cash."

"Betty, you've really got some problems. There have to be some changes soon. This debt's going to run over you like one of Ben's giant earth movers. Or worse, Ben is going to get sick and collapse."

"That's what I'm really worried about, Bob. I go to bed every night thinking he's going to get sick. Where would we be then?"

"You'd be in trouble."

Betty looked wistful. "You know, a lot of people think that just because some folks have money, they're rich. Know what I mean? We have fancy cars. We have a big house. We go on vacations. So everybody thinks we got money, money. Well, bull. We can buy anything we want with a credit card, and Ben does just that. It doesn't matter whether we really have the money or not. The bank gives us more. I know we owe lots of money. My family back on the East Side, they don't have any credit cards. They're more secure than we are."

Betty paused for a moment. "I don't know if we'll be able to retire and live happily ever after. I'm worried about being able to do that. Bob, Ben isn't a kid anymore. I'm not either. In a couple of years I'd like to see Ben retire, but we won't be able to if he keeps blowing our money. He's got to stop spending so much money."

"And get rid of the debt," Bob added. "How about the business? Is he grooming an heir apparent? You know, someone to take over?"

"No. He tries once in a while, but he won't give anyone a real chance. He has to run everything. He keeps his finger in everything."

"That's terrible. He has to let go. He has to delegate. He has to learn to hire good people."

"He does hire good people. But he just doesn't let them have enough slack to run on their own."

Ben's voice began to boom louder, shouting into the phone. He chewed harder on his cigar. Bob and Betty stopped their conversation to listen.

"You what!" he bellowed to his marketing manager. "Roger, I want the 305 system, not the 303. The 303 is too slow. I don't care if you have to put it together from scratch.

"One more thing. When you write your specifications, make sure everything is typed double-spaced. I want room to edit what you do."

Ben was silent for a moment. Then he spoke into the phone.

"Don't tell me that's too much. I'm sorry if you think I'm working you too hard. Don't all of you know that people are a dime a dozen? If you don't like it, then go work somewhere else. Now, I want you to call me back in an hour. Let me know where you are on this project, got it?"

Ben slammed down the phone against the picnic table and then looked at Bob and Betty and shook his head.

Bob and Betty stared back at Ben, shaken by the violence of Ben's hostility on the phone.

Ben said tersely, "You have to push people if you want to get the best out of them. Like a horse, you have to kick 'em and prod 'em." He took a couple of hard drags on his cigar, blowing clouds of strong smoke in front of him.

Betty timidly offered, "Ben, Roger is talented. You know that. I don't know why he keeps working for you, the way you treat him."

"Roger is good, but he's got a lot to learn. Besides, there's no room for mistakes in this business. Roger couldn't make as much money somewhere else. So he'll take all the yelling and screaming I give him."

Bob stepped in. "Ben, what would happen if you weren't around to tell him what to do?"

"Oh, the company would probably fall on its rump," said Ben.

"Would you want that to happen? You know, you're not going to be around forever. While you're here, don't you want to spend more time with your family? With your daughter and your son, with Betty? You're always working. When you're not working you're still working, because you've got business on your mind. If you want to build your company, you've got to bring in talented people. Give them responsibility and let them run with it. You know, you're not working out of your garage anymore. You've built a successful company."

"I know, Bob. That's because I drive hard and demand the best. I don't tolerate mistakes. In this business, you can't afford to be wrong."

"I know it's a tough business. But what if something happens to you? What if you're flying your plane in a storm and you crash?"

"I'm a good pilot."

Betty said, "Ben, you've flown in all kinds of storms. Storms so bad that most people wouldn't fly in them."

Ben chomped on his cigar.

Bob gently chided, "Ben, your number's going to come up. You just can't keep living on the edge. One of these days, you're going to go too far. You don't take care of yourself. You're overweight. You smoke. You don't exercise. You're a Type A personality."

Betty looked at Bob and shook her head sadly. "He's a heart attack waiting to happen."

$ $ $ $ $ $

No one else had shown up for the card game yet, so Ben, Bob, and Betty played a few practice rounds for pennies and nickels. It gave the three a chance to talk about investments.

Ben relit his cigar. He took a few puffs, then spoke proudly of the commodities account he had just opened. "Bob, commodity futures is where you can really make the big money. You can make it fast."

Bob replied, "You're right. In commodities, you can make big money fast and you can lose it fast, and lose big, big money. You could lose all your money real fast. In fact, Ben, did you know you could lose more money than you actually put into your account?"

"What are you talkin' about? I know I can lose a lot of money. But more than I put in?"

"That's right."

"Well, you have to risk it if you want to make it big."

"How much is in your new account?"

"50 grand."

"And you have more accounts like this?"

"Many more."

"Let me show you what can happen," said Bob. "You put $50,000 in, you could lose $100,000. Or $200,000."

"More than I invested. How's that?" questioned Ben.

"Because when you go into a commodity account, most of the time you're buying on margin."

"I know about margin," Ben snapped back.

"Let me give you an example," said Bob. "Let's say gold is selling for somewhere around $400 an ounce. If I wanted to buy 100 ounces of gold bullion, it would cost $40,000."

"I'm with you so far. But I don't want to buy the gold. I just want to make money by speculating."

"Right, Ben. You're speculating when you have a commodity account. So the margin they require on gold futures is only about 10%, or $4,000."

Ben said, "Right. So I can have 10 or 15 or 20 gold contracts going with only $50,000. Or, I could only buy one 100-ounce gold bar for 40 grand. It's a much better deal to have a commodity account."

"Wait a minute. I'm not through, Ben."

"Okay, I'm listening."

"If gold goes up $10 per ounce, the person who owns the 100-ounce gold bar makes $1,000. Right, Ben?"

"Right, Bob, but here's where commodities are so good. All I have to put up is $4,000 to make the $100 for every $1 move in the price. So if gold goes up $10 per ounce, I make $1,000 on a $4,000 investment."

"Yeah, but Ben, what if the per-ounce price goes down $10?"

"Well, then I lose a thousand."

"What if it goes down $30 or $50 or $70?"

"Well, then I lose more. No problem."

"Yeah, you lose more. But you only put in $4,000 per contract. If it went down $50 to $350 an ounce, you'd lose $5,000 per contract. And you only put up $4,000 per contract. So if you had 10 gold contracts, you would lose $50,000."

"Wow, I never looked at it that way. But I would get out before it goes down."

"Maybe and maybe not. Sometimes the commodity markets move so fast that you can't get out in time. The commodity exchange calls those kinds of markets fast-moving markets. They don't guarantee that you're going to be able to get in or get out where you want—or when you want. The market may be moving too fast."

"I didn't know that, Bob."

"Commodity futures are based on margin. If the money

you've put up for margin runs out, and the market still keeps moving in the opposite direction from what you speculated would happen, you'll owe more money. I know of cases where people have put $100,000 in the market and have lost over $1 million."

"Really?"

"Yes. Believe me, it can happen. In fact, Ben, if you had 30 gold contracts going and the market went down $50, you would lose $150,000."

"Wait a minute. I only put up $50,000."

"That's okay, you signed the commodity account papers. This allows the commodity broker to collect for additional losses. They'll come after you for the additional $100,000," said Bob.

"I'd better talk to my broker in the morning," said Ben.

"Yes, you'd better talk to him. When it comes to commodities, my advice is to invest only money that you can afford to lose."

"Well, I can afford to lose it."

"What are you talking about, Ben?" Betty said. "We can't afford to lose any money. We need to be saving money, not speculating with it."

"Okay, okay, Betty. I'll talk to Bill in the morning and find out if he says the same thing." Ben looked at Bob. "He's my broker."

Betty stated, "Bill will say the same thing. Bob knows what he's talking about."

"I don't see any problem with it," Ben said. "Bob, I'm not going to sit around and put my money into CDs or double E bonds. I can't make any money doing that."

Bob said, "You're right. At today's rates, the returns are low. But again, those investments are guaranteed. Ben, you need to have some of your money in guaranteed investments."

"Yeah, but there isn't anything really guaranteed in this world. Look at how the government's going down the tubes. Do you really think Treasury bills are safe?" asked Ben.

"The United States government is not going to topple tomorrow," Bob shot back.

"Yeah, but those politicians know how to spend. Now, on the other hand, there's this guy calling me from Brazil about a diamond mine. Now that sounds like a deal. And there's another guy in Utah talking about a gold mine in Canada. Don't you think diamonds and gold are a good way to go? There'll always be a market for them."

"Ben, those are mines, not gold and diamonds themselves. They're high-risk investments. You can lose all of your money overnight."

Ben's cigar had gone out. He impatiently pulled it out of his mouth, looked at it, and relit it.

Bob continued. "Ben, here's what I think you need to do. Start saving. You need to set aside money to invest. Now, have you ever heard of the financial pyramid?"

"No, but I've heard of pyramid investments," said Ben.

"No, Ben. I'm talking about building your investments on a firm foundation. Setting up your investments is like a pyramid."

"Is that like those pyramid schemes where you buy into something, then get 10 other suckers to buy in, then they get 10 other suckers, and everyone makes a profit off the next guy?"

"No, Ben. Do you really think I'd suggest something like that?"

"No, you're too conservative. You don't know how to make the big money. You may never be poor, but you'll never be rich."

Bob said with conviction, "I'm a millionaire, Ben."

"Oh, come on, now. By saving your pennies?" said Ben.

"Yes. And investing wisely. I diversify my investing by the financial pyramid."

"All right. I can't believe you're a millionaire. You? Tell me about this pyramid."

Bob reached into his pocket and pulled out a tattered, folded piece of paper. He opened it, and on it was a drawing of a pyramid.

"Here's a picture of the financial pyramid. See how it's set up in layers. The base layer is guaranteed investments like certificates of deposit, Treasury bills, and double E bonds. These are secure investments that you can count on. Also, the first layer includes making sure all your insurance needs are covered."

"All insurance needs?" said Ben.

"Yes. Life insurance, disability, disability income, hospitalization, casualty, homeowners, all of that," counted out Bob.

"My basic needs."

"Right. Once that's set, then you can start speculating a little. You can add a little risk, with the prospect of a higher return," said Bob.

"Now you're talking." Ben smiled.

"The next layers of risk above guarantees are investments like money market funds, mutual funds, rare coins, guaranteed annunities, and your home."

"Not enough risk for me," said Ben.

"As you progress through each layer, you raise the level of risk. You can see that commodities are at the top of the pyramid. They are the most volatile in terms of potential returns and losses. The value of highly speculative investments can run up and down like a roller coaster."

Ben looked at the pyramid and pointed to the top. "That's where I like to be. At the top."

"My point is, Ben, that you have to build from the base up. You can't just jump to the top and have only high-risk investments. You have to diversify. You have to start your investment portfolio with secure investments, at the base of the pyramid, and build your way up."

"I like the high-risk investments. They're for people who want to make it *big*."

Ignoring Ben's remark, Bob continued. "There's also a great chance you could lose big. That's why a smart investor builds from the base up."

Bob's Investment Pyramid

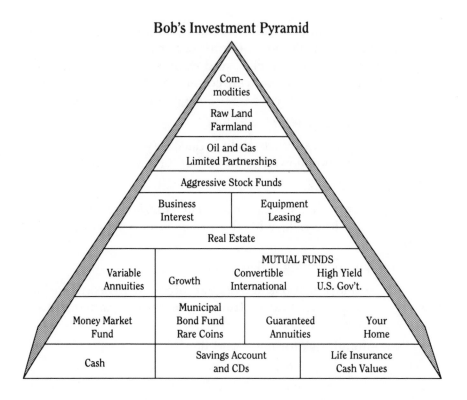

Betty added, "We're really lucky we haven't lost big. Bob, I really like your financial pyramid. It makes sense."

Bob said, "Ben, you need to start thinking about retirement. You're making plenty of money right now. It's just that you aren't puting away anything. The only thing you're thinking about is today. That's wrong."

Ben said nothing but continued to chomp on his cigar.

"Here's what you need to do," Bob said. "Have financial goals. Figure out how much money you'll need down the line. Track your expenses. Start a savings program. You can achieve financial success because you're a driver."

"Thanks, Bob," said Ben.

"That's right. You're a driver, and you're going to be successful. But you're on the wrong path right now. You're headed for financial disaster."

"Bob, I have a very successful company," said Ben.

"Is it in debt, Ben?"

"Well, every successful company has some debt."

"What if you get sick? What if you don't get those contracts? What if you die? What's going to happen?"

"I have to get those contracts so everybody gets paid."

"See what I mean, Ben? You've got to make sure you know what you're doing."

"Well, I don't need to think about that right now. Let's have fun at this picnic. Besides, I have two jacks and two tens. Can you beat that?"

Betty threw her cards down and so did Bob.

"No, you've won that round," Bob said.

"I win all the rounds." He collected a handful of coins from Betty and Bob.

"Let's not talk about debt or investments or investment secrets now, Bob. Your investment secrets'll be around when we need them. I just want to enjoy myself."

"Ben, you need to know my *secrets* now."

"Why now?" asked Ben.

"Because retirement is a lot closer than you think."

"Bob, I'm going to be working from now on. I'm not gonna retire."

"But what if you have to?"

"You mean if I'm sick or something?"

"Yes. What if you get sick? What if you become disabled? What if you start losing all those bids instead of winning them? It sounds to me as though you have a lot of overhead. How are you going to pay your employees? Will they stay if you're sick? The way you yell at them all the time, I wouldn't be surprised if some of them aren't looking for other jobs already."

Ben chomped harder on his cigar.

"Just because you work and just because you work hard doesn't mean you're paying all the bills," Bob continued. "Many breadwinners think that hard work is enough. Do you know what your expenses are?"

"Of course," Ben replied. "Betty takes care of paying the bills."

Betty interrupted, "Ben, we pay over $1,500 a month just on our cars. We have mortgages on two homes—our home here and the house in Aspen. Plus, there is half ownership on the airplane. The overhead at the office. You've said yourself, Ben, we've got to win at least two bids a month just to stay even."

Bob jumped in. "Ben, what if you don't win two bids? What if you just get one? What if you don't win any?"

"I'll always win some. I know how to bid projects. And beat the pants off the competition."

"But what if you don't win?"

Ben said, "Big deal, so what if our expenses are high? We make plenty of money. That's America. You work real hard, you make a lot of money, and you spend it on anything you want."

$ $ $ $ $ $

They continued dealing cards and playing poker as they talked. Ben was ahead, but not by much.

Bob went on, "Ben, you enjoy spending your money. It's great that you work hard. You should enjoy your money. But here's something to think about. It's not the size of your assets that counts. It's how much you *own* that counts. Your situation is just the opposite of what you want."

"How's that?" asked Ben.

"You have big assets, but you don't own very much of what you have. You have debt on most of what you've got. Ben, you actually own very little."

"So, we have things. We'll pay for them later."

"Ben, do you know your total net worth?"

"Sure," Ben said, nodding his head.

"I mean," said Bob, "if you added up all of your assets—your company, your house, your toys, everything—and subtracted what you owe . . ."

Ben broke in, "Bob, you said toys. What do you mean, toys?"

"People have toys, Ben. Everyone has toys. I drive a car that has four wheels, a steering wheel, a glove compartment, a front and back seat, and a trunk. You drive a car that has those same things, but your car probably cost $150,000 more than mine."

"Well, that's because I have a Rolls Royce."

"That's great, but does it get you where you're going any better than my car does?"

"Aw, Bob, that's foolish. My car looks great."

"I understand that, Ben. I think it's terrific that you can afford a Rolls. But do you own it?"

"No. We lease it through the company," said Betty.

Ben picked up his cellular phone to make a call, looked at Bob, and said, "So what's the point about my toys? I like 'em."

"Ben, don't think you're wealthy just because you've got a lot of toys. It's better to own everything you have. If you own all your toys, you won't have to worry about being in debt when you retire. What will give you worries is debt. You see, Ben, if you retire with debt, here's what happens. You might think you're retired, but your debts aren't. They're going to keep staring you in the face every day and every night. They're going to say, 'Pay me off.' And if you can't pay them, someone may come to your front door one day and say, 'Ben, you've got to move out of this house.' "

"Oh, Bob. This is nonsense."

Betty blurted out, "Ben, I've heard stories about people who have lost everything."

"Honey, we're not going to lose everything. We're not going to lose anything."

"I'm not saying you will, Ben, but you better start thinking about getting out of debt and saving your money now. If you still owe bills when you retire, you may not really be able to retire regardless of how much you're worth. Your bills might be so big, like they are now, that you're not going to be able to retire—ever. Toys are important, but why don't you try to *own* all your toys? Now you buy them whenever you want, and pay for them over a long period of time. Buy only what you need and pay with cash, not plastic."

"Bob, isn't being in debt the American way?"

"A lot of people in the United States have large debts. Many times it doesn't bother them until they retire. Then they find out they can't retire and live the same lifestyle they have grown accustomed to. Here's the bottom line: If you want to retire successfully, you can't have any debt."

Bob looked at his cards for a minute. He discarded four and drew four.

He continued, "Did you know that some people who earn a lot less money than you retire in much better shape than you?"

"How is that possible?" questioned Ben.

"How? Because they don't have debt."

"So what?"

"So, Ben, they don't have financial obligations to worry about every night. They only spend what they need to spend. They don't have debt payments in their budgets. They know exactly what their expenses are. They pay their bills, and they have money left over to save. On the other hand, people with debt really can't retire. Ben, you're headed in that direction."

On the second round of betting, Bob raised Ben by five nickels. He continued talking as he played.

"You might have to work the rest of your life. You might have to keep doing what you're doing now when you're in your 60s or 70s. Maybe in your 80s. If you don't get out of debt soon, you won't ever be able to retire."

Betty said, "Honey, that's not what we want. You've worked too hard and too long for us not to be able to travel and smell the flowers when we want."

"You're right. We're going to have to do something about it. This time, Uncle Bob's investment secrets may have hit home. You've made your point," said Ben.

"That's good. I'm glad I'm making some sense, Ben." Then, Bob laid down four kings. He won a pile of nickels and pennies, and he was nearly even with Ben.

"Don't worry, I'll get you back," said Ben. "Now, back to this investing. When's the best time to start?"

"The best time to start investing is now," Bob answered.

$$\$ \$ \$ \$ \$ \$$

Betty and Bob knew that if they were ever to get through Ben's hard head, now was the time. Bob also wondered how long Ben's patience would hold out. This hand, Bob drew only one card even though he only held a pair of deuces.

Betty continued the money talk. "You bring home over a quarter of a million dollars a year, and we are spending more than that."

"How can we be spending more than I make?"

"Ben, we spend money on everything," said Betty.

"We buy everything we want, don't we, honey?" Ben shot back.

"Yes, we do. I appreciate that, but there's got to be a stop to it. Let's just buy the things we really need."

"That's all we buy anyway."

"No, Ben. We spend money, here, there, and everywhere. We don't hesitate to drop $200 on a dinner for the two of us. If it's diamonds or clothes or a new stove I want, it's there. We buy what we like and what we want. We pay for it with plastic."

Bob bet three nickels on his pair of deuces. He hoped Ben had something better. Bob said, "Buy only what you need. Pay for it in cash."

Betty looked over to Bob. "You know how we pay the bills? I tell Ben to bonus himself more money. You bonus yourself and borrow more money from the company. Then I turn around and pay off some of the bills, and the taxes are unbelievable."

"Ben, just think, if you had a benefits plan at the office, you wouldn't pay as much taxes. You'd automatically be saving money. You'd be paying yourself first."

"Cutting taxes, I like that. Now, pay myself first? What does that mean?" said Ben.

"You always want to pay yourself before you pay the bills. Betty, whenever that paycheck comes home, write a check to yourself," said Bob.

"How do I do that?"

"Open up another checking account. Then, put a couple of thousand dollars in it. Every time Ben brings a paycheck home, put $2,000 into your new checking account."

"What do I do with it?" asked Betty.

"You're going to let it grow. Put it in a CD. Or, Ben can call that investment adviser who keeps calling him. Tell him you want to get together and find out more about investing. Remember the investment pyramid I talked about earlier."

Ben had three kings and won the hand. He was safely ahead of Betty and Bob in pennies and nickels.

$ $ $ $ $ $

Ben pulled out a fresh cigar and lit it. He seemed to enjoy those first puffs.

"Company benefits packages? Who needs them? My people work hard and get paid good. I pay them more than they'd make anyplace else. I pay them more than they deserve."

"But don't you want to keep your employees?" asked Bob. "Don't you want them to be happy with their jobs? Don't you want them to respect you? If you lose people, it's hard to replace them."

"Sure. Turnover is expensive. But with me, they've got the best job they can get."

"There are benefits programs your company can provide for

you and your employees. It'll save money for you, the company, and the employees," said Bob.

"Give me some examples."

"Health insurance, for one. If you buy it through the company, your employees don't have to pay any taxes on it. It's much more expensive for your employees to buy insurance privately. Your employees will appreciate health insurance benefits. They're a must."

Ben puffed the cigar as Bob continued.

"The 401(k) is a great vehicle for employees to save money. All the money that goes into the program accumulates tax-deferred. Pension and profit-sharing programs are good, too."

"Big deal. How much can I put in there?" Ben asked.

"Well, for starters you can probably put up to 15% of your income, or $30,000, whichever is the lesser amount. And look at it this way, Ben, if you didn't put that money into the pension plan, most of it would just go to Uncle Same in taxes anyway. So you're really way ahead."

Ben paused and looked at his cards as he chewed his cigar. "Why should I do all this for them? I'm the heart and soul of the company."

"You need to develop a team. One way is with long-term financial rewards, so that employees know they can benefit from the company's success. Maybe, if your employees were happier with you and you gave them some motivation besides a whip, they might just do better work. You wouldn't have to harass them so much!"

Everyone was quiet for a moment as they placed their bets. They opened with two nickels. Betty raised three, and Ben and Bob matched this.

Bob continued. "Life insurance can be a needed part of your company benefits plan. Certain types of insurance have built-in savings programs and death protection. If the employee doesn't die before retirement, the policy can go with the employee. The cash is theirs. There could be more money in the policy for retirement than you paid for the insurance."

"You can get your money back?" said Betty.

"Yes, Betty, you not only get your money back, but you still have some life insurance. You win. The employee wins. The company wins. It's a win-win situation. You can't lose. You should start this type of program as soon as possible."

"Bob, I've had insurance agents bug me before. They're always pushing something. Everybody wants me to buy insurance. I'll buy it when I need it."

"Ben, you can't wait until you need it to buy it."

"Why's that?"

"Because then it's too late to get it. When you need it, you're either disabled, dying, or dead. It would be great if we could wait until the day before we die or become disabled and say, 'Hey, Insurance Person, I want to buy some insurance.' Ben, don't be stupid. You can't do it then. You've got to do it now when you're in good health. Maybe you should listen to your insurance agent."

"Well, maybe you're right, Bob. But I don't need it now. Maybe in the future, but I'm not going to worry about it now."

Ben's phone rang again with the same electronic warble.

Bob talked over the sound of the phone ringing. "Don't talk about waiting. You're going to have to get this done now, Ben. You said you'd do this a couple of years ago. Will you get this taken care of tomorrow?"

The phone rang again.

Ben said, "Well, maybe I'll think about it."

"You thought about it last time and you have done nothing about it," said Bob.

$ $ $ $ $ $

Ben put the phone to his ear. On this call, his tone was decidedly different.

"Roger, thanks for calling. . . . Sounds like you're on the right track. . . . Good job."

Betty looked at Bob and, facing away from Ben, said, "My

goodness. I've never heard him talk that nice to any of his employees for at least three or four years."

Bob whispered, "Well, maybe we've lit up his light!"

"I hope so. He needs to turn it around. He's never home. He never gets any sleep. He's working, working, working."

"Roger, you've been working very hard. So have the other guys. Let's do this. Tell everyone, next weekend we're off. We're on vacation. In fact, I want everybody to go out to dinner and a show next Saturday night. With families. The night's on me."

Ben paused as he listened. He began to smile. "Well, thanks, Roger. I appreciate that. I'll talk to you again."

Ben hung up the phone. Bob and Betty smiled. Ben cracked a small smile.

"You know, if I talk to people nice, they really appreciate it. I thanked Roger, and he said he'd stay longer today if I wanted him to."

"Good for you, Ben! There's more to life than competition and win, win, win. There's sleeping and enjoying your family and having people who enjoy their work. It's having a real team that works together. A real team has fun together when they work. With a team, you'll always pull through the tough times."

"The idea of a team is a little hard to get used to. That's because I've always done it myself, with hard work. It's hard to let go. But I'll try. In fact, I'll do it."

Bob added, "Ben, just because you work hard doesn't mean you're going to win. You know, if that were all it took, then most people would just work hard and be successful. But it not only takes hard work, it takes smarts, it takes being a team, it takes working together and all the things we've already discussed."

"Strength as a team," Ben boasted. "A tough team."

"You also build your team with company benefits, Ben. Health insurance, pension plan, life insurance. It's being nice to your employees and respecting them that develops a team."

$ $ $ $ $ $

"Let's take a break for a minute." Betty put her cards on the table. Ben remained safely ahead in winnings, with the help of Bob's dropping out of the game when he had two pair. Bob wanted to make sure Ben stayed in a good mood.

Bob was ready for more money talk discussion.

"What is the size of your estate?" asked Bob.

"Oh, gosh, I don't know," said Ben.

"How much do you think Bigway Construction is worth?"

"Probably $5 million."

Bob asked more questions. How much does Bigway owe on its buildings and machinery? How much does the company owe in total? What is its revolving line of credit? When Bob was finished, Ben and Betty estimated liabilities at $4 million. That left assets of $1 million.

"What about your house?"

"The house is worth about $600,000," said Betty.

"And your winter home in Aspen?"

"Oh, it's beautiful. Its value is over $1 million."

"What do you owe on them?" asked Bob.

Betty replied, "About $200,000 on our main house and about $660,000 on the Aspen place."

"When you subtract what you owe on these homes, there's about $740,000 left in net assets. Add that to the net worth of Bigway Construction, and that brings your estate to about $1,740,000. What else is there?"

"I have about $50,000 worth of stock," said Ben.

"Are they good solid stocks, or high risk?" asked Bob.

"I guess you might call them high risk. I call them growing companies. The future companies of America."

"How much were the stocks worth when you bought them?"

"About $200,000."

Bob just sighed and shook his head in desperation.

"They'll be worth something someday," said Ben sheepishly.

"How much do you still owe on your cars?" asked Bob.

"Aw, probably $60,000. But they're worth at least $200,000."

"And jewelry?"

"Ben gives me all kinds of jewelry. I guess it's easily worth over $300,000."

"Is it paid for?"

"No, I'm paying it off each month," said Betty.

"Well, what do you think it would be worth if you had to cash it in? What do you think you would get for it?"

"Aw, we'd get over half a million. You know jewelry appreciates."

"No, that's not true. In fact, Ben, jewelry doesn't appreciate. It usually goes down in value. Especially when there's a fire sale."

"What's a fire sale?" asked Betty.

"A fire sale is when you're forced to sell something. People will probably give you pennies on the dollar for it. Chances are your $300,000 worth of jewelry wouldn't get $100,000 if you had to sell it immediately. You probably owe more than that on it, so you wouldn't keep any money from the sale of your jewelry."

Ben and Betty looked at each other in amazement.

"So what other assets do you have?" asked Bob.

They ran off a list. Paintings, antiques, silverware, china, crystal—all worth somewhere around $100,000, on which they owed $40,000. There was more—a couple of snowmobiles, a boat at the yacht club, and Ben's biggest toys, his sports cars and his airplane.

"I have a collection of sports cars. They're all over 25 years old, and they're worth about $2 million."

"Do you owe anything on them?" asked Bob.

Betty jumped in. "Are we doing better with the cars?"

Ben answered reluctantly, "We owe about $1.5 million." He continued, "By the way, the cars are beautiful. All in mint condition. You should see them some time. I have three Corvettes, a '54, a '60, and a '65. Then there's a '57 T-bird, and a Lamborghini, and three Ferraris. And a Jaguar roadster and an MG. Then there's my favorites, the muscle cars—a '68 Plymouth Roadrunner hemi, a '66 Shelby GT Mustang, and a '64 Chevy Super Sport."

"Can I take one out for a drive some Sunday? I do have a thing for Corvettes. Those big V-8s. Three hundred horsepower."

"I don't know, Bob. I want my car back in one piece. Do you know how to drive a stick shift?" Ben teased. "They go four speeds."

Bob looked puzzled. "You know, stick shift. On the floor. Four speeds." Ben motioned like he was driving a stick shift.

"Oh, sure," said Bob. "By the way, where do you keep all your cars? Do you have a warehouse in your backyard?"

"I keep them at the office. In one of our buildings."

"Are the cars insured?"

"Why should they be insured? I keep them in my office building. There's someone there all the time."

"What if the building burns down, Ben?"

"The building isn't going to burn down."

"But what if it did?"

"If it did, I'd lose all my cars."

"You better look into getting them insured. Ask your insurance man tomorrow about casualty and fire insurance."

Bob added up the list of assets and liabilities, and Ben was elated with the result. Bob said the estate was worth well over $9 million.

"See, we don't have anything to worry about."

But Bob came back and said, "Yes, you have $9 million worth of assets. Subtract your debt of $6,560,000 and your assets are about $2,440,000."

"That's impossible, Bob."

"It's not impossible, Ben, it's the truth. You're living like a millionaire. When you get your debt paid off, then you'll really be a millionaire."

"You said we don't have anything liquid?" questioned Betty.

"You don't have any cash. If you became disabled and couldn't work, would there be any income?"

"Bigway Construction will pay for it," snapped Ben.

"What if Bigway closes because no one else can run the business?"

"Well, I guess I wouldn't have any income."

"And if you die, what is Betty going to do with your company if there's no one around to run it?"

"I'm sure my employees would run it for her."

"Do you think they would under the current conditions? No benefits, no hospitalization, no life insurance, no savings plan? And a bad attitude to top it off?"

"Well, maybe you're right, Bob."

"You better talk to that investment adviser about a company benefits plan. One plan for home and one for the office," said Bob.

"You know, Bob, I work awfully hard. I've always wanted to be a millionaire. Betty, let's do get out of debt before we retire. We'll live the good life and retire in a style we deserve."

"I'm with you all the way, honey. Let's start tomorrow. And I'll raise the bet five," said Betty.

"Call and raise two," said Ben.

"Call," said Bob, throwing in his coins.

"Call," said Betty.

Bob showed his cards. "Two pair, aces and tens."

"Three kings," said Ben proudly, as he began to reach for the pile of coins in the center of the table.

"Full house," said Betty, showing two queens and three jacks. She pushed Ben's hands aside and took the biggest jackpot of the day.

"I'll take this money, men, thank you," she said.

$$\$ \, \$ \, \$ \, \$ \, \$ \, \$$$

"Ben, what would happen if you or Betty died or became disabled? What are you going to do with your estate?"

"Our kids will get it."

"Would they know what to do with a million dollars, several homes, some real estate, and your business?"

Ben started to answer, but Bob continued. "How is Ben, Jr., going to be taken care of? Would your daughter know what to do with the money?"

Neither Ben nor Betty said anything. They just looked at Bob in utter amazement. Then Ben spoke up.

"Oh, we're not going to die."

"But what if you do? What if you die on the way home from this picnic? Do you have a will?"

"Yes, we have a will," said Ben.

"When was it dated?" asked Bob.

Ben thought for a moment. "Back in the early 1980s, I think," he said.

"Ben, it's probably outdated. There were rules changes in the 1980s that might make your will outdated. In fact, Ben, if you and Betty get your debt paid off and then you and Betty die, your federal estate taxes could be over $1 million."

"$1 million! That's ridiculous."

"Probate fees will have to be paid on your estate. Then there will be federal estate taxes. And, federal estate taxes are the bigest tax in the United States," said Bob. "The rates start at 37% and go all the way up to 55%."

"55%?"

"That's right."

"Uncle Sam can't take that much money."

"He certainly can and he does. I've heard of cases in which parents have died and the children have had to sell off half the estate or more just to pay the federal estate taxes and probate fees. Can you see your daughter selling off your home and your business to try to get the estate and probate taxes paid?"

"That doesn't seem fair. That would be awful," said Betty. "Is there anything we can do to avoid having our children pay all those taxes?"

"First, update your will. Then, get a living trust."

"What's that?" questioned Ben.

"A living trust allows you to take advantage of the federal estate tax exemption. There isn't any federal estate tax on an estate if it's worth less than $600,000. And married couples each get a $600,000 exemption. So you see, you and Betty can avoid probate and federal estate taxes up to $1.2 million. So, if you have a trust, there are no probate fees or federal estate taxes on your first $1.2 million."

Betty asks, "What happens to the rest of our estate?"

Bob answers, "The federal estate taxes on a $4 million estate are over $1 million."

"I understand, Bob, but how are they paid?"

"Your daughter and your son may have to clear out the estate and sell some of the assets. Here's where your financial planner will help you. You'll be shown a way your children can have 100% of your estate without paying any federal estate tax or probate fees whatsoever. Ben, you know how?"

"No, Bob. How?"

"Your financial planner will explain to you how, through a combination of trusts and a life insurance policy, you will enable all of your estate to go to your loved ones when you want and how you want."

"How can insurance and a trust do that?" asked Betty.

"There's a new type of insurance called survivorship, or second to die insurance. It's actually one policy that covers both of your lives, and it's cheaper than one policy on each of you."

"Both of our lives?" asked Betty.

"Yes," said Bob. "One policy covers both of you. It doesn't make any difference who dies first. The death benefit is paid only after the second spouse dies. You see, federal estate taxes won't be due after the first death if you have a trust, or if everything you own is titled in both names."

"So, there is a value to life insurance," said Ben. "It can be used to pay off my federal estate taxes so that my estate goes to my loved ones."

"That's right. But let me warn you, that life insurance policy has to be owned a certain way."

"What do you mean, a certain way?" Ben questioned.

"You can have a trust made which is called a life insurance trust or an irrevocable life insurance trust. Or, you can have it owned by someone other than you and your spouse."

"Who could that be?"

"Possibly your daughter Bridget could own it. Her estate is outside of your estate. Here's how that would work: Each year, you could gift the premiums to her. You can gift up to $10,000 to each person per year. I'm sure a $1.5 million survivorship life insurance policy would probably cost less than $20,000 a year. You could each gift $10,000 to your daughter. She takes the money and pays the insurance premium. Then there are benefits to having your life insurance trust own the policy. If the kids ever got into a financial problem or were sued for some reason, the insurance policy could be attached as part of their estate."

Bob pointed out another insurance need.

"Betty needs to have liquid cash when you die, or your kids do if both of you die. Ben, there's no liquidity in your estate at all right now. There's too much debt."

Ben said, "It seems like I'm gonna be spending all my money on insurance. I won't be able to save any money. I'll be spending it all on insurance. I'll be insurance poor. All this insurance is going to kill me."

"Well, if you don't have the insurance, Ben, it's probably going to kill your estate and put your family into a situation where they're forced to liquidate. You don't want that, do you?"

"No, but Bob, how can I afford all this insurance?"

"Talk to your financial adviser—remember, that person who keeps calling you."

"Yeah, but won't it be expensive?"

"Life insurance might seem expensive, but I'm sure you and

Betty will find a way. Some of the insurance can be paid by your company. Your financial planner will explain everything to you."

Ben said, "Bob, it does sound like it's definitely something we should consider."

"And you know you have to do it when you're in good health," stated Bob.

"Well, what happens if we're not in good health?" asked Betty.

"Then you might be rated or have to pay an extra amount for the insurance. Or you might not be able to get any insurance at all. Then you're really in trouble because when you die, your estate will be liquidated. Wouldn't that be a pity after all your hard work?"

"Wouldn't it, honey?" Betty said, looking at Ben.

$ $ $ $ $ $

Bob recommended that Ben and Betty meet with their investment adviser and develop a financial plan with specific financial goals.

"Ben, I know that if you have a financial goal, you'll reach it. You're a winner. Here's one thing to keep in mind. Winning in investments takes a long time. It's like your business. It took you a long time to get where you are."

"I have to stay on top of my business daily," said Ben.

"The same holds true for investments," said Bob. "It's a marathon run. You've got to save and save, and plan and plan, and look far ahead. Don't worry about deviations in the marketplace on a day-to-day basis. Don't worry about a loss here or a loss there. Look long term.

"Remember, the more you save and the sooner you start saving, the more you have for retirement. And as time passes, we all get closer to retirement. If we don't save, time will pass us by. Retirement will be reaching for you, but you won't be able to grab on.

"Time is the most valuable asset we have. Save today and

plan for tomorrow. Get that trust taken care of. Get those company benefits. And get your insurance needs taken care of as soon as possible. There's something else that's extremely important."

"What's that, Bob?"

"Set up some special bequests in your trust for your son."

"What do you mean, special bequests?"

"If anything happens to you and Betty, who's going to take care of Ben, Jr.? Who's going to take care of your son's special needs down the line, when the two of you are gone? Maybe your daughter Bridget will take care of him, but you can't count on that."

"Right, Bob. Some day Bridget is going to get married. She may move away. She loves her brother, but she'll have her own family."

"That's right," Bob chimed in. "She shouldn't have to be responsible for taking care of her brother. Who knows, some day his medical expenses could eat up your entire estate. You've got to set up your estate and trust properly, so he will always be taken care of. And you need to do it now. What do you say, Ben?"

Betty, staring at Ben, asked, "Yes, Ben, are we going to keep wasting time or are we going to plan today for tomorrow?"

Ben was thinking, but he said nothing.

$$\$ \$ \$ \$ \$ \$$

Bob asked Ben about bringing his daughter Bridget into the business.

"I know she'd like it. She tells me all the time that she wants to learn about the business. But, she's just a kid. And, besides, she's a girl."

"But, honey," Betty protested, "you buy her cars, jewelry, clothes; you've sent her to the best schools. You give her everything, but you won't bring her into the business."

"That's because she's a girl."

"Now she's a young woman," Bob countered. "And a

woman can run a business just as well as a man. This summer, when she's off from school, give her a job. Put her in a position where she can learn about the company. Give the employees a chance to get to know her. See how she does."

"That's an idea, Bob. I'll certainly give it some consideration."

"That sounds great, honey," Betty smiled.

Ben's phone rang again.

"How's it going? Everything wrapped up? Great. I want to let you know how much I appreciate everyone giving their extra effort to work, not only during the week, but the weekends, too."

Ben hung up his phone and tucked it away in his bag. Betty applauded Ben's change of approach to his workers. "Ben, this is the right time to develop your family estate and provide your employees with assurances that you appreciate them. What do you say, Ben?" asked Bob.

"Ben, let's do something," suggested Betty.

"I think you're right. I've been slow to make these important decisions, and I've been slow to see how really important all of these items are to me and Betty, our family, and our business. But I need some time to think about it," said Ben.

"Ben, I have an idea. Let's you and me take a stroll around the ball fields and think about it," Betty said.

"Okay, honey, let's do it."

"And, Ben, how about letting me know your decision before you leave the picnic today?"

Ben nodded to Bob.

Bob announced, "Now, I've got good news and bad news. The good news is, there's no question in my mind that you're on the road to financial success."

"That's great, Bob, but what's the bad news?"

"The bad news, Ben and Betty, is that I have four aces. I'll take the whole pot, please."

"You win, Uncle Bob," said Betty.

"No, Ben and Betty, you win from now on."

8

George and Gail Gotittogether: Enjoying the Empty Nest

FULL FROM A BIG DINNER, Bob was ready to settle down for the last few hours of the picnic. The temperature cooled slightly as the sun moved into the western sky.

As Bob stood next to the picnic shelter looking over the valley and the green, rolling hills, he was greeted by George and Gail. Like the picnic day, George and Gail were coasting into the final phase of their lives. Now in their late 60s, both George and Gail had just retired. The ultimate empty nesters, George and Gail enjoyed a life that was orderly and stress-free. They were financially secure, their children were grown, and they were ready to sit back and enjoy life.

To the picnic, George and Gail wore matching outfits: red and blue plaid shirts and yellow shorts with black belts. They had similar glasses with auburn plastic frames. They seemed alike in many ways, showing signs of a couple that had been together for many years.

"Hey, Bob, how'd you like to walk off some of that dinner?" asked George. "There's a three-mile hiking trail through the woods."

Bob replied, "I don't know if I can keep up with you two."

George and Gail walked five miles every morning along the

tree-lined streets in the comfortable suburban neighborhood where they'd lived since their children were young.

Now their three children were grown and living on their own. Their oldest daughter, Gina, was married and had two children. Middle daughter Glenna had just had a baby, giving George and Gail their newest grandchild. Son Gregory was two years out of college, and worked in the marketing department of a large consumer products company.

"Congratulations are in order. Is it a boy or a girl?"

"It's a girl, Bob. Her name is Jennifer. Glenna is always bringing her over. She's so cute," Gail humbly admitted.

"She stayed overnight once while Glenna and Tom went away for the weekend."

"You sound like happy grandparents."

"You might say we're just a little happy," Gail said beamingly, with a tone of understatement.

"All of the pleasure and none of the responsibility, right?" queried Bob.

"You got it!" Gail replied.

For George and Gail, everything seemed to be together in their lives. They lived in a good neighborhood, and their house was in immaculate condition. They ate out several times a week. They enjoyed going to the theater, and they traveled a lot.

George had worked as an engineer for the telephone company for 35 years. He had retired five years ago and was now 68. Gail, 67, had retired the same year George did. She had been an elementary schoolteacher.

The couple enjoyed being doting grandparents and indulging baby Jennifer. And, they expected more grandkids in the next few years.

"With Jennifer and the grandkids, we want to make sure we can take care of ourselves financially. We don't want to be a burden to our kids, and we want to be able to leave something for them," George said. "We were hoping to talk to you at the picnic today about a financial problem we have."

Bob said, "Let's talk while we walk. Just don't go at too fast a pace or this old guy won't be able to keep up." They all laughed.

$ $ $ $ $ $

The trail started in a valley along a creek. Tree-covered hills rose on either side. The trail was completely shaded, and birds were singing.

"What a nice day." Gail's voice almost sang.

"It certainly has been a good day," Bob agreed. "It's been great to see everyone."

"So, Bob, are you doing any of that money talk with people?" asked George.

"Of course. That's a lot of why it's been such a great day."

"Bob, dear, I can't imagine you coming to a picnic and not talking money," Gail said.

"Some people had some things they needed to think about. We talked it over. I think we made some progress. The only thing I haven't done yet it play horseshoes. Maybe we can do that after our walk."

"We'll see if we can get back in time." George looked at his watch.

The trail turned uphill. When Bob saw how high the hill was, he asked, "We have to walk all the way up there?"

"It's not bad. You'll make it," Gail encouraged him.

"You do this all the time."

"We'll look out for you," George assured him.

"Okay."

While the three walked at a steady pace, George looked over at Bob. "Say, Bob, we've listened to your advice over the years. We've done well. But, you know, there is one thing I'm wondering about."

"There are always financial things to wonder about. You know, the older you get, the more complicated financial planning becomes, especially when you retire."

"Well, Bob, we've planned carefully to get where we are. But I do have a concern."

"What's that?"

"Our CDs aren't paying what they used to. We've never been big risk takers, so we've stayed with secure investments like CDs. That worked fine 10 years ago, when CDs were paying 13%. The problem is, now the rates have gone down, so we're not making as much money. We want to keep our same lifestyle. We're at the point where we can pay all our bills, but we have to watch closely on extras like entertainment and vacations. I don't understand how this happened. All of a sudden, we're in a tight situation."

Bob began to breathe a little harder as he climbed the hill. Between his huffing and puffing, he tried to answer. "Lower interest rates have caught a lot of people in a squeeze. They were depending on income from their CDs. Now their income has gone way down."

George continued, "Also, everything costs so much more today. Prices keep going up. We want to provide for our children and our grandchildren. We want to help them out. But at the same time, we'd like to continue to live a good life, the kind of life we've become accustomed to."

"George, I've heard the same concerns from a lot of other retired people. Don't think that you're the only retired people who are in this situation. Remember when I talked to you about inflation? I said that with interest rates down, you might need to take a little more risk with some of your investments, to keep up with inflation."

"Yes, I remember. But back then I didn't like the idea of risk. I still don't like it today. Then, we had a good income. We didn't have any debt, and we still don't have any debt, and we're never going to have any debt. But we could use a little more income."

"I agree. Most retirees do need more income."

"In the past, we just wanted to save some money and put it someplace safe. We just wanted it to make a little money. And at 10, 12, and 13% interest, we could pay all the bills. It's a different story today. Then, we weren't taking any risk. Everything was guaranteed by the government. The rates now are so low that the interest income won't cover our bills."

"But, George, don't you remember, I told you there was no such thing as a risk-free investment?"

"Yes, but we didn't understand what you meant."

"Okay, let's do this." Bob breathed harder as the uphill incline got steeper. "Let's cover that important fact right now. There's no such thing as a risk-free investment. You see, every year—regardless of what you're making on your money, whether it's in Treasury bills, Treasury bonds, CDs, double E bonds, or whatever—there's a nemesis out there that's constantly pecking away at our money's buying power."

"What's that, Bob?"

"That, George, is *inflation*."

"Oh, you've told us that before. But I really don't understand how it works. I can't see it. I can't hear it. I can't feel it. But you say it's there."

"Yes, George. Most people don't ever see inflation. When they're working, they have income coming in. They think that if they're paying the bills, they're probably ahead of the game and ahead of most other people, so why worry about doing anything more? They're paying the bills, they're getting along. They're going from day to day, so what else is there to worry about?"

"And that's exactly what we did, Bob. We paid all the bills and thought it was always going to be like that, but now it's not. We're at the point now where we're barely covering our expenses."

"So things haven't quite worked out the way you wanted."

"I'm very pleased with us for staying out of debt. But I'm concerned that if our expenses keep skyrocketing as they have over the last five years since we retired, we may find ourselves having to live a different lifestyle in the future. Things have really been great for us up to now. But now we're both concerned."

Gail stopped for a moment at a bench about halfway up the hill. Bob sat on the bench, sighed, and wiped perspiration from his forehead. From the bench, they had a beautiful view of the valley. While the walkers paused momentarily, the conversation continued.

"Well, I'm glad that you're finally seeing the true picture. The inflation rate has averaged about 4% a year for a long time. Do you know what that means, George?"

"Well, yeah, sure. Things cost more."

"Let's talk about it. If inflation is 4%, everything goes up in price by an average of 4% every year. A loaf of bread may go up 6%. Milk may only increase 2%. However, the increase in prices will probably average 4%. Do you know what that could do to your buying power over the next 10 years?"

"We're going to have a 40% increase in our expenses," Gail offered.

"And that means that at least 40% of your buying power today will be gone 10 years from now. A dollar today buys a dollar's worth of goods. In 10 years, that same dollar will only buy you about 60 cents worth of goods. That's a lot to lose, Gail. You really should be gaining on your money rather than losing on it. Don't you think so, George?"

"That's a big chunk." George shook his head in agreement.

"Here's another way to put it. Whatever your income is today, in 10 years it will buy only about 60% of what it buys today."

"Only 60%?"

"Yes, that's right. And you folks are young, in your late 60s. Hopefully you're going to be here when you're in your 80s and 90s. What do you think your dollar will buy then?"

"If inflation's going to eat up 40% of our buying power over the next 10 years, goodness, Bob, we're going to need twice as much money 15 to 20 years from now just to be able to buy the same things we buy today."

"That's right, George, and that's not counting higher taxes. And if you don't think that's going to happen, you're missing the boat."

Gail joined in. "It looks like if we live to be 85 our principal is going to be gone completely as far as buying power. We'll have to double our money by then just to break even."

She stood up and said, "Shall we walk some more?"

George got up as he said, "I'm beginning to see more clearly what inflation really is. It just constantly eats at your money until it's gone. I guess people just get to the point where they've got to spend all of their principal. What happens then?"

Bob groaned as he slowly raised himself from the bench. "Spending your principal can be disastrous. A lot of people say that they don't care about their principal continuing to grow as they get older. They don't think they'll be around too much longer. All they want is to have enough income to pay all their expenses and live a good life. They're the kind who have the bumper stickers that say, 'I'm spending my grandkids' money.'"

The three resumed walking.

"Well, I guess in some sense that's not a bad thing to do. You might as well spend it while you've got it," Gail suggested.

"No, it's the worst thing you can do," Bob differed. "You see, those same people who say they don't care about their money growing, wake up one morning and find out that they've outlived their money."

"What do you mean, Bob?"

"They wake up one day and they don't have any principal left. The money has been spent. Now they're in a terrible situation. They're retired, they've got a little money coming in from Social Security and maybe a company benefits plan, but their principal is gone. They have spent it. Now they can no longer live the lifestyle they've grown accustomed to living. They're left to make a decision on living with their children, borrowing from their children, or just living uncomfortably the rest of their lives."

"That sounds terrible," Gail concluded.

"George and Gail, please, never outlive your money. Let's all three of us make a promise right now. Let's make our money grow, beat the inflation rate by investing prudently, and have some of it left over for our loved ones when we are no longer here."

"It sounds good to me." Gail sighed. "You know, this is exasperating."

"The walk?" asked Bob.

"No, what we're hearing. I like to think we're in a good financial situation now in our retirement years—that everything will be a downhill coast. But the idea of outliving our money is scary. We could run out of money some day."

Bob replied, "A lot of people tell me that they really don't care what happens when they're 85 or 90. They say, 'Bob, why should I worry about that? I'm not even going to be around then. Who cares? I want to invest in short-term investments. Because long-term I won't be here. I just want to make sure I've got enough income for the next 10 years. That'll take care of my expenses. It'll allow me to live easy, and that's all I'm concerned with.' That's what most people think. But do you know what happens to many of those people?"

"No, what?"

"One day they wake up, they're 85 years old, and they don't have any money. They didn't plan to be 85, they planned to die before then. They used up all their money and all their principal and all their earnings just getting there. They wake up one day, and they're 85 years old and broke. They're alive, but their money has passed away."

"A very scary thought," said George.

"That's not where we want to be, Bob," Gail agreed.

"If you don't do something with your investments now, that's just where you could be. Maybe not at 85, maybe not at 75, but sometime in the future. How about this? Make a game plan to live to 100. People are retiring earlier and earlier today, *and* they're living longer. With all the advances in health care, chances are you will live well into your late 80s, and maybe they'll print your picture in the newspaper when you turn 100."

"That would be great, Bob, but in our current situation, I don't know if our money is going to last as long as we do."

"You're right," Bob agreed. The climb up the hill was getting steeper. "Most people today will outlive their retirement dollars.

That's something we can't let happen to us. You've worked together all through your lives. You've stayed out of debt and saved
your money. You have a good life. You've paid off your home and
sent your kids through college. You're retired, you thought everything was going to be terrific, and now you find that the inflation
rate and higher taxes are going to put you behind the eight ball
rather than in front of it. Plus, you want to figure out a way you
can help your grandkids, and also leave something behind for
your children."

"Yes, yes!" yelled George and Gail. "That's right."

"Well, the way to help your grandkids is to take care of yourselves financially first. Plan to have more money than you need
when you're in your 70s, 80s, and 90s. Plan to live to 100, but
make sure you've got enough money to last through 110."

"Bob, we can't even be sure we're going to have money in 10
years. We're probably going to be spending our principal down."

$ $ $ $ $ $

They reached a stone picnic table at an overlook. The three
sat down.

"Let's look at what you have and what you're spending,"
Bob began.

George offered, "We have $350,000, all of it sitting in CDs and
money market accounts."

"That's your principal, what you hope to live off of."

"Right."

"Now, what are your expenses? Have you been keeping
track?" asked Bob.

George said, "Bob, years ago you told us about your Cookie
Jar Expense Checklist. You taught us to do a financial profile and
keep it updated. We've been doing those things ever since. I can
tell you almost to the dollar. Our expenses are about $65,000 a
year."

"What is your income?"

"From our money market accounts and CDs, we have about
$12,000 a year coming in."

"Okay. What about your pension plan?"

"I've got $23,000 a year coming in, and Gail has about $15,000."

"So far, that adds up to $50,000. How much do you have coming in from Social Security?"

"About $1,800 a month."

"That's another $21,000. Add that up, you've got $71,000 in income. That's more than your expenses. Not much more, but more."

"Yeah, but Bob, something doesn't make sense. It seems like we're spending all of our income."

"Yeah, Bob, there's nothing left over," said Gail.

"When was the last time you did your Cookie Jar Expense Checklist?" Bob asked.

"Well, not for a while," said Gail. "I know we have the same bills—utilities, food, entertainment, and the grandkids."

"What about the grandkids? Do you give them any additional holiday presents?"

"Yes."

"And birthday presents?"

"Yes."

"And do you slip your kids some money when they ask for it?"

"Well, yes."

"Do you count that?"

"Oh, George, I don't think we do count that money."

"So you probably don't know what your total expenses are now. You haven't kept really up to date. I'd bet that instead of having $60,000 to $65,000 worth of expenses, you have over $75,000 of expenses. Don't forget that everything costs more today than it did when you were working."

"Bob, that's when we stopped doing our Cookie Jar Expense Checklist," said George.

"And that's when you should have been really sharpening

your figures," said Bob. "So, you've got about $71,000 a year coming in. You've got $65,000 a year going out. That leaves you very, very tight. Yet you're both in the prime of life. You're just starting your retirement. At a 4% inflation rate, that $65,000 of expenses will surpass your $71,000 income within the next couple of years."

"That's a very scary thought." Gail grimaced. "We're retired, on fixed incomes that won't pay our bills down the line."

With that, the three hikers headed on up the path.

$ $ $ $ $ $

The uphill grade leveled out slightly as the walkers continued their climb. The trail had snaked up the side of the hill and was now straight as the grade leveled off. The walkers emerged from the woods into an open field. Bob was still puffing.

"Oh, my goodness, Bob, that's terrible. I'm starting to get tired already and we've only walked half as far as we usually walk every day," Gail admitted.

"Yeah, I guess it's the utter frustration of this whole investment situation. I'm getting tired, too," George added.

"I'm just not sure I'll make it to the top of this hill," Bob declared as he puffed harder.

"Well, Bob, I'm not worried about this trail. We'll get to the top of the hill soon. But we're in trouble when we're talking about getting to the top of our financial hill."

"I'm glad I got your attention. But really, George and Gail, it's not as bad as you think. You think we can manage this hill; I think you can manage your money."

$ $ $ $ $ $

"Here's the way you can beat inflation," Bob offered. "Change your Sleep Syndrome. Take a little more risk."

"But you know we're conservative," George protested.

"If you want your money to grow, you're going to have to take a little more risk," Bob stated again.

"We've heard you talk about Sleep Syndrome before. I've always said I wanted to sleep as soundly as possible. But explain it again, would you?"

"Simply put, your Sleep Syndrome is the ability to go to bed at night and sleep soundly without worrying about your investments. Sleep Syndrome means that you're not going to worry about your investments during the daytime. You're not going to follow the stock market each day, or read the mutual fund quotes to see if your shares are up or down. You're not going to worry about your investments on a day-by-day basis. You're certainly not going to think about them when you go to bed at night. You've got to be able to make your investments and go to sleep at night and not worry. Get a diversified investment program of guaranteed investments like you have, but add some fixed and variable investments. That should give you more growth on your principal over the next 10 years. The more principal you have, the more income it will provide. Diversify."

"Well, Bob, we don't want investments that make us nervous. We'll never sleep at night," said Gail.

"Sleep Syndrome involves many considerations. The first thing for you to consider is what kind of risk taker you are. Let's consider returns for a moment. If you're making 10% to 15% per year in a CD, Treasury bill, or Treasury bond, you're going to say, 'Who cares about any other investments?' Right? That's what you said 10 years ago."

"You're right, Bob; that's exactly what we said."

"Remember, if you make 10% a year and it compounds, you'll double your money in 7.2 years. If you make 15% a year, you'll double your money in 5 years. There are two types of Magic Windows that are going to make you money."

"Magic Windows? Bob, what are you talking about now?"

"One is a time Magic Window, and one is a percentage of growth Magic Window."

"Okay," said George. "What are you talking about?"

"If money doubles in 7.2 years at 10% a year and money doubles in 5 years at 15% a year, there are your two windows."

"Oh, I see."

Gail interjected, "All we do is figure out what percentage of return we want to make. That'll tell us how long it'll take to double our money," said Gail.

"Right, Gail, you've got it. So in a 5- to 7.2-year period, you should double your money if you can make somewhere between 10% and 15% a year."

"But I can't make 10% to 15% a year right now," George complained.

"Oh, yes, you can. You're just going to have to take a little more risk with some of your money."

"Bob, don't start talking to us about things like commodities. That's for people like Ben. He's a gambler. You know, I heard him bragging about the diamond mine he bought into. That's not me or Gail," George said.   ·

"I know it's not you. And I don't think there are many people like Ben. I'm not suggesting that you gamble with your money. I'm just suggesting you find something with a little more risk than you have now."

"We want things secure," Gail emphasized.

"There's a lot of room for you to take some risk without sacrificing security."

"So we need to move at least a little in that direction." Gail began to understand.

"You have to. Here's the picture. Leaving all your money in guaranteed investments isn't going to give you the kind of income you need right now. It's not going to give you the growth and principal that'll build the income you need down the line."

"You're probably right, Bob, but we don't want to risk all our money," George protested.

"So, don't risk all your money. Take a small amount. Put it into something with a small to moderate level of risk, and watch it for a period of six months to a year. If you feel comfortable, if it's growing, if it's giving you more income than your guaranteed returns, invest a little more. You don't have to do it all in one day."

"That sounds more palatable," George agreed.

"Let's see," Bob calculated. "If you took $5,000 of your money today at your age of 68, George, and you made 15% a year, you would double it to $10,000 by age 73, and to $20,000 by 78. At age 83, you'd have $40,000, and at age 88 you'd have $80,000. By 93, you'd have close to $160,000 just off that initial $5,000 investment."

"Yeah, Bob, that sounds good. But we're still having to take a risk."

"George, you're going to have to take some kind of risk. If you leave your money in guaranteed investments, inflation is going to eat up your money. In my mind, that's a bad risk. Or, you can take what I think is a better risk, and try to make more money than the guarantees can give you now. And remember, I'm not saying that you should gamble and take unnecessary risk."

Bob added, "You see, you either take a risk with some of your money and try to get a greater return, or you stay right where you are with low rates and guaranteed returns. If you choose low returns, realize that, one, you're barely covering the inflation rate and paying your bills, and two, your principal is really not growing."

"Yes, I see what you mean, Bob. That's exactly what has happened over the last 10 years. Back then, 12% or 13% was great, but at the current rates we're just kind of standing in place."

"And don't forget, you were both working, so you didn't need any more income."

"We depend on the income from our investments. It's our major source," Gail agreed.

Bob paused and took a deep breath.

"Are you okay, Bob?" asked George.

"I'm fine." Bob looked over his shoulder down the hill. "But what happens if I stumble. Am I going to roll backwards all the way down there?"

George pointed down the hill. "See that boulder? That'll stop you."

They all laughed.

"Bob, you're not going anywhere until you tell us what to do with these investments," Gail insisted. "Here we're retired, and all of sudden inflation is hitting us right where it hurts. We need to make more money, but we're retired, so we don't want to lose the money we've worked so hard all our life to save."

"*Now* you need to make more money and take the least amount of risk. You've got to change your Sleep Syndrome. You've got to be able to go to bed at night and say that the world will be here tomorrow. Chicken Little is not going to come running into your bedroom in the morning and say that the sky has fallen. You've got to sleep soundly and realize that there's a certain amount of risk in every investment. You've got to think long term."

"Can't I stay in some of my guaranteed investments?"

"Of course. I'm not saying get out of all your guaranteed investments. No matter whether the returns are as little as 1%, 2%, or 3%, a certain amount of your money should always stay in guaranteed investments. But you also need to take some of that money and put it into investments that are going to give you more growth and more income so that you can stay ahead of inflation and make your principal grow."

"How can we do that, Bob?"

$ $ $ $ $ $

Gail spotted another overlook with a pair of benches. "Let's sit down for a few minutes and let Bob catch his breath."

"Isn't that an eagle flying out there?" George pointed off to the right.

"Yes!" Gail pointed to another one.

"They say eagles mate for life." Bob smiled warmly at George and Gail.

The three enjoyed the beautiful view from the hillside as they talked investments.

Bob began again. "First of all, I said *think long term*. We've talked about Sleep Syndrome. We've discussed taking a little more risk. Keep most of your money in guaranteed returns. There's no stronger guarantee than our government. I'm not saying take all of your money out of the guaranteed investments. Take some of your money and put it in something long term that's variable."

"What do you mean, variable?"

"A variable investment is one where we're not sure what the return will be. It may be a stock. It may be a variable annuity. It may be a unit trust. It may be a mutual fund."

"We've never had anything like that."

"Well, a variable investment is exactly what it says. Instead of something like a CD that gives you a specific rate of return over a specific period of time, you invest in something that can return more or less. You're taking a risk, but remember, we're trying to beat inflation."

George and Gail held hands and looked around at the scenery as they listened.

"Many of these variable investments provide a pamphlet called a 'prospectus.' You can read the prospectus and find out the risk you're taking, the length of time that you're required to keep your money in the investment, the objectives of the investment, who is managing the money, how long the investment has existed, and many other investment considerations. It should give you all the infromation you need to make an informed decision about the investment."

"They have a lot of fine print."

"Yes, a lot of that small print written by legal departments is hard to understand. But don't start any investment until you understand the risk involved and you feel comfortable with it. Most importantly, the prospectus should tell you what kind of risk you're taking. There are industry rules about what must go into a prospectus. The prospectus is there to help you, so you don't get into something that you're not suited for. *Suitability* is the term used by the securities agencies to judge whether your comfort level will tolerate a specific investment. I call that Sleep Syndrome."

"How does suitability work?"

"Well, you might have to have a certain amount of assets to get into a specific investment. You have to understand risk and the possibility that you might lose some or all of your money in that particular investment."

"Oh, my goodness, Bob. I hate to hear you say that."

"And, you've got to know the time factor of the investment. Is it short term? Is it medium term? Or is it long term? What specific length of time are they referring to? Six months? Three years? Ten years? You have to know whether the investment is a growth-type or income-type investment. With some investments, only the value of the principal increases, whereas others pay dividends or interest.

"Today, you need growth from your investments. You shouldn't look for investments with tax benefits only. Tax benefits by themselves are not important to you now. You have to know ahead of time what your financial goals are."

"Bob, you mentioned tax benefits. We want to stop paying taxes, don't we, George?"

"You bet, Gail."

"That's good," said Bob. "Given an equal choice, I'd choose the investment with tax benefits over one without them. However, that's usually the last item I look for in any investment. There are many other things that are more important."

"Why's that, Bob?"

"Well, first let's go back to risk. That's the most important consideration. Then, you've got to look at the time factor: short, medium, or long term. Then, whether the investment is growth or income. Then, after you've looked at all those factors, you want to check to see if there are any tax benefits. You have to look at every one of those factors before you make your investment. I call these *investment considerations*."

"That scares me, Bob, just thinking about it," Gail admitted.

"What scares me, Gail, is thinking about you and George at the age of 80 without any money."

"You're right, Bob. I'm scared about the idea of risk. But I'm even more scared about the idea of running out of money. It's not like we can go back to work when we're in our 80s. So my big question to you is, How do we earn more money and get rid of inflation?"

"You're never going to be able to get rid of inflation. But what you can do is slow it down by earning more money on your investments than inflation eats away. The only way I know of to do that is to take a little more risk with some of your money. That's especially true when guaranteed rates of return are as low as they are now."

"Okay, so what should we look for, Bob?"

"Well, you need your money to grow, right, George?"

"Yes."

"But you don't need income now. You've got $71,000 a year coming in. You've got $65,000 going out. What you need right now is growth and some tax benefits."

"So what do we do?"

"You put your dollars into investments that will give you growth and tax benefits today, plus income down the line."

"Is there such an animal?"

"There are several. One is stocks. Over the last 20-year period, stocks have outperformed CDs. Your next best bet over CDs is bonds."

"What about precious metals, like gold, silver, or platinum? I hear they're going to start moving up soon. Ben says he's making a lot of money in gold futures."

"Well, they aren't going to pay any income. They may build your principal, but now you're speculating. Do you want to speculate?"

"No, we don't want to speculate."

"Well, then, if you don't want to speculate, don't bother with high-risk investments, especially those that don't yield an income. Remember the financial pyramid. Build your foundation and then invest up to your Sleep Syndrome level."

"Okay, then, you're saying we should buy bonds or individual stocks?"

"Well, you might buy some stock. But remember, if you own one stock and it goes up, that's good; you make money quickly."

"But what if it goes down, Bob?"

"If it goes down, you're going to lose money quickly. Which means you've lost some of your principal quickly."

"Okay, so stocks are out."

"No, stocks aren't necessarily out. You just have to understand the risk."

"Well, then, what do we do?"

"You could buy a municipal bond, which is backed by its municipality. Some of these investments have tax benefits and accumulate on a tax-deferred basis, which is what you want."

"Sounds good."

"One thing to keep in mind, riskwise, is what happens if you need to get your money back before the bond matures."

"They won't let us have our money back whenever we want it?"

"You may not be able to get all of it. There may be a penalty for getting out early. The bond can fluctuate in value before it matures. These are just more considerations you need to think about before you invest."

"So, we're back to taking a risk."

"Yes, you're back to taking a risk. However, there's risk in everything. There's risk in taking this walk. One of us might trip and fall. A tree limb might land on someone's head. The real question is, what is appropriate risk for you? If it was winter and this path was covered with ice, one of us probably would fall. So walking would be a bad risk. Today, it's unlikely that anything will happen. I may have a coronary and keel over, but that's because I'm not in as good physical condition as you two. But still, walking here today so far is low risk."

"That helps to explain risk. Now, what about those bonds?" asked Gail.

"Well, there are some good things about bonds. But you should hold bonds until maturity; otherwise you might get back less money than you invested."

"You mean if we needed the money before the time was up?"

"That's right."

"I thought bonds were guaranteed."

"Government bonds are guaranteed to return at least the principal if you hold until maturity. But municipal bonds and corporate bonds are backed by their respective municipality or corporation. As long as it's strong and successful, chances are you'll get all of your money back. But if it fails, or you pull your money out early, you might lose some of your principal. Bonds fluctuate up and down during their growth period, so you may have to sell low rather than sell high."

"Bob, we've never been in the market. We don't know anything about it. We're not brokers. We don't have any inside information," George said, bewildered.

Gail too appeared overwhelmed, "Yeah, it seems as if we're getting into something we really don't know much about. I've heard a lot of people say that as soon as they got into the market, it went down. They became instant losers. I'm sure the same thing would happen to us. We'd invest all our money, and it would go right down the tubes."

Bob responded, "I've heard that, too, but it's just an old myth. You have to be willing to take at least some risk if you're going to try to get better returns than you're getting now. You need growth in principal now, so you have more income down the line."

"So what do we do? Do we buy bonds?"

"Well, you can. But I don't advise putting all your money in bonds."

"Well, then, what, Bob? Tell us. You talked about stocks, you talked about bonds. Where should we invest our money?"

"There's an investment that's a combination of stocks, bonds, Treasuries, and money market accounts."

"What's that?"

"It's mutual funds."

"You've talked to us about mutual funds before, but I don't understand them."

"Let me give you an example. It's like a pool of money. Let's say each of us puts $100 into the pot. You give the money to me to manage. I buy stocks, bonds, money market accounts, and maybe some Treasuries. I decide to hold some of the investments long term. I decide to sell some when they're profitable. Or, I sell some as soon as a small loss occurs. At the end of the year, our pot is worth so much money—hopefully, more than it was at the start of the year. Each of us owns the same percentage of the pot. Right?"

"Right, Bob."

"We all put the same amount of money in, so we'd each own one-third of the pot. Now, there's one other item to factor in."

"What's that?"

"Well, you told me to manage the money. Do you think I'd manage the money for free?"

"Well, no. But I know there are mutual funds that don't have any charges. I hear people talking all the time about buying no-loads. Those are free investments. That's what I want to buy. Why pay commission?"

"There's no such thing as a mutual fund or any investment that I know of that's free," Bob explained. "George, don't you think the people who run these funds are in business to make money?"

"Well, yes, of course, I guess."

"So, do you think they'd really let you invest with them for free?"

"Probably not. But I heard there are no-loads, where there are no charges."

"That's not how they work. Some mutual funds have charges

and fees that you see. But there also are inside fees that you might not see."

"What do you mean, inside?"

"Well, there are expense ratio fees, management fees, and percent of profit fees. People have to get paid for their work. The portfolio manager gets paid a fee. The company makes a certain amount for putting the mutual fund together. The company has employees. George, do you think those people work for free?"

"No, I don't think so."

"So don't look at investments and conclude that they don't have any costs."

"Well, what should we look at?"

"Look at the prospectus or the pamphlet about the investment. It shows what the fund invests in, and who is managing the fund. It will give the fund's past results. Now keep in mind that previous results don't guarantee future returns. There's a lot of information in a prospectus."

"I understand that, Bob. But how can I tell what the mutual fund or investment is going to do after I get in it?"

"There are no guarantees, George. There's no way to know. What you've got to do is feel comfortable with the previous results and the objectives of the investment. Previous results cannot guarantee future returns, though, so for your Sleep Syndrome it is very important that you choose the variable investment that you feel most comfortable with."

"So, what kind of risk should we take?"

"Here's how I look at it. Someone who is in their 20s or early 30s might purchase a mutual fund that has an aggressive investment strategy. That would probably be a fund that purchases mostly stocks that appreciate quickly in a rising market, but could fall even more quickly in a declining market."

"Yeah, but we're not in our 20s, Bob."

"That's right. People in their 20s or early 30s have time to make up any losses that they may incur in their early investment years. They have another 30 or 40 years to recoup and have their money grow before they retire. By getting into aggressive growth investments, they have the opportunity to make a lot of money over a long period of time. Can you imagine your kids making 15% a year from the age of 30 all the way to age 65? Wow! Just think, they could double their money seven times."

"That's fine for the kids, Bob. But what about us?"

"I'm getting there. If you were in your 30s or 40s, I'd suggest a good growth fund. Maybe not very aggressive, but a growth fund where you would have A-rated bonds, Treasury bills, maybe some CD-type investments, and stocks. The stocks probably wouldn't be highly aggressive—maybe the stocks of large, solid companies, called blue chips."

"What's a blue-chip stock, Bob?"

"Blue-chip stocks have been around a long time and have given good returns in the past."

Gail said, "But past success is no guarantee of the future."

"Right," agreed Bob. "The blue chips simply are those companies that have good track records and get good ratings from agencies like Standard & Poor's or Moody's."

"What do these rating agencies do?"

"They rate and rank companies. They will rate the company on risk, size, management ability, and other important issues."

Gail moved to another subject. "You know, the view sure is great here. But we've been sitting here for a while. Time is passing us by. We need to finish this walk before it gets too late."

Bob got up slowly, his bones creaking. He noticed a solid, four-foot-long stick beside the path. He picked it up and began using it as a walking stick. It was comforting to know that they weren't far from the top.

"These are some scary thoughts," said Gail.

"You two will do just fine," Bob said. "Just follow my tips."

"You mean your secrets, Bob." George smiled knowingly. "All of us always talk about Uncle Bob's Investment Secrets."

"Okay, if you want to call them secrets, but they're easy to follow. You just have to take a little risk at certain times to hopefully get the best returns."

"I hope so, Bob. I hope so."

Bob got philosophical. "You know, investing is a lot like hiking this hill. You can run up totally out of control and almost get to the top, only to stumble and fall all the way back down. Or if you take a lot of risk in your investments, you can make a lot of money very fast, but then turn around and lose it even more quickly. In my opinion, the best way to climb this hill is exactly as we've just done. Easy does it. Not rushing. Just taking our time, enjoying the sights, smelling the roses.

"And look, we've made it to the top!"

$ $ $ $ $ $

The path wandered along a ridge. The walkers stopped momentarily at a bench with a spectacular view overlooking the valley and the lake. The bench was full of initials carved by the many people who had visited the spot in days and years past.

"Isn't this peaceful?" asked George.

"This is the way we want our life in retirement to be, peaceful." Gail seemed very content.

An eagle swept across the hilltop and landed in a tree within 50 yards of Bob, George, and Gail. They stood breathless, looking at the beautiful bird, then began the last leg of their journey.

"Okay, Bob, where do we go from here?" asked George.

"Well, I'd suggest we start down."

"I don't mean that, Bob."

"I'm just trying to be funny, George."

"I know, I know. But, Bob, we want to start making some money now."

"Well, there are a number of professionals who can help you."

"Like whom?"

"Let's start at your bank. You've done business there for a while, haven't you?"

"26 years."

"Sit down with your banker and figure out some ways your banker can get you better returns. Maybe a reverse mortgage."

"What's a reverse mortgage?"

"A reverse mortgage enables you to work out a situation with the bank where they pay you an income based on the borrowing power of your home. That income could last as long as you live. Then, after both of you die, the home is sold and that amount the bank paid you is returned to them."

"Hey, that sounds neat. Do we get to continue to live in the house?"

"The house is still yours in every way as long as you're alive."

"Okay, what else?"

"Then, sit down with your CPA and figure out what your tax situation is. Your CPA will advise you whether you need tax benefits in your investment or not."

"All right, Bob, that sounds pretty good."

"Well, your professionals won't have all the answers for you. But they have a lot. They're a storehouse of information. If you work with your professionals, you'll find out a lot more about investing than if you try to do it all on your own."

"Who else should we talk to?"

"A financial planner."

"What's a financial planner, Bob? Is it my broker, is it an agent, is it a person who sells stocks?"

"All of the above. Let me explain. A financial planner is a professional in the investment field who works with all kinds of investments, such as stocks, bonds, mutual funds, partnerships, and all kinds of insurance. A financial planner can sit down with you and help you pick the investments you need. Financial planners help you figure out where you really are today, and where you want to be tomorrow. Then they help you choose the right investments to help you reach your financial goals. Working with your financial planner should give you a better chance to reach and accomplish all of your financial goals."

"Where do we find a financial planner?"

"Talk to your friends. Listen to the investment programs on the radio. Watch investment programs on television. Go to investment seminars. When you hear the same financial adviser's name mentioned over and over, make an appointment. You're under no obligation. Just go in and sit down and be prepared to answer all kinds of questions."

"What kinds of questions, Bob?"

"Nothing that we haven't gone over today and over the last 10 years."

"You mean like the financial profile we did?"

"That's correct. They'll do a financial profile and ask you where you think you are right now financially, and where you want to be 10 years from now financially. What type of risk taker are you? How much income do you make? What are your expenses? Do you have any debt? They'll gather all that information and make some suggestions to you on how to reach your financial goals."

"And then we're finished, Bob?"

"No, then your work has just begun. You take all that information home, and think about what you want to do. Read as much about investments as you possibly can. Watch and listen to investment programs. Talk to your friends about investments. Find out what everyone is thinking and doing. Make sure you run everything by your attorney."

"My attorney doesn't have anything to do with investments."

"Yes, but your attorney can assure you that the investments you've considered are legally correct and can be purchased legally in our state."

"Oh, I never thought about that."

"You also need to go to an attorney for another reason."

"Why?"

"To make sure that your estate is set up properly."

"What do you mean, Bob?"

"Do you have a will?"

"Yes. You told us to do that 10 or 15 years ago, Bob. Around 1978."

"Uh-oh," Bob said as he shook his head defensively. "Your will is probably out of date. In fact, chances are that with the size of your estate, you're not only going to need a will but you should look into a living trust."

"What do you mean, a living trust?"

"It's a special trust account that governs how your estate will be distributed. An attorney can help you set it up."

"Okay, Bob, so now we have a will, we've got a trust, we've talked to our professionals, we've done a financial profile. We're continuing to do our Cookie Jar Expense Checklist, so we know exactly what our expenses are, and we're continuing to stay out of debt. We must be way ahead of most investors."

"Yes. You're doing very well. But there's one more stumbling block that befalls some investors."

"What's that?"

"The P word. Procrastination."

"Putting things off," said Gail.

"People can keep saying that they're going to save and invest, but they're going to wait until they get a big lump sum or they're going to save their money until the end of the year and then invest it when they get their bonus or that tax refund. Do you know what happens?"

"No, Bob. What happens?"

"An emergency comes up. The roof gets a leak, the car breaks down, or a medical expense crops up. They've got to spend those savings. By the end of the year, they're right where they were at the beginning of the year: nothing saved, nothing invested. So they've got to start all over again."

Gail looked at George. "It sounds to me like we don't have plenty of time anymore. We certainly can't procrastinate. We've got to go to work today on building our financial future. We've got to make our money grow now, so that when we need more income, we'll have more principal to make us more income."

"Yes, Gail. If you don't do it now, it's going to be too late tomorrow. You've got to act now."

George smiled. "Bob, you know, I feel better already. You've really cleared the air for us on inflation, savings, planning, risk, and everything else that we've discussed on our walk."

"Yeah, Bob, thanks a lot. I do feel a lot better," added Gail.

About then, Bob stumbled over a rock. George caught him and helped him up. They all laughed. As he dusted off his pants, Bob said, "See, I thought I was under control, but I was getting tired from walking too fast. It's something like what happens when we don't have direction in our investment portfolio. It can fall apart quickly. We've got to have 'fiscal fitness' with our investments."

"Fiscal fitness?"

"Yes, we have to keep our investments up to date and in good shape. Focus them on meeting current financial needs and achieving our financial goals for the future. Throughout our walk, we've stayed on course. In your investments, stay on course toward your financial goals."

$ $ $ $ $ $

The walkers wound down the hill. The end of the path was in view.

"Well, Bob, you and Gail and I have done three miles. We've made it to the top of the hill and back down without breaking a leg."

"And I'm probably going to be huffing and puffing for the rest of the day. And it looks to me and sounds to me like you, George and Gail, are going to be able to make it to the top of the hill financially, and stay there for the rest of your lives."

"We sure hope so, Bob. I know one thing for sure. I'm going to sleep more soundly knowing that we're keeping ourselves fiscally fit, and that we're not going to wake up one day and find our money dead.

"We're going to stay on top of this hill, making our money grow more. And Bob, I'm going to sleep a lot more soundly knowing that the additional risk I'm taking is for the purpose of beating that nemesis, inflation. Gail and I owe you a lot."

Soon they came out of the woods and into a grassy area. They could see the picnic shelter a short distance away.

"Well, I think I'm going to sit down for a few minutes and get something to drink. Would you both care to join me?"

"Thanks, Bob," they answered. "We need to check on the grandkids."

Bob was so tired from the walk that he forgot to ask them to play a game of horseshoes.

9

Grandma: Managing the Final Years

BOB SAT AT THE PICNIC SHELTER, his legs sore from the walk with George and Gail. "I don't think I'll be able to move tomorrow," he thought to himself.

He looked at the evening sky. A band of dark clouds was rolling in quickly, and everything was getting darker. It was still about two hours before sunset. "Looks like a storm," he thought.

He saw lightning to the west. He heard a rumbling sound, and it wasn't Scott Youth's motorcycle. It was thunder.

Within minutes, the skies over Prosperity Park became dark. Heavy raindrops started to fall and quickly became a full downpour. Softball players and volleyball players grabbed their gear and ran for cover. Ben stood in the rain shouting at Betty and pointing to the Rolls Royce. She ran to the car and closed the sunroof. At the same time, Larry Lost was raising the top on his convertible. All the picnickers eventually ended up at the shelter, from where they watched the summer shower.

While the downpour fell from the sky, the floodgates of discussion inside the shelter were opened with these words:

"Hey, how is Grandma doing?"

Grandma was one loved family member who was not at the picnic.

Sally responded to the question. "Not too well. It's terrible what's happening to her."

"We really need all the help we can get for her," said Sam.

"So, what's going on?" asked Dan.

"Well, she's 84 years old now," Sally added. "She's frail, and she's sick most of the time. Her health is failing."

"That's too bad. We've got a lot of great memories of Grandma," Gail said wistfully.

George reminded the group, "Well, you know, it's been five years since Grandpa died. I know she misses him a lot. She's never really gotten over it."

"She was so spry and energetic," Denise added.

Uncle Bob held a horseshoe in his hand as he listened attentively to the conversation.

"We've been helping her a lot," admitted Sally, "but I don't see how she can possibly live on her own much longer. It's too much for any of us to take care of her. We all have things to do. Our careers, our jobs, our kids. I want to keep on helping, but it's getting to be a 24-hour-a-day job. It's real tough on our entire family. She stays in her home for several weeks, and then she'll stay with us for days to weeks at a time."

"We really should help more. We just haven't. We're too busy," said Denise.

"To say the least," agreed Sam, turning to Denise. "It seems like one or two people in the family carry most of the load, and Sally and Gail are doing that. They're just as busy as you are."

"We've been working on the house, and taking Darin to soccer camp. Darlene's in high school. You know how much running around you do with a high school student," Denise said defensively.

"Well, Grandma is quite a load," agreed Sally. "And, Dan and Denise, you guys haven't done much of anything."

Dan shot back, "We sent her a big bouquet of flowers at Christmas. And we bought her an exercise bike. Don't tell us we haven't done anything."

"All right, you guys. Stop bickering," interjected Ben.

Sally apologized. "It's just really hard being with Grandma.

For all those years they were married, Grandpa did everything he could to make it easy for Grandma."

"Yeah, that's the problem," Sam said. "He did everything for Grandma. He insisted that he was the man of the house and that there were certain things that he should do and certain things that Grandma should do."

Gail added, "Grandpa did everything for her. He went to the store. He bought the groceries. He wrote the checks. He bought the car."

"Oh, remember," Denise recalled, "Grandma didn't even know about Grandpa selling their house and buying another one. He had them moving before Grandma even knew what was going on. Can you believe that? No one would do things like that today."

"They were traditional, old-fashioned people," said Gail. "They placed a lot of value on tradition. I'm not sure the way we do things today is really any better."

George reminisced, "Remember how when we were young, Grandma and Grandpa would have those long conversations, and we'd all sit around and listen? Grandpa would say, 'Your grandmother has been a good mother. She's taken care of the kids. She's helped keep the house clean, she's cooked the meals, she's washed and ironed the clothes, and that's all I've wanted her to do. She's done a great job of it. I do everything else. It's a man's job to write the checks, pay the bills, buy the groceries, and provide for his wife and children. That's what I've always done. That's the way I'll always do it.' And Grandpa and Grandma did live happily together for many years."

"They never had any problems. I never remember them arguing," concurred Gail. "They just always seemed to get along. Yes, they were a perfect couple."

"That is, until Grandpa got sick with his first heart attack," observed Denise. "Grandma was hysterical. She didn't know what to do. She stayed by him at the hospital every day. She slept in the chair next to him. They loved each other so much, but she didn't know what to do on her own. She thought she had lost the love of her lifetime. And then Grandpa got better and got out of the hospital and everything seemed to be going just great. The next three years seemed to be the happiest years of their lives, until Grandpa had another heart attack and never came out of the hospital."

"Yeah, that was terrible, wasn't it?" George said, shaking his head. "I mean the funeral, and Grandma grieving. She was completely lost. And now we find that Grandpa really didn't do Grandma or us any favors. He shouldn't have been doing all those things for Grandma. She was completely dependent on him. She didn't even know how to write a check."

"Yeah, remember, she was looking for some money," recalled Sam. "We said, 'Just write a check.' But she replied, 'Grandpa always wrote the checks. Grandpa always paid the bills. Grandpa always went to the grocery store. I don't know how to do that. I don't know how to pay the bills.' She was really confused. She didn't think she had any money."

Sally interjected, "She said, 'How can I keep living in my house?' She'd tell us that over and over again. Even though it's been five years, she still says the same thing. Now she's crying most of the time when she talks about Grandpa."

It was a sad situation, thought Bob. He too had fond memories of Grandma. Bob and Marge had moved from Goodvillage before Grandpa had died.

Gail explained, "Grandpa would always tell Grandma that everything was going to be fine. She believed it. Now, that's not the way it has turned out. I mean, it's like we've had to take Grandma and treat her like she's in first grade. Remember when we took her to the bank?"

Sally remembered, "Yeah, she was so embarrassed, she just sat there. The teller asked her if she wanted to write a check. She had never written a check. She had never touched the checkbook. She just kept looking at me with tears in her eyes, saying, 'Will you help me? Will you write the checks? You will go to the grocery store with me, won't you, honey?' All I could say was, 'Of course, Granny. Of course.' Gosh, that was a terrible feeling. She was petrified. And what's worse, she's still petrified. You know, a simple thing like figuring out the grocery list was beyond her. She didn't know what she needed. She didn't know what to buy."

"So all of us pitched in," Gail explained. "We took turns going to the grocery store and buying her things. She shouldn't have had any problems. But then we found out she wasn't eating. She said she just wasn't hungry. She'd eat breakfast and no lunch. She'd just snack for dinner. Some days she wouldn't eat anything. She just sat there and looked out the window. She was completely lost. She had no idea what the value of her money really was, or how she could get it. It's got to be a terrible feeling. Every once in a while, she'd get on my nerves, and I'd say things that I wish I hadn't said. Then I'd go into the other room and cry. I made her cry, and what I said made me cry. It's a terrible feeling. I wish there was something we could do."

All conversation quickly stopped as a bolt of lightning touched the treetop near the pavilion. "Wow, that was close!" said George. Then the conversation began again.

"I don't think there's anything we can do about Grandma right now," said Sally, sighing deeply. "Most of us have been sharing her care. She's been living with one of us for three or four months and then moving on to someone else. I know she really doesn't want to do that. But she just doesn't feel she has any other alternative. There's no one for her to hold onto. She continues to feel like she's all alone. We were going to a show last week, and we asked Grandma if she wanted to come with us. She said no. Then we started to leave. She said, 'Are you going to be gone very long? When are you coming back? What happens if the phone rings? What if someone knocks on the door?' She was petrified. We've got to do something."

Gail turned to Sally. "We took care of her basically from the time Grandpa died until you took her for a long spell. But now, on top of everything else, she's getting feeble and very weak. She's starting to forget things, and every once in a while she can't hold her bowels."

"You mean she's wetting her pants?" asked Denise.

"Yes, that, too."

"Oh, my goodness. And it's our turn to take care of her next." Dan winced. "I don't know how we can do that."

"Dan, don't be so selfish," Denise countered. "Everyone else has taken care of Grandma but us. It's our turn."

"Yeah, but I don't want someone like that in the house."

"Dan, you're talking about grandmother."

Gail replied, "I'm sorry, but it just seems like there should be something else we could all do, something that would be good for Grandma and for everyone else. Remember last year, when she tripped and fell and broke her hip?"

"Wasn't she in the hospital for over a month?" asked George.

"Yeah. In fact, she was in the hospital for three and a half months because she wouldn't heal. She just lay there in bed. She'd push the nurses' call button and just ask someone to come in and talk to her all the time. She was so lonely. Then she stopped eating."

"Yeah," said Dan. "That's when all of us started doing a routine where we'd go and stay with her for a couple of hours. At least we kept her happy during the daytime."

"Dan, you act like it was a big pain," said Denise.

"Well, it was kind of a pain."

"Well, that's what we have to do when our loved ones, especially our older loved ones, get sick."

"That's not what happens today, Denise. People go to nursing homes today," Dan replied.

"Well, all I can say," said Gail, "is, the hospital bill was scary. Her hospitalization policy paid for most of it. But there were over $5,600 worth of bills that we had to take out of her savings. You know, Grandpa said there would always be money to take care of Grandma." She looked at Sally and Denise. "Remember, he would say, 'Granny, if anything ever happens to me, there'll be plenty of money for you and the kids.' "

"What a mistake!" Dan blurted out. "There's never enough money."

Gail nodded. "You know, Dan, you might be right on that

one. There's only so much money left. If anything happens to her health now, I'm worried that we might completely deplete her savings over the next couple of years."

"How is she mentally?" asked Dan.

Sally said, "One day she's terrific, mentally alert and very happy. Then she'll go through days and weeks where she can't remember anything. Last week we were talking and all of a sudden her lower jaw dropped open and she had a stare that was frightening. I asked her, 'Granny, what's wrong?' She said, 'What's your name? Who are you? Where are we? What are we doing here?' I was shocked. I was stunned. I got big tears in my eyes. I didn't know what was happening."

"What did you do?" asked Denise.

"Well, I tried to hide my feelings and said reassuringly, 'I'm Sally, dear, and I'm here to help you. Now it's time to go to bed.' So, I just helped her up to her bedroom and I told her to lie down for a while. She lay down and slept for about three hours."

"How was she when she woke up?"

"She was fine. She didn't remember a thing about our conversation, and, thank God, she knew who I was and she knew who she was. The next day I called her doctor. Well, I guess no one is going to like what he said."

"What did he say, Sally?" asked Denise. Everyone else waited for Sally's answer.

"First, I told the doctor it's getting harder and harder for us to take care of her."

"Did you tell the doctor about Granny forgetting?" asked Denise.

"Yes, I told him about her memory loss and how fragile she's getting and how she doesn't want to eat."

"Well, what did he say?"

"He said that we should really consider having her move into a nursing home."

"Oh, gosh, that would be terrible."

"Yeah," said Dan. "Not only terrible, but it's going to cost a lot of money."

"I know, but what are we going to do?" Sally asked. "Are we going to keep passing Grandma around from one home to another? Can we afford to keep paying babysitters to come and take care of her when we're not there? I'm afraid she might fall or hurt herself really badly next time."

"Is she really that bad, Sally?"

"Yes, she really is. She gets in these moods where she doesn't remember anything. She doesn't know what's going on. She's left the house a couple of times, only to have one of our neighbors call us from a couple of blocks away and say they saw Grandma walking in the street. When we go to pick her up, she acts like nothing was wrong. She says she got lost and couldn't find her way back home, and she knew that if she just sat down on the curb, we would come by and find her."

"Oh, my gosh. We've got to do something about this situation. It's going to drive us all crazy," complained Dan.

"Dan, why don't you calm down?" said Ben. "All you ever think of is yourself."

"Hey, watch it, Ben. What about you driving around in that fancy car?" said Dan.

"And what about you buying all those things you can't afford?" yelled Ben.

"Guys!" interjected Bob, who had been quiet up to this point. "Take it easy! This is very important. It's not about you, it's about Grandma."

"Granny's sick and we have to do something about it now," explained Sally. "You know, it gets really difficult. Sometimes she won't even take care of herself. She just doesn't understand what's happening. It really makes it difficult for whoever is taking care of her."

Denise said, "It's our turn next. I don't know how we can do it. We've got a lot of our own bills. It's going to have to come out of her money, because we can't spend ours. I certainly don't want to change the way I live."

"But it's our obligation to take care of Grandma," Gail insisted.

"It was Grandpa's obligation to take care of Grandma," Dan countered. "Let someone else take care of her. We don't have any money right now to take care of her."

"You want the rest of us to pay for it?" asked Sam.

"Well, we aren't going to," Dan said. "I don't know what we'll do. We didn't realize that Grandma was that bad."

"That's because you never come over to see her. You're always on a vacation or a trip someplace," complained Sally. "If you'd see her more often, you'd realize how difficult the situation is."

"Yeah, Dan." Ben was being sarcastic. "Why don't you drop over with your fancy gadgets?"

"Hey, Ben, I've had enough out of you."

"Okay, guys, let's get back to our concerns for Grandma." Bob tried soothing them.

$$\$ \$ \$ \$ \$ \$$

"Sounds like it's best now for Grandma to go to a nursing home," Dan concluded.

"Why's that?" asked Sam.

"Because if she goes in the hospital, the bill is paid. If she comes to our house or to your house, we've got to pay the bill. It's a better deal if she goes into the nursing home."

"Wait a minute!" Sally objected. "That's not the way it works, Dan."

"What do you mean? She'd be in the hospital, wouldn't she?"

"No. A nursing home isn't a hospital. Hospitalization insurance programs don't cover nursing homes."

"Why not?"

"I don't know why not," Sally said, "but you have to have a special kind of nursing home insurance in order to have the bill paid in a nursing home."

"Well, before she goes in, let's buy the nursing care insurance program for her. In fact, let's get it for her right now," said Dan.

Bob fiddled with the horseshoe in his hand as he spoke up. Everyone listened.

"Long-term nursing care insurance is just like life insurance or hospitalization insurance. Once you need it, you can't get it."

"What do you mean, Bob?" asked Dan.

"If you're in good health, you probably don't think you need any type of insurance. That's when the insurance company is very willing to issue you the protection. But they are not going to sell you a policy after you're ready to start collecting on it. You usually can only get insurance when you're in good health, and can pass their physicals.

"Long-term nursing care works on the same principle," Bob continued. "Grandma will never ever be able to get nursing home coverage. She's already in a state of confusion mentally, and most of the insurance companies would figure she might be in the beginning stages of Alzheimer's."

"Alzheimer's! Hey, she could be around forever," blurted out Dan.

"There you go again, opening your mouth before you think," said Ben.

Both just stared at each other.

George interrupted. "It sounds like we have one of two choices to make. Either we take care of Grandma with all of us sharing, or we're going to have to look into the possibilities of placing Grandma in a nursing home. And that first option sounds to me like it would be pretty much a full-time job."

Uncle Bob reminded everyone, "You know, in the old days when a parent got sick, he or she would just move in with the children and the children would take care of the parent."

"Bob," Denise defended herself, "we're not saying we don't want to take care of Grandma. But we have our own lives; we have our kids and our bills and our own expenses. Not only don't we have the time to take care of Grandma 24 hours a day, but the added expenses could put our expenses over the top. It would just be better if Grandma were taken care of professionally."

"I remember when I was a little boy and one of our relatives was very sick and had a stroke," Bob continued. "Everyone took care of her. But again, I understand what you're saying. The family was a closer-knit unit then. If some members got sick, the family took care of them."

Dan interrupted. "Now, a lot of times families don't even live close to their parents or grandparents."

"I understand what you're saying," Bob said. "I'm not arguing with you. I'm just telling you that's the way it was then."

"Thing have changed," said Dan defensively.

"I'm just saying, Dan, that that was the way it was with most families in the old days. Financially, families are the same today as they were then. They put off buying insurance until they needed it. Once they needed it, they couldn't get it. When the need came up, it was too late to buy the insurance, so they just took care of their loved ones until they passed away."

Sally explained, "Grandma will call me and ask what's on TV tonight because she has such a hard time reading. I'll tell her, then she'll call me back an hour later and ask me the same question. She may call me five or six times a day and ask me the same questions."

Bob went on, "She's not stupid; she's just slowing down, both physically and mentally. It happens a lot to older people. All the warning signs are there. She's lived a long life, and it's our duty, as her family, to make sure she lives the rest of her life comfortably and as worry-free as possible. I didn't realize Grandma had deteriorated so quickly. If I lived here in town, I could have helped. It's just as much Marge's and my fault as it is anyone else's."

George sounded very concerned. "Bob, this is really getting serious. Her finances have slowly dwindled over the last couple of years until now she's only got about $125,000."

Dan muttered, "I wish I had $125,000."

"Seriously, $125,000 doesn't go far when you're talking about hospital and nursing home expenses," explained Bob. "And I bet Grandma hasn't allowed you to invest any of her money."

Gail nodded. "You're right. Grandpa did all the investing. She didn't know anything about what he did with the money except that Grandpa always had it in CDs. So, she wants us to leave everything in CDs. Well, that was great when interest rates were high. But now they're real low and she's hardly making any money. The result is, we've been spending her principal."

"And that's a no-no," Bob said, shaking his head.

"I know, but what are we going to do?" asked Gail. "She's not making any money, so we have to spend her principal. And now $125,000 left? Help! I just don't know how long that's going to last."

"How much do nursing homes cost, Bob?" asked Denise.

"Well, it depends on the nursing home, and in what part of the country the nursing home is located. Many nursing homes in the Northeast cost up to $8,000 a month; some in the Midwest cost $2,000 a month. It really depends on where you live and what kind of care you're getting. Most nursing homes with what I consider very good care—that is, doctors and a complete nursing staff, good employees, and a clean and safe facility—would cost about $100 a day."

"$100 a day?" stammered Dan. "That's $3,000 a month."

"That's right," said Bob. "It's going to run about $36,000 a year. On average."

"$36,000? For what?" asked Sam.

"Well, there are a lot of people who'll be working with Grandma from now on if she does go into a nursing home. Registered nurses, doctors, licensed practical nurses, physical therapists, aides, maintenance people. And in addition there's her food, her bed, the room, and many other amenities. All of that totals about $100 a day."

"That's nice, but we can't afford $3,000 a month," Dan moaned.

Denise admonished her husband. "Don't say that, Dan.

We've got to give Grandma everything she needs. We want her to live her last few years comfortably."

"Yeah, but that means the money will be coming out of our pockets, honey," complained Dan. "That's $36,000 a year. We're going to have to spend our money or Grandma's money."

"Yeah," George added. "But before we know it, Grandma will probably be out of money. Let's see, $36,000 a year and she has $125,000 . . . in four years she'll be broke, and then we'll have to pay all the bills."

"What happens if she doesn't have any funds?" asked Sam.

Bob, who had been quiet and pensive, suggested, "We could apply for Medicaid coverage."

"What do you mean, Medicaid? I thought you said Medicaid doesn't cover long-term nursing care," said Dan.

"No, I said Medicare or regular hospitalization programs don't cover long-term nursing care," Bob explained. "But if someone is destitute, then Medicaid coverage could be applied for."

"So the difference between Medicare and Medicaid, just to make it real simple," Dan figured out loud, "is, if someone still has money, they have to pay the bill, and if they don't have the money, Medicaid could help pay the bill."

"Well, there's a lot more to it than that," Bob said, "but that's basically correct."

"Yes, but Grandma has money," protested Dan. "So we're going to have to pay the bills until her money is gone."

"That's right, Dan. We're all going to have to spend her money until she's worth about nothing," Bob agreed.

"Just think," Sally remembered, "all those years that Grandpa worked to build his estate, as he called it. He was so proud. He would always say that he came from humble beginnings, and he was able to build his estate to the point where he had accumulated over $250,000, plus their home!"

"Yeah, and you know what's sad?" said Sam. "Grandma didn't even know what the value of their money was then."

"She still doesn't," Dan added.

Looking over at Bob, George said, "Well, Bob, let me ask you this: What happens after Grandma's money is gone?"

"You mean, in three years when we've used up all her money for the nursing home?"

"Yeah. Let's agree to putting Grandma in the nursing home and getting her the best care. Let's say everyone agrees to get Grandma the best care possible."

Dan said, "Yeah, you're right, we need to take care of Grandma. She's been a wonderful person. In some way she has taken care of all of us, and we want to make sure that her remaining years are easy for her."

"Well, Dan," said Ben, "it sounds like you've really come around."

"Okay, Ben. I've come around. Let's make sure the two of us come around and see eye to eye on this."

"That's fine with me," agreed Ben.

"Okay." Bob seemed pleased with both Ben and Dan. "Let's talk about what happens after Grandma's money is gone. First of all, each of us could chip in and pay the bills each month."

"You know," Sally concurred, "that really wouldn't be too bad. Chances are it would be less than $400 a month per family."

"$400 a month doesn't sound like much," Dan reminded them, "but you know it mounts up."

Denise spoke up. "Dan, we don't even know what our expenses are now. Bob told us that. We have to figure out what we're spending. We might not even have $400 left over each month."

"Come on." Ben smiled. "You've got your big cars, your beautiful home. Surely you have $400 a month."

"Now, Ben," Dan responded. "Let's not get into that. Bob showed us we were doing some things wrong, and one of them was probably spending too much money."

"Yeah." Ben backed down. "It seems like Bob can really key in on the real issues."

George agreed, "There's no doubt about that."

Everyone else around the table nodded their heads in agreement.

$$\$\,\$\,\$\,\$\,\$\,\$$$

It rained harder, and hail the size of peas began to fall. A bolt of lightning hit a tree across the field, and a section of the tree fell to the ground. Everyone shuddered but the kids. They thought it was awesome! "I'll be happy when this storm is over," said Gail.

"Bob, what happens if we can't pay the bills?" asked Dan.

Bob said, "Well, Medicaid coverage would be the next step."

"How does that work? A lot of red tape?"

"Some. First we could try to have Grandma qualify for Medicaid. They would probably tell us that she wouldn't qualify until we have all the necessary forms filled out and she's passed the nursing home and medical doctors' qualifications."

"What do you mean, qualifications?"

"Well, she has to be in a certain state of health before she can qualify. The doctor gives her a complete examination. She has to qualify under a point system."

"A point system?" said Gail.

"So many points. She has to have so many things wrong with her before she can qualify. In other words, she's got to be really sick and really out of it, and destitute, before Medicaid will help pay for her nursing home expenses."

"I see," said Sally. "If she qualifies, then Medicaid could pay the bill from then on."

"So we wouldn't have to chip in to pay," George added.

Bob continued. "Correct, *if* Grandma qualifies. If she does, the bill would be paid through Medicaid. Maybe not all of it, but at least a portion."

"That doesn't sound too bad," said Sam.

"But, there is a second test. She can't have any assets except for some personal items and about $1,000 in cash."

"Does that mean she can't keep her house?"

"Possibly. Only people who have a spouse or have someone living with them, like a child, can keep the house. Every state has its own qualification rules. We'll have to check into all of the regulations."

"Well, what if she gives everything away?" Sam asked.

"Hey, that's a great idea!" agreed Dan.

"The government thought of that trick. If she gives everything away, there is up to a 36-month waiting period. It could be less. That depends upon how much she gives away and how much the nursing home costs."

"That's complicated!" said Sally.

"It is," agreed Bob. "And, if you apply for Medicaid too soon after giving everything away, the waiting period could be longer than 36 months. That's why it's really important that we see an attorney who does this sort of work."

"That could be expensive!"

"Not nearly as expensive as if things are done wrong," Bob stated. "On the other hand, she could simply spend all of her money before applying."

"You mean Grandma would be broke?"

"She'd be destitute?"

"Now you're with me!" said Bob.

"How do we avoid spending all of her money?"

Ben asked, "Is there anything we can do right now?"

"Yes, in fact there is. One, Grandma could gift her money away."

"You mean like that $10,000 a year deal? That would take 12½ years," said Dan.

"No, not really, Dan. She could gift each one of us and the grandkids $10,000 each," said Bob.

"I thought you could only gift $10,000 a year." George seemed puzzled.

"No, a lot of people think that. But it's a better situation than that. You can gift $10,000 a year to as many people as you want."

George said, "So Grandma could gift each one of us $10,000 in one year? Let's see—my goodness, if we look at everyone in the group here, that would . . ."

"And don't forget," said Bob, "you can gift your children."

"Granny could gift all her money away today," said George.

"You're probably right," said Bob.

"So we could put her in a nursing home. And the bill would be paid by Medicaid," said Sally.

"No. Remember, the 36-month waiting period?" said Bob. "The money has to be out of her estate for 36 months before Medicaid will consider paying the long-term nursing care bill."

"Oh, that's right. So if she gifts all the money today, we still have to pay the bill over the next 36 months."

"Yes, plus, there's no guarantee that Medicaid will ever pay the bill," Bob reminded them. "Remember, Grandma has to qualify by taking a medical test given by the professionals."

"Wow, this is really complicated. How do other people do it? What if people don't have any money?" asked Sally.

"It's really tough financially on families today," replied Bob. "It's as I said earlier: in the old days, when parents or grandparents got sick, they just moved in with the kids. It's a different story today. People live all over the country. They have moved away from home, and many of them don't have the time or money to take care of their parents. They still love their parents, but for many families today, taking care of the aged loved ones just isn't the thing to do."

"That's a shame," Sally sympathized.

"It just isn't something that people are choosing to do," Bob continued. "For one thing, many families have both spouses working. No one is home during the day to care for the aging relative."

"What about adult day care?" asked Betty.

"That's another option. There are day care centers that take care of elderly or disabled adults during the daytime. Their families drop them off at the center during the day, and pick them up and bring them home at night. For many, it is a good alternative to nursing home care. The centers have professional nurses and physical and occupational therapists on staff. They have organized social activities. It's something to consider."

"But we're still going to have to be ready financially for a nursing home," said Gail.

"Unfortunately, yes."

"Isn't there anything else that can be done?" asked Sam.

"Well, there are some things that we might do with Granny's money. We could invest it in a certain type of annuity that Medicaid officials might accept, and by doing so, let her qualify sooner than the 36-month waiting period. But that's chancy."

"We need to look into various options. We should ask an attorney," said Sally. "But there's no question now in all our minds that Grandma is probably going to have to go into a nursing home."

"Isn't there something we could've done before now?" asked Sam.

"Sure. We could've made sure that Grandma bought a long-term nursing care program," answered Bob. "Of course, it's something all of us should be looking into now."

"Well, we don't all need nursing care insurance," Dan countered. "Maybe you do, Bob. Maybe you do, George and Gail. But not the rest of us."

"Don't be so sure about that, Dan," Bob went on. "I know of people younger than you who have had a massive stroke or some kind of serious health problem or accident. The family couldn't take care of them anymore and had to put them in a nursing home. And believe me, the bill can get into the hundreds of thousands of dollars."

"You mean hospitalization wouldn't cover that?" asked Dan.

"Hospitalization doesn't cover long-term nursing care in most instances, regardless of what age you are, Dan."

"Oh, my gosh, that's terrible."

Sally added, "I've read about people in their 40s who had

accidents or strokes and have been in nursing homes for over 15 years. But I didn't even think about the cost involved. I just took it for granted that it was take care of by the hospitalization insurance."

"Yeah, that's what most people think," Bob agreed. "But can you imagine what that did to their estates? Those families may have been very wealthy, but at $36,000 a year for 10 to 15 years, you're spending down $300,000 to $500,000. It's terrible. And don't forget, the spouse still needs money to pay expenses at home."

"I never even thought about that," said Dan wistfully. "Just think, even wealthy people can lose all of their assets."

"Right," Bob agreed. "Don't think nursing care protection is for someone in their 70s, 80s, or 90s. It has to be looked at by everyone. If we're not yet 50, then we definitely have to make sure that we and our parents are informed about long-term nursing care needs. If we're over 50, not only do we need to have our parents and grandparents consider the consequences of not having long-term nursing care coverage, but we have to consider it for ourselves. It's getting to the point that with our lifestyles today, we have to look at long-term nursing care protection at a much younger age. Even earlier than 50."

"So the answer for all of us," Sally concluded, "is to consider purchasing a long-term nursing care program."

"And as I understand it," Bob assured them, "long-term nursing care coverage isn't all that expensive when you're younger."

"So it pays to buy it when you're younger?"

"The younger you are, the less money the policy costs."

"Well, what do you buy?"

"Well, there are different types of policies and there are different kinds of coverages for long-term nursing care. But what you want to do is get the type of nursing care insurance that doesn't have any exclusions."

"What are exclusions, Bob?"

"Areas that aren't covered."

"Like what?"

"Well, some long-term nursing care policies won't pay unless you go from a hospital to the nursing home. Others won't pay for certain types of nurses or visits from the doctor. Or, they don't pay the entire cost of the room per day."

"Why would they offer the insurance if they don't cover everything?" asked Sally.

"The insurance companies place certain exclusions in policies in order to keep the premium down."

"That's terrible, Bob. If you buy a policy, it should be all-inclusive. It should cover everything," Sally insisted.

"Well, maybe you're right, but there are different cost levels associated with different types of protection. You just have to make sure you know what you're buying before you buy it. Read your contract thoroughly."

$ $ $ $ $ $

"So, Bob, what can we do now?" Sally asked.

"Several things. First, we need to have some kind of a family meeting."

"Well, that's what we're doing right now, Bob," said Ben.

"Yes, but I mean with Grandma."

"Do you mean you're going to tell Grandma?" asked Ben.

"Well, of course we're going to tell Grandma," Sally answered. "We're not going to do it without her knowing about it, Ben."

"But will she go along with it?" asked Ben.

"If she's coherent when we get together, I think she'll agree to it."

"Well, what will we say, Bob?" asked Gail.

"We could explain to Grandma that we're concerned about her health and we want to make sure that she gets the best care possible."

"Bob, that's going to be difficult with Grandma. Do people want to move into nursing homes?" asked Gail.

"In most cases, Gail, they don't. They always feel they can take care of themselves."

"Yeah, but Grandma keeps falling and she keeps forgetting."

"The fact that she keeps forgetting things is one of the difficulties of having her realize how important it is for her to go into a nursing home."

"Gosh, you know, Bob, this is terrible," groaned Gail. "We're standing around here talking about Grandma as if she were already in a nursing home."

"It's almost as if she were already dead," said Ben.

"I know," agreed Bob. "This is a difficult situation. But again, remember, we're her family. We're the ones who have to deal with this."

"You're right," Dan concurred. "We're just going to have to tell Grandma. I agree with Bob, that we should do it with all of us present."

"Then we explain to Grandma that we want to look at a new place for her to live," Bob went on, "A place where she could get very good care all the time. We'd tell her that she could learn to like it. There would be other people there who were her age, who liked what she liked. We'd visit her all the time."

"Well, what about telling Grandma about the cost?" asked Sally.

"We'll tell her how we can maintain her money for her by moving it into our names. If she keeps the money in her name, it might all get eaten up by expenses. We'll tell her that Grandpa wouldn't want that to happen to their money. We're going to use it for her, for whatever she wants and whatever is best for her. We'll explain to her that the nursing home costs could be very expensive. The medical bills could eat up all of her estate if she doesn't gift the money."

"She'll agree to that," Sally said. "Grandpa always said he wanted their estate to grow so that it could take care of Grandma and Grandpa in their later years. Then, when he was no longer around, it would take care of Grandma. When she was gone, whatever was left would go to their loved ones."

"You're right, Bob, she'll agree to this," said Gail. "It's in line with what Grandpa wanted. So that's exactly what Grandma will want and do."

"Gosh," pondered Sally, "I don't know if I feel better or worse. This is really a tough decision."

"It is, Sally," Gail agreed. "It's a tough decision for everyone. It's going to be very tough mentally for Grandma. We're all going to have to pitch in and help as much as possible. We all need to see Grandma as much as possible over the next month or so, or at least until we agree that what's best for Grandma is a nursing home. If that's the case, then we'll have our meeting and explain everything to her."

"Is everyone in agreement?" asked Bob.

Everyone agreed.

"As always, Bob's secrets come through," said Ben.

$ $ $ $ $ $

"Well, I don't know about secrets, but I'll tell you what. If you're going to call them secrets, I've got another secret that we'd better talk about."

"What's that?" asked Sam.

"This is about Grandma also. You know, I don't think Grandpa ever updated his will before he died. Did they ever do a trust, Sally?"

"A trust? Um, I don't think so. Why would she need a trust? There's only Grandma."

"The rules on wills changed back in the early 1980s. Even with an updated will, if she owns anything in her name alone, her estate will have to go through probate court."

"I thought if you had a will, Bob, your estate didn't go to probate court," said Dan.

"No, that's not the case if you own anything in your name alone."

"Well, what if Grandma dies?" asked Dan.

"That's a good question. What happens if Grandma doesn't live through the next three or four years? There would still be money in her estate. What if she dies next month? There's still $125,000 in her estate," said George.

"Well, then it's just going to be shared with all of us, isn't it?" said Dan.

"Well, it will after it goes through probate court," said Bob.

"Can we avoid probate?" Dan asked.

"Yes, there are several ways you can avoid probate costs. You can set up Grandma's estate properly by having all her assets in a trust. At least in Grandma's case, you can avoid probate. You see, probate fees are based on your assets—your automobile, your house, your savings, your savings bonds, CDs, Treasury bills, all of your investments. The court just totals these up and charges a certain fee."

"What kind of fee would there be on Grandma's estate? There couldn't be very much."

"Well, probate fees on $125,000 could run anywhere from $6,000 to maybe $10,000."

"What?" stammered Dan. "How is that possible?"

"That's just what the rules are."

"Well, what can we do?" asked Gail.

"We can get Grandma to update her estate plan and do a trust."

"What's so good about a trust as opposed to a will for Grandma?"

"If she sets up her estate properly in a trust, then there won't be any probate fees."

"You mean when Grandma dies, Bob, the money will just be divided up among all of us?"

"That's right, Gail. If Grandma does a trust, then it can be set up exactly the way she wants it. The money will go to whom she wants, when she wants, and how she wants. All the money will avoid probate fees."

"Wait a minute, Bob," said Gail. "I remember Grandpa saying that he had everything taken care of. He had put all of their assets, including the house, in joint names. I remember him distinctly saying he had taken care of everything. When he died, everything would go to Grandma."

"And it did," offered Dan. "Right, Bob?"

"Right. No question about that. When an estate is set up in both persons' names, there aren't any probate fees on the first death."

"Well, then, what are we talking about here, Bob?" asked George.

"Grandpa is already dead. When Grandma dies, the probate fees will be charged after the second death, not the first death."

Sally suggested, "Bob, why don't we put everything in joint accounts now? Then, when Grandma dies, it will pass right on to us without going through probate court."

"Not necessarily, Sally. It's not for sure, and there could be serious consequences. Our best bet for Grandma is to update her estate by setting up a trust."

"Oh, my goodness. I didn't realize that," said Gail.

"It's something that most people don't understand," Bob continued. "What all of us have to do is sit down and talk with an attorney, and figure out what is best for our families. Your attorney might suggest a will or a trust. Just find out as soon as you can what's best for your situation. Don't procrastinate."

"There's that 'P' word you were talking about," recalled George.

"Don't put off until tomorrow what you can do today," Bob reiterated.

"Have you got yours set up properly, Bob?" asked Dan.

"Oh, yes! I have a trust. All of my assets will go to my wife if I die first, or vice versa if she dies first. When the surviving spouse dies, everything will go to all of the loved ones exactly as we had wished it to be distributed."

"That's neat, Bob. Maybe we should look into a trust not only for Grandma but for me, too," said Scott.

Everyone laughed.

"Don't laugh," Bob cautioned. "Scott's starting a savings program, and eventually he'll have his own business."

Everyone was quiet then.

"What would happen if Grandma were to die right now, today?" asked Ben.

"You mean as far as probate fees?" Ben nodded. "They're paid before the estate is closed. That could take about nine months to two years or more," answered Bob.

"That's when the money is paid?" asked Ben.

"Right. You know, if Grandma's estate is worth over $600,000, there will also be federal estate taxes. Those taxes start at 37% and go up to 55% on every estate, starting from $600,000."

"Gosh," Gail remarked, "people work so hard all their lives to make a good living and provide for their family. Look what Grandma and Grandpa did. They provided most of us with some kind of financial help during their lifetime, and all they wanted to do was live a good life. They didn't have any bills, they didn't buy things on credit, they never had any debt, they did everything right."

"They did everything right," Bob agreed, "except set up their estate properly and provide for emergencies such as long-term nursing care insurance. They didn't share decision making, either. That was probably their biggest mistake."

George asked, "Okay, so if Grandma were to die today, what would happen to the money in her estate during the next nine months? Do we just sit around and wait?"

Bob replied, "We don't know how much and what the probate fees will be. We'll have a rough idea. But in most cases, it's best to estimate probate fees on the high side."

"That could cause a problem, couldn't it?" asked George. "What about expenses that might be incurred for Grandma if she goes into the hospital or nursing home before she dies?"

"Yes, it causes a lot of problems. That's why I think we need to get this entire matter taken care of immediately," said Bob. "Let me point out one other thing. If we don't get Grandma to do a living trust, you'll never believe who will divide up the estate after the probate fees are paid."

"You mean, Bob, we won't divide up the money ourselves?" asked Dan.

"No way, Dan. The courts are going to divide up the money for us."

"And naturally, that's going to cost more money."

"That's right. You have to pay for the work that's done."

"You know, Grandma promised me her wedding ring," interrupted Denise.

"And she told me I could have their bedroom set," added Gail.

"Now, look, let's not get selfish," Bob continued. "Hopefully, we can work out a way to take care of Grandma. Let's figure out how we can financially give Grandma what is best for her and at the same time not have all her assets eaten up."

"We were talking about Grandma gifting her money to us," reminded George.

Bob said, "Gifting the money is a good idea, so if we do that now, then 36 months from now maybe she could qualify for Medicaid."

"And if Grandma qualifies for Medicaid coverage, wouldn't most of her expense problems be taken care of?" asked Sam.

"That's right. So, we need to observe Grandma very closely during the next month so that all of us feel comfortable with our decision."

"I agree," said Gail. "Then, we need to have the meeting with Grandma and make sure she feels comfortable."

Sally suggested, "What we need to do is have Grandma start distributing her assets through gifting."

"And also," Bob concluded, "we've got to meet with an attorney and set up her trust."

$$$$$$

The storm had subsided into a gentle light rain. The sun was attempting to peek out.

"Bob, while we're talking about Grandma, I've got another question for you," said Sally.

"Shoot," said Bob.

"For the past year, whoever is taking care of Grandma handles her investments. I don't know if that's such a good idea. She insists on keeping all her money in a money market account or CDs like Grandpa did. She said Grandpa kept his money there, and they never had any problems. Besides, she doesn't want to take any risks. She constantly talks about the Great Depression and how terrible things were then. She said her dad was making about a nickel an hour when he worked, but he didn't work much. No one had anything. People lost their money. Many lost their money when their banks failed. She doesn't want to get to that point."

Sally paused. "Bob, it's really hard to talk to her about a lot of things, but especially money. She just gets real scared and starts crying."

"Yeah, money market accounts aren't paying anything," commented Dan.

"Bob, what kind of investments do you suggest for Grandma?" asked Gail.

"Good question. Let's talk about it. Most retired people don't want to touch their principal. In fact, I recommend that no one spend their principal. It's not a good idea. And for retired people, their principal is all they have. They don't have any way of making new money or building upon their principal in any way other than investing. They can't go back to work or they don't want to.

"So I understand what Grandma is saying. She should have a certain amount of her money in guaranteed investments, such as CDs, Treasury bills, double E bonds, and money market accounts. They're all safe investments. Naturally, with interest rates as low as they are now, they're not going to be paying high rates of return. At least the principal is guaranteed. But if you're going to need to make her principal grow, and produce income that's going to help you pay the bills, then you're going to have to take some kind of risk and invest it elsewhere."

Sally said, "Grandma is so nervous. She's always saying the stock market is going to collapse. She's afraid she'll lose everything just like her parents did during the Depression."

George added, "That's what happens when people get older. We're more concerned now about our money than ever before. It's tougher to take a risk now than when we were younger. Since we don't have any more earned income, we're satisfied with our money doing less, as long as we can ensure the safety of our principal. We're afraid to make investments that have any risk, because we're afraid we're going to lose all of our money."

"Yeah, Bob," Gail agreed. "Grandma is always talking about when her mother and father lost everything in the Depression. They stood in bread lines and soup lines, and that was all they had. She doesn't ever want to be in that situation again. That's why she doesn't want us to invest her money. She's afraid she's going to be in a bread and soup line like her parents."

"That's ridiculous," objected Dan.

"It may sound ridiculous," said Bob, "but that's how Grandma feels and that's how a lot of retired people feel. That's what happened to many families in the Depression."

"I can understand exactly how she feels," George sympathized. "It's scary in the investment world when you know that all your money is at risk."

"Then what do we do, Bob?" asked Gail.

"Well, I suggest that you find an outside person. Find a financial planner who has worked with other retired people like Grandma, and understands their needs and how they feel. Hopefully, this person can give us some good advice. Perhaps he or she will recommend mutual funds or annuities or bonds. But let's see what the planner thinks, first. The professionals are the ones we should be talking to. This is too important to Grandma for us to make her financial decisions for her without the help of professionals."

"Grandma will probably go along with that, too," Ben added.

'Well, I'm glad we got together to talk about this." Gail smiled. "It took a rain shower to do it. So, everyone, please, go see Grandma some time in the next few weeks."

Bob said, "Then we can start contacting the various professionals we need for help. An attorney. A financial adviser. A banker. A CPA. Grandpa liked baseball; let's talk to her about covering all the bases." Everyone agreed.

Gail said, "We need to do this as soon as possible, while Grandma is still pretty alert."

"Right," said Bob. "Once she's not alert anymore, the attorney will refuse to do a will or a trust because of liability."

$$\$\,\$\,\$\,\$\,\$\,\$$

"I sure don't want to end up like Grandma," said Gail. "Grandpa kept her out of decision making because he thought he was protecting her."

"It actually made it much rougher on her and on us," said Sam.

Bob agreed. "Finances and investments are for both the husband and the wife to work on together. We need to know everything that's going on, whether we're talking about finances, investments, grocery shopping, buying furniture, real estate, or whatever. If an emergency comes up, both the husband and the wife need to participate in the decision-making process. Then, if something happens to one spouse, the other spouse is not in the dark.

"Now, how about a great game of horseshoes?" asked Bob. "We can set up teams and have a championship round!"

"Not yet," said Sally. "There's still a lot of food from dinner out on the tables. And the rain made a mess of everything. We'd better clean up first. Let's clean up, then play. Sound okay to everyone?"

She turned to Bob. "Should we do anything else, Bob?"

"We've already accomplished a lot today, but let's each of us do something specific. We need to find a good financial planner. I'll call our planner," stated Sam. "We've really been happy with our results."

"Let's plan a date when all of us can be together at some time with Grandma," said Bob.

"I'll coordinate with everybody on that, Bob," stated Gail.

"Let me call the attorney and Grandma's doctor and I'll have the information for everyone before we all meet with Grandma," commented George.

Walking outside the shelter and looking up at the sky, Bob remarked, "Everything is going to work out for the best. We all need to keep communicating more and helping each other." Everyone nodded in agreement. Bob's game of horseshoes had been delayed again.

10

The Animals of Fortune Forest

THE RAIN LET UP and the evening sun began to peek out. All the grass and trees carried a fresh coating of moisture, having just been washed by the rain.

"Look! A rainbow!" exclaimed Sarah as she pointed to the sky. Darin ran to join her in admiring the beautiful sight. Seeing the commotion, Jennifer and Jason (Larry's children) ran over, as did other children. Uncle Bob stepped into the wet grass and looked at the rainbow with the children.

"Sarah, isn't this pretty?" said Uncle Bob. "The rainbow is arching over Prosperity Park."

"Yeah. A rainbow! Hey, Uncle Bob, can we hear the story about Billy Bear, Dan Donkey, and Willie Wolf now? Can we? Everybody's here. And we're all gonna have to go soon. Can we?"

"Well, okay, Sarah."

"Horray!" She jumped up and down. "Darin, come on. Uncle Bob's gonna tell us his animal story now!" She looked at Uncle Bob. "Uncle Bob, I've got an idea. Let's invite everybody to listen in. We can make a big circle."

"Okay."

"Hey, everybody! Uncle Bob's gonna tell us a story."

"Kids, gather 'round. I'm gonna tell you a story. Anybody who wants to listen, come on over."

Ten kids came over and sat on two picnic tables. Then parents came over and stood behind them. Seeing a crowd, nearly everyone came—Dan and Denise, Sam and Sally, Larry, Scott, Wilma, Ben and Betty, George and Gail, and all their children.

Sarah sat on the picnic table right next to Uncle Bob. Darin sat on the other side of Uncle Bob.

Uncle Bob began.

"One night there was a tremendous storm in Fortune Forest. The wind blew with a giant force, and it rained and rained. The wind picked up the birds and the squirrels along with their nests, and whisked them through the forest. It rained so hard that the rain started a great flood. The flood washed all the ground animals like bears and foxes from their nests. It was a disaster. It all happened very fast.

"All night the rains came down. The flood waters rushed through Fortune Forest, picking up everything in their path. Every animal fought for its life to keep above the flood waters. If only they had known that something like this was going to happen, maybe they could have prepared for it. They tumbled and rolled and bumped into trees as the flood waters washed them away. Then, in the early hours of the morning, the rain became a drizzle, and the flood waters slowly receded.

"The storm had ended. The sun was out, and the sky was clear and calm. The animals awoke to find themselves scattered throughout Fortune Forest. They were safe, but their homes were gone. So was their food and the other supplies some of them had stored.

"They were amazed at how much damage had been done by the storm. Fortune Forest didn't even look the same. All of the animals either had been washed away or were flooded out. Some of the animals couldn't even get to their homes.

"Now, to make things worse, winter was just a few weeks away. The animals quickly would have to rebuild their homes, gather food and supplies, and get ready for the cold, gray days and nights of winter. Not much food could be found in winter, so the supplies would have to be replenished now. The animals didn't have much time.

"Ollie Owl was one of the first to wake up. He was a handsome owl, with dark brown feathers and big, intelligent-looking eyes. He flew to a perch in a tree overlooking the valley. He watched the other animals as they awoke.

"First, he saw Billy Bear. Cute and cuddly, Billy Bear had soft brown fur. He woke up and noticed he was next to a beehive. How lucky could he get? He was already hungry. His tongue was smacking up against his lips. Oh, was he going to have a great breakfast!

" 'I'm hungry,' he said. 'I'm hungry for honey.' Without thinking of the consequences, he picked up the beehive and started licking the honey as it dripped from the comb. It was really exciting and great fun.

"Billy Bear was having so much fun, he didn't notice that he had awakened the bees and they were stinging him. Then, all of a sudden, he howled, leaped, and screamed. He took off running through the woods. The bees flew after him. They were angry. He had invaded their home without even asking. As he ran from the bees, he realized how stupid he had been. He hadn't planned ahead. Billy Bear was greedy to get into the beehive, and he didn't even think that he might get stung. Have you ever done anything without thinking about the consequences?" Uncle Bob asked his story listeners. He continued without waiting for an answer. Several heads bobbed up and down.

"Billy Bear tried to have the whole hive's worth of honey. He wanted it, but he didn't think about whether he really needed all of it. He didn't think about what might happen, that he might get stung. Leaping and screaming, he finally reached a pond, jumped in, and disappeared under the water. The bees circled around Billy's entrance into the water for a while, but then left. Slowly, Billy lifted his nose and then his face out of the water.

"Ollie Owl yelled down from his perch to Billy, 'You are so silly. Chances are, if you had asked the bees for some honey, they might have given you some. You just do things without thinking of the consequences. Billy, you know better than that. You've got to plan ahead. And you were silly to go and take things that you really don't need. You were going to eat the whole hive rather than just take a lick.'

" 'Yeah, I know,' said Billy Bear. 'I always do that. I just forget to plan ahead. I tell myself I'm going to change, but I keep forgetting. And what looks good to me today may not really be what I'm after anyway. And long-term down the line, it may not be good for me at all.'

" 'Well,' said Ollie, 'You'd better get started.'

" 'Get started doing what?'

" 'Building yourself a new home.'

" 'Oh, that's right. My home was washed away. Well, I'll do that soon.'

" 'Billy, there you go again. Procrastinating,' said Ollie.

" 'Pro, what?' asked Billy.

" 'Procrastinating. Putting off important things until tomorrow that you should do today.' "

Uncle Bob said to the children, "Now, isn't that the way some people are? They don't really do today what they should do. They don't fix things and make them right. They don't plan ahead."

Sarah reached around behind Bob and nudged Darin. Dan and Denise looked at each other. Larry and Scott thought of how they'd been sort of like Billy Bear.

$ $ $ $ $ $

"Who else is in Fortune Forest?" yelled Sarah.

Uncle Bob continued. "Ollie saw Willie Wolf. He had gray and white fur, and big sharp teeth. He was strong, smart, and fast. Now, Willie walked gracefully across the top of the hill. He wanted to find out what the storm and the flood had done to Fortune Forest. He wanted to see how Fortune Forest had changed. And, he was looking for new places to find food and shelter.

" 'Willie, what do you see?' asked Ollie.

" 'This was quite a storm. I see a big tree that was knocked over on the hillside. That could be a good place for a home. And it looks like the hunting will be very good in the valley. You might say that what I'm doing is planning ahead.'

" 'Good!' said Ollie. 'Say, could you lend Billy a hand? He's really confused. And all full of bee stings.' "

Wilma and George and Gail thought about how they, like Willie Wolf, had planned ahead so they could adjust to changing situations.

$$\$ \, \$ \, \$ \, \$ \, \$ \, \$$

"Just about then, there was a loud shuffling in the grass. Something was rushing through the thicket. Was it something strange that the flood had washed in? No, it was Robbie Rabbit. Then there was a big thump. Robbie had run right into a tree stump.

" 'Oh, my head!' said Robbie. He looked up and saw Ollie, Willie, and Billy laughing at him. 'I've got to get busy. I've got to make a new home. I'm in a hurry. I have to do it fast.'

"Robbie had big bunny ears and a round, white, furry tail. He sat in place with his legs curled up. But when he ran, you could see that his legs were longer than his whole body. He ran real fast.

" 'You're always doing things fast, Robbie,' said Ollie. 'Why don't you slow down? Why don't you plan ahead?'

"Looking out from behind the whiskers on his face, Robbie said, 'I haven't got any time to plan ahead. I've got to think about today. Today is the only day, right now is the only time. Tomorrow might not come.' "

Dan and Denise reflected on those words.

" 'Well, for sure, Robbie,' said Willie, 'if you don't plan for tomorrow, you're certainly going to be in a lot of trouble when tomorrow comes.'

" 'Yeah, but I'm fast. I'm speedy. I never get behind.'

" 'Well, Robbie,' said Ollie, 'I don't know that you're getting behind. But I don't think you're getting too far ahead, either. The way you run around, you're always bumping into something or falling over. By the time you finally get done with whatever you want to get done, it's always a lot later than you think.'

" 'Well, I get sidetracked.'

" 'No, I don't think you get sidetracked. I just don't think you're organized. You need to pull yourself together and make a game plan. Think about what you really need.'

" 'But I do that. And then all of a sudden something else catches my eye. Then I go after that. Then another thing comes up, and I chase after it. I do one thing, then I do something else, then something else. Before long, I've forgotten what I started out to do in the first place.'

" 'See what I mean, Robbie? Changing things all the time just isn't worth it. You have to have a game plan. You have to plan ahead. You have to decide what you're going to do, and stay with it.'

"Willie said, 'In the long run, Robbie, planning really helps. You'll be able to run around this forest faster than you ever imagined. And, you'll be able to do it without bumping into tree stumps.'

" 'All right, I'll think about it.'

"Ollie said, 'Robbie, do think about it. Please, plan ahead. Do only what's important, only what you need to do. Make a plan. Set a course and then follow it.'

"Robbie sprang up and said, 'Gotta run, everybody. I've got things to do, places to be. I've got to find a new home. I've got to . . . well, I forgot what else I've got to do. What did I say I was going to do?' "

The children laughed.

" 'Anyway, I'm on my way somewhere.'

"Robbie dashed down a muddy path. He sped around a corner, then suddenly, right in front of him, an object was blocking the path. He dug in his feet and screeched to a halt, but his speeding force was so strong that he rolled over a couple of times. He came up looking right in the eyes of Tina Turtle.

"Tina Turtle said, 'Robbie, you crazy driver! You almost ran over me.'

"Robbie got up and shook himself off. Tina had short, fat, dark green legs that stuck out from her brown shell. Popping up from the front of her shell was her long neck and head. Tina had a pretty face and a nice smile.

"Tina said, 'You know, Robbie, I might not be as fast as you, but I always know where I'm going. It might take me a little longer to get where I'm going, but I've got a game plan and I stick to it.' "

As Wilma listened, she thought to herself, "I like what this turtle has to say."

Bob went on with the story. "Tina said, 'Say, did you ever hear that story about the tortoise and the hare?'

" 'No. A story about a tortoise and a hare?'

" 'Well, it's sort of like us. The tortoise and the hare are having a race. The tortoise has a slow pace and the hare runs real fast.'

" 'That is like us,' said Robbie. 'Pretty awesome. There's a fairy tale about us?'

" 'Yes. The story has taught a good lesson to millions of children for years and years,' said Tina. 'Robbie, you need to learn a lesson from the story, too.'

"Tina continued, 'I always follow my game plan, and I do only what I need to do. I don't follow every impulse. I go after what's most important, what I really need to get done. I set a course and stay with it. And, by the way Robbie, do you know how the story of the tortoise and the hare ends?'

" 'Uh, no.'

" 'The hare forgets his game plan, falls asleep, and loses the race.'

$$ \$ \, \$ \, \$ \, \$ \, \$ \, \$ $$

"Just then, a walnut came crashing down from the tall tree next to Tina and Robbie. It smacked Robbie right on his tail.

" 'Ouch,' he said. 'The sky is falling. I've got to go. I've got to go.'

" 'Robbie! Don't be silly. The sky isn't falling,' said Tina. 'Look up in the tree. It's Sam Squirrel. Sam, what are you doing up there?'

" 'I've found a new home. I'm making a nest, and I'm stocking it with nuts.' Sam was gray and was standing on his hind legs on one of the high tree limbs. Most of the time, he held a nut in his front paws. He had attentive eyes that observed what was going on around him.

"Billy Bear said, 'Isn't it early to be stocking up? There'll be plenty of food. We'll get it later. Come on down and let's have some fun!'

"Sam replied, 'Winter is just a couple of weeks away. What if there's another storm? And Billy, what if your bees fly away and you don't have any more beehives to raid?' "

Sarah smiled and looked at Darin. Sam and Sally, Wilma, and George and Gail thought how they were like the squirrel.

"Sam Squirrel asked Billy, 'What if you can't find any food this winter? What are you going to do?'

" 'I never thought about that. I don't think that far ahead,' said Billy.

"Sam turned to Robbie Rabbit. 'Robbie, what are you going to do? You keep running around without any game plan. You never plan for tomorrow. You think that just because you're faster than everyone else, you're always going to be able to get the job done.'

" 'Well, I am faster than everyone else,' said Robbie.

" 'But that doesn't mean you're better than everyone else,' said Sam.

"Ollie interrupted. 'Sam's right, and he's also smart. Sam, I've always noticed that when you pick up your nuts and food, the first thing you do is store some away.'

" 'That's right,' said Sam. 'I'm not going to eat it all. I'm going to store some away for later so I always know I'll have some food. I never want to go hungry. I want to plan for tomorrow. I want something down the line. In fact, I'm interested in having a good time today, but I'm more interested in having a better time in the future.' "

Sarah and her parents nodded in approval. Ben thought while he listened that he should be more like Sam Squirrel than Robbie Rabbit.

"Sam continued, 'I might not be able to climb trees when I'm older like I can now. If I can't do that, then I might not be able to get food. The nuts may not always drop where or when I want them to. I've got to plan ahead. If I always store something away, then I know I'll never go hungry. I'm always saving something.'

" 'That's great,' said Ollie.

$ $ $ $ $ $

"Just then, Cranston Crow swooped down from the sky. He landed in Sam Squirrel's tree and slowly started moving over towards Sam's warehouse of savings. He grabbed some walnuts that Sam had just cracked.

"Sam yelled, 'Get out of here, Cranston. You're always trying to take something that isn't yours. You're strong enough to gather your own food.'

"Cranston just looked at Sam through his black eyes shrouded in black feathers. He said nothing. Cranston was jet black. He was big and fat and flew slowly.

"Then Cranston spoke. 'I look around. If I'm hungry and I see something, I'll eat it.'

"Sam Squirrel replied, 'Why are you always trying to take somebody else's food? You never want to work hard. You never try to save things. You never plan ahead. You're going to let everyone else do the work, then you're going to pick at it and tear it apart and take whatever you want. You take from others.'

" 'I don't know any other way to do it. That's just the way crows are. That's the way I'm always going to be.' "

Dan and Denise listened attentively. This reminded them of the grilling they had received from Uncle Bob and Sam and Sally.

Larry and Scott thought about how they were mortgaging their futures with credit cards, and living off tomorrow's money.

Ollie said, 'You don't have to be this way, Cranston. You can learn to store your food and save it just like others. Then, when you get hungry, you'll have something right there in your own warehouse. You can nibble on it, and you won't have to go out and take from somebody else's nest. You're going to have to learn not to take anything from others. If you succeed, you'll earn our respect.'

" 'If you don't have any food, then don't expect to get any more from us,' said Willie. 'Don't take anything that isn't yours. Don't take anything that you certainly don't need.'

" 'Well, what am I supposed to do when I get hungry?' asked Cranston.

"Tina said, "You have to figure out how to get your own food. You're going to have to plan ahead. You can't just act on a whim and do whatever you want. If you learn to get your own food, and then only eat a little and store away the rest like Sam Squirrel does, you'll never be hungry.'

" 'Really?' said Cranston.

"All the other animals said in unison, 'Really, Cranston!' "

The children laughed louder. All the adults smiled.

$ $ $ $ $ $

"Then, they heard a commotion nearby. The trees were shaking. Leaves were falling. There was a lot of screaming and hollering. It was Charlie and Ceal Chimp. They were yelling and screaming again. They were always fighting. They never agreed on anything. This time they were fighting over what sticks to use for their nest.

"Sam Squirrel shook his head in disbelief. He said, 'Why can't they ever sit down together and decide what they want to do? Why can't they work together?'

"Billy said, 'I don't know. It seems like whatever Charlie wants to do, Ceal doesn't. He tells her that she doesn't know anything, so he goes out and does whatever he wants.'

"Charlie and Ceal were lanky, almost gangly. Their arms and legs seemed too long for their bodies. Their gray-brown fur was matted and stuck out in places, looking sort of like a bad haircut. And, since they screamed all the time, they both had their mouths open and their teeth showing. They looked frazzled.

"Billy said, 'When Charlie is gone, Ceal goes out and does whatever she wants to do. They never work together. They never plan ahead. They don't have any direction at all, do they, Ollie?'

"Ollie said, 'No, they sure don't. They need to plan ahead just like all of us need to do.'

"Ollie noticed Dan Donkey standing around daydreaming when he should have been preparing to build a new home and gather food supplies. Dan Donkey was just standing there looking up at the sky. One couldn't tell whether he was alive or dead. He stood with a blank look on his face. His donkey ears were sticking straight up. Every few minutes, he would shake his long, stringy tail as if to prove he was alive.

" 'Dan, aren't you going to get busy and start building your new home?' asked Ollie.

" 'Don't know. Haven't decided. There's no hurry. I'll get it done.'

"Ollie and the rest of the animals knew Dan well. They knew he could be sitting around the same place a month from now, still not having moved."

Ben and Betty especially, and all the other parents, thought about times they had put off decisions, the way Dan Donkey was doing.

$$\$\,\$\,\$\,\$\,\$\,\$$$

"Suddenly a loud hissing noise was heard. No one could tell quite where it was coming from. It was getting louder. All the animals stopped what they were doing. They froze in place, wondering what this scary sound was, and where it was coming from.

"Then, out from behind some swampy, thick grass crawled Hardy the Snake. He was hideous looking. His scaly skin was a chain-like pattern of brown, yellow, green, and white. He was coiled up, with his neck and jaws blown up. He looked around, as if he were ready to pounce on a victim. He kept hissing.

"From up in a tree, Sam Squirrel saw Hardy. 'Oh, it's just you again, Hardy,' said Sam. Sam scampered down the tree, right past Hardy, and across the field to another tree.

" 'It's just Hardy,' yelled Robbie Rabbit, who then ran circles around Hardy, knowing that the intruder was just Hardy the Snake. All the other animals relaxed and went back to their business.

"Tina Turtle walked up to the snake. 'Oh, Hardy, why do you always have to act like that?' she asked. 'You're all bluff. You hiss and scream and holler and make all kinds of noise and look real bad. You're just a big bag of hot air. You try to frighten everyone. You act tough, but you're not really tough at all. In fact, I bet that behind all that hissing, you're one scared snake.'

" 'Who says I'm scared of anything?' said Hardy. 'It's just that when I hiss and coil up, other animals get scared of me. Then I can get anything I want!' "

Ben recalled how many times he had talked like a bully to his family and his employees. He thought about how he did a lot of hissing and coiling to get his way.

"Ollie Owl flew over and landed next to Hardy and Tina. He said, 'Hardy, there are many ways that you can get what you want without having to scare others.'

" 'But it works!'

" 'Well, let's try something different,' said Ollie. 'First, try not being such a bully. Start being nice to the other animals. You know we're all friends in this forest?'

" 'Really? I never thought of it that way. Everybody always runs from me when I come around.'

" 'That's because you scare us.'

" 'Okay, I'll try to act nice from now on, and not scare anybody,' said Hardy.

" 'Good!' said Tina."

Ben smiled in agreement.

$ $ $ $ $ $

"From way above the woods, Eli and Ellie Eagle soared in the sky. Their wings spread wide as they gracefully and effortlessly circled above. They had dark brown feathers, and their heads sported the beautiful white mange of an eagle. Both looked down into the woods and waved to their friends below. They then swooped down to greet everyone.

"Ollie said, 'Hi, friends. Have you found a new home yet?'

" 'Not yet,' said Eli, 'but we've looked at several possibilities.'

"Ellie said, 'It'll take us a while to make a decision. But when we do, we'll make the right one, and we'll make the decision together.'

"Ollie said, 'Eli and Ellie, you always do things right. You've been best friends forever. You've raised your chicks together. You've hunted together. You've built your home together. You've always planned your next move together.'

"Eli said, 'There's another secret, friends. We make small adjustments along the way. It's just like when we fly over Fortune Forest. We turn and mold our wings slowly. We bend our feathers, or tuck our feathers next to our bodies. We go from gliding to speeding to landing. It looks easy, but it takes many years of training. Small changes, small adjustments.'

"Ellie said, 'We don't make big changes. We always plan together and make small adjustments along the way.' "

Gail nudged George as if to say, "That's like us."

$ $ $ $ $ $

Uncle Bob continued, "Ollie looked around as if he had something else on his mind.

" 'Ollie, what's wrong?' asked Ellie Eagle. 'What are you doing?'

" 'I'm looking for someone.'

" 'Who are you looking for?'

"Ollie said, 'I'm looking for Mrs. Red Fox. She's been so different ever since Mr. Red Fox left the forest last year. She's very scared. He left her unable to take care of herself. He always did the hunting and everything for her.'

" 'I remember watching them,' Willie Wolf said. 'Mrs. Fox would always stay at home and Red would build the summer home, and then when fall ended he would leave to find a good piece of property and build their winter home. He would gather all the food. He protected her in every way. Then he left one day and never came back. When she finally realized he wasn't coming back, she just fell apart.'

" 'There she is,' pointed Billy.

" 'Oh, Mrs. Fox, over here. How are you?'

" 'Oh, I don't know how I am. My home is gone. I don't know what to do anymore since Mr. Fox left. He told me he would always take care of me. But now that he's gone, I'm afraid to do things on my own.'

" 'Mrs. Fox,' said Ollie, 'You must build a home before winter.'

" 'But I don't know how to build a home.'

"Willie Wolf said, 'We'll help you, Mrs. Fox. But you're going to have to learn, so that next year you can do it on your own.'

" 'Oh, thank you. I just need all the help I can get right now. I've never been in this situation before. I'm so lonely. I can't make any decisions. I'm afraid I'll be wrong, so I don't do anything. I'm all alone.'

" 'Well, you've got us, Mrs. Fox,' said Willie Wolf. 'We'll make sure you learn how to do everything on your own.'

" 'Oh, thank you.'

"Well, soon winter came. And it got real cold. Most of the food that was hanging on the trees and growing in the ground had disappeared."

Uncle Bob looked around the picnic tables at all of the family members and asked, "Guess which animals ended up making it through the winter?"

"Which ones, Uncle Bob? Which ones?" asked Jennifer, sitting next to her dad Larry and her brother Jason.

Uncle Bob looked over at her and said, "Those who planned ahead, of course. Willie Wolf had a comfortable home and lots of food. So did Sam Squirrel, and Eli and Ellie Eagle, and Tina Turtle. They all had a comfortable winter and plenty to eat."

Darin asked, "But what about the others, Uncle Bob?"

"The others didn't do as well. Robbie Rabbit, Billy Bear, and Hardy the Snake didn't make their homes in time for the first snow. Without the help of their friends, they wouldn't have made it through the winter.

"Dan Donkey, Mrs. Red Fox, and Charlie and Ceal Chimp also had miserable, miserable winters. They barely made it through winter, and only with help from their friends. But they soon learned how to make a good home to live in, and how to fill their bins with food for the rest of the winter."

"What about Cranston Crow?" asked Sarah.

"Oh, yes. He never did stop scavenging. He never found a home, he never stored any food. He didn't have any friends, and he spent the entire winter trying to fill his belly by taking the easy way out. He never did plan ahead, he kept on just taking care of one day at a time. He was a very unhappy crow. Then one day, he left Fortune Forest, never to be seen again. But all the other animals learned to plan ahead, and work together and share.

"So, the moral of the story of the Animals of Fortune Forest is . . ."

"Uncle Bob, Uncle Bob! Let me tell it!" cried Sarah.

He nodded. "Okay, Sarah. You tell everyone."

"The moral is that you have to plan ahead and start doing the right things today so you don't find yourself in trouble tomorrow. Plan today and save for tomorrow."

"Well put, Sarah. That's exactly what the animals learned to do. That's exactly what all of us have to learn to do.

"The end."

The kids clapped and cheered. The parents smiled and thought, "What a great story."

Bob thought about playing horseshoes.

11

Twilight Time

TWILIGHT TIME WAS FLEETING. All that was left of the sun was a bright orange glow on the western horizon. The moisture on the grass sparkled in the dim light of twilight. Lights came on automatically in the picnic shelter, and now it was lighter in the shelter than outside. The crickets and cicadas began singing. A park ranger drove up and reminded the remaining picknickers that the park was closing for the day.

"Uncle Bob, I'm outta here," announced Scott. "This picnic is history, man."

Bob answered, "Scott, take care. When's the grand opening of Scott's Skillet?"

"In a few years. Know what I'm going to do now? I'm going to cruise by Fast Freddie's and tell my boss I want to get into management as quickly as possible."

"Great!"

"And tomorrow, I'm going back to State U. to find out about management classes. I'm going to look into taking classes while I work."

"Good for you. Scott!"

"Uncle Bob, I'm going to just make small adjustments, small changes along the way. But there's no doubt, Scott's Skillet is going to be known by everybody! Uncle Bob, you can have the first burger off the grill!"

"Gee, thanks."

"Thank *you*, Uncle Bob. You've helped me a lot today. I'm gonna be a millionaire some day."

"Stick to it, Scott. Keep me up to date on what's happening."

"I'm history," exclaimed Scott, as he strapped on his helmet and fired up the Harley. The rumble of the motorcycle drowned out the sound of the crickets and cicadas momentarily, as Scott drove out of the park.

$ $ $ $ $ $

Sarah gave Uncle Bob a hug. "Thanks for telling the animal story, Uncle Bob. It was the best ever. Do you know what?"

"What, Sarah?"

"Darin says he's going to start saving his money. He's not going to buy so much candy. He's going to be a millionaire just like me! Everyone will call him Darin the Baseball Card Millionaire."

"Oh, that's great, Sarah. Make sure *you* keep that savings account growing. I'll have some real surprises for you next year."

"Oh, Uncle Bob, tell me now, tell me now."

"Well, here's what I'm going to tell you. If you save as much money as you possibly can, and you show me that your savings account has really grown during the next year, I'll tell you even more secrets next year at the picnic."

"Ooh, boy, that's great!"

Sarah's mother Sally called out to her, "Come on, Sarah. It's time to go."

Sam yelled, "Hey, Bob, thanks for all the help. I hope she wasn't too much of a pest today."

"She was terrific. You've got a great girl there. She's teaching Darin to be a good saver, too."

$ $ $ $ $ $

As Sarah ran along and jumped in her family's car, Bob felt a tap on his shoulder. He turned around and looked up at Benjamin. A well-worn cigar extended out one side of his mouth.

"Well, Ben, have you made the big decision?" Then Bob saw Bigtimer's face melt into a big, wide grin that a truck could drive through.

Ben said, "Bob, I really thank you for all the help. You said some good stuff. You gave me something to think about. That animal story was great. I need to get a plan in order, like those squirrels and wolves and eagles do. I'll stop hissing at people like the snake. Next year, you'll see a different Benjamin. Betty and I have decided to call that insurance planner tomorrow. We're going to start building our investment savings plan now so we can meet all our emergencies, give the kids the best education, and retire with the same lifestyle we've grown accustomed to. Then we'll make sure that our estate is set up so that when we're no longer here, everything we have will go to our loved ones—how we want and when we want."

"This is good news. You've got everything it takes to be successful, and now you're going to make sure you keep what you make, and enjoy your life knowing that if and when an emergency occurs, everything will work out fine. You'll be helping other people become successful, too."

"Helping other people?"

"Yes, Ben. You know how to do it. Stop pushing your employees. Teach them. Make them a team."

"Bob, let's have lunch sometime."

"You're going to take a lunch break?"

"Yeah. Might be good."

Betty hugged Bob and thanked him for all the help. Betty and Ben held hands as they walked back to the Rolls Royce, where Ben, Jr., and Bridget had been patiently waiting to go home.

$ $ $ $ $ $

Bob noticed Larry standing with Jennifer and Jason in the parking lot by the shelter.

"There's Mom!" Jennifer shouted, pointing to her mom's car entering the park.

The kids picked up their bags as the car pulled up. Then they pulled on Larry's arms.

"Come on, Dad, come with us. Let's tell Mom what a great picnic this was."

Larry walked to the car with the kids. They gave him hugs and got in the car. He stood next to the driver's door and talked. The conversation continued for a while. He appeared to be smiling. He stuck his head in the car's back window to give each child another hug and kiss. Larry waved as the car drove away.

$ $ $ $ $ $

Dan and Denise packed up their coolers with what was left of the soda and ice.

"What are we going to do with these three new coolers?" asked Dan.

"I wanted to have a garage sale next month."

"Sounds good. We'll get rid of some of the things we don't use anymore."

"I've got an idea," interjected Bob. "Why don't you check with Sam and Sally or with George and Gail? Maybe they could use a cooler. That way, we'd keep them in the family. Next year, when picnic time rolls around, we'll have enough coolers."

"And we won't have to run out and buy more." Dan smiled.

"Right!"

"Buy only what we need, not what we want. Buy only what we need, not what we want. I'm going to have to keep saying these words over and over again." Dan looked at Bob for approval.

"Experts say it takes six weeks to change a habit," Bob suggested.

"Well, we're really going to try," Denise added.

"Don't just try. Do it. Decide that now is the time to change. Commit yourself," said Bob.

"Thanks for all your help," said Dan. "You really helped Denise and me see more clearly how stupid we've been."

"I don't know that you've been stupid, Dan, but maybe you haven't thought things through enough. Maybe you just haven't planned ahead. You've only been thinking about today."

"You've helped us a lot today," Denise added. "Those animals, Cranston Crow and the chimps, maybe we've been like them. That's not how we want to be."

"Good. Just start figuring things out day by day. Work on your plan a little every day until you've got it right. Then start working to reach your long-term goals. Most important, get free of debt."

Darin held up his quarter. "This is the start of my savings account. Some day, this will grow to a million dollars! They'll call me Darin the Baseball Card Millionaire."

"That's wonderful, Darin. Remember, only the quality cards!"

"Right, Uncle Bob. Right."

Darin and his parents gave Bob the thumbs-up sign and walked to their car.

$ $ $ $ $ $

"Great walk, Bob. Hope we didn't wear you out too much," said George.

"I'll know better in the morning."

"You ought to walk more often. It would be really good for you. Get you in shape. Keep those arteries clear."

"Maybe I can join you two for a walk the next time we're in Goodvillage."

"We'll probably be seeing you soon about Grandma," Gail suggested.

"That's right. Let's all work together to help her."

"Yes. And thanks for your help with our finances, too," she said.

George looked over at Gail. "Honey, I have an idea."

"What's that?"

"You know how we walk the same three-mile course every day?"

"Yes."

"Maybe we should try some new courses. You know, take a little risk. Get off the same path."

"Are you sure? Around the other side of the neighborhood, isn't it too hilly? Will we get back in time? Oh, wait a minute, look at what I'm doing. I'm giving all the reasons not to make a small adjustment, a little change."

"I've thought of all the same reasons myself," George admitted.

"Let's try a new course tomorrow!" said Gail triumphantly. "Not a big change, just a little change. A small adjustment."

"Go for it," Bob said as he patted them both on the back and sent them on their way.

$ $ $ $ $ $

Marge rejoined Bob. Now everyone was gone except the two of them. They sat on the picnic table and looked at the moon. He put his right arm around her while he held a horseshoe in his left hand. "Bob, I'm going to drive Sis's car back to her house. I'll see you there.

"By the way, I didn't see you play horseshoes today. I think you're going to owe me a dinner out."

"Well, I almost got out there, but then it started raining."

"Doesn't count. You didn't say anything about rainouts. Let's see. *Phantom of the Opera* is coming. And *Evita*."

Just then the park ranger walked up.

"Excuse me, young lovers, the park is closed."

"Okay, we'll be going soon." Bob smiled.

"Young lovers. Thanks for the compliment." Marge felt good about that!

The ranger munched on an apple. "Say, you folks have this picnic every year, don't you?"

"Yes. Did you know this park is named after my great-grand-father, Phillip Prosperity?"

"No, that's amazing. Amazing that you're his descendant. I always wanted to find out more about him."

"Well, the first thing about Old Phillip was that he was a fantastic horseshoe player. He made his money playing horseshoes. I know some of his secrets."

"Can you show me?"

"Sure."

Bob winked at Marge. She leaned over and kissed Bob on the cheek. "I'll leave you two to your horseshoes." Marge then got up and walked to her sister's car.

Bob and the park ranger strolled over the horseshoe pit and began pitching in the twilight.

Finally, Bob got in his game. But he'd still give Marge the dinner and theater night out on the town. He appreciated all her cooperation and support. Yes, he had spent the day talking about money. She had won the bet fair and square. She deserved the night out anyway.

The day had been worthwhile, he thought. He had really planted some seeds. He had shared some of his secrets that he knew he needed to pass on. He hoped the secrets would help. Those secrets were simple; they kept playing over and over again in his head.

"We know what our expenses are, and we keep them far below our income."

"We don't buy things we want. We only buy those things we need."

"We only buy with cash."

"We don't buy on credit or time payments or credit cards— and if we do, we pay the bill completely before any interest charges start."

"We stay out of debt."

"We save by paying ourself first, and we save as much money as we possibly can, every day, every month, every year."

He thought how important it was to share the secrets about his Cookie Jar Expense Checklist. People have to know what their expenses are. If we know exactly what our expenses are, we can develop a plan for financial success. By making small adjustments along the way, we can pick that correct path that guides us down the road to financial success and becoming millionaires.

The park ranger thanked Bob for the game and got in his Jeep. He drove back to the ranger station.

Bob took one last look at the horseshoe pit. "What a great day," he thought. He was still holding one horseshoe. He looked around. No one was there. He was alone in the park. There was one thing left to do. "Now all I need is one perfect ringer," he said to himself.

He got into his stance, he bent his knees, and placing his feet side by side, he positioned the horseshoe out in front of his face. He aimed at the horseshoe pole in the middle of the far horseshoe pit. He had the angle. He planned perfectly on the arch of his toss. He brought his arm back behind him, and held it there for a split second. Striding forward with one leg in front of the other, he swung the horseshoe forward in a perfect pendulum swing and let it go. It sailed through the air, end over end, side over side and then fell straight down to wrap around the pole.

"A ringer," he shouted. His words echoed around the park as if he wanted the animals in the forest to hear him. He shouted again, "A ringer, a perfect ringer. What a perfect way to end a perfect picnic.

"Yes, I've shared the secrets today, and I've also played horseshoes."

With that, he walked up the path leading into Fortune Forest, where Billy Bear, Dan Donkey, Willie Wolf, and the other animals were waiting.

Postscript

Uncle Bob is alive and well!

And you can meet with him or an Uncle Bob look-alike in any of the fifty states. At first glance, he may not be easily recognized since he appears using many different names and titles: Mary, James, Abdul, Raj, Alice, John, and so many more. And he has loads of titles and various names on his office door and on his business card: Financial Planner, Accountant, Tax Specialist, Registered Investment Advisor, Life Insurance Agent, Chartered Life Underwriter (C.L.U.), Chartered Financial Consultant (ChFC), and on and on. And you may find an Uncle Bob who is a member of an organization called International Association of Financial Planners. In fact, if you flip the dial of your radio, you may hear his or her voice talking about money and financing.

And when you need Uncle Bob, you may be able to contact him at his private office or in an office that he shares with others. You may be able to talk with him or her on an investment talk show, meet him at his seminar, or read investment articles written by him or her in local newspapers or magazines. You might also discover that he regularly publishes an investment or money newsletter. You might also join the thousands of others who have gone with him on his investment cruises.

Or, then, you also may meet him at the family picnic!

When you see Uncle Bob, say hello for me!